Columbia University

Contributions to Education

Teachers College Series

No. 537

AMS PRESS
NEW YORK

SURVEY STUDY OF TEACHER TRAINING IN TEXAS, AND A SUGGESTED PROGRAM

By

GEORGE M. CRUTSINGER, Ph.D.

Teachers College, Columbia University
Contributions to Education No. 537

Bureau of Publications
Teachers College, Columbia University
NEW YORK CITY
1933

Library of Congress Cataloging in Publication Data

Crutsinger, George Mahan, 1886-
Survey study of teacher training in Texas.

Reprint of the 1933 ed., issued in series: Teachers College, Columbia University. Contributions to education, no. 537.
Originally presented as the author's thesis, Columbia.
Bibliography: p.
1. Teachers, Training of--Texas. 2. Teachers colleges--Texas. 3. Teachers--Texas. I. Title. II. Series: Columbia University. Teachers College. Contributions to education, no. 537.
LB1962.C7 1972 370'.73'09764 79-176680
ISBN 0-404-55537-3

Reprinted by Special Arrangement with Teachers College Press, New York, New York

From the edition of 1933, New York
First AMS edition published in 1972
Manufactured in the United States

AMS PRESS, INC.
NEW YORK, N. Y. 10003

To

Doctor William Herschel Bruce
President Emeritus of the North Texas State Teachers College
gentleman, scholar, constructive leader, friend,
who has made a permanent contribution
to the development of education
in Texas and elsewhere

ACKNOWLEDGMENTS

It is impossible to carry to completion a study of the nature of the one herewith presented without the unselfish assistance of many individuals. The number of those who have helped with this study is so great that it is impossible adequately to acknowledge either the assistance rendered or the fine coöperative spirit shown by each one. For encouragement and indispensable help in securing original data the author is especially grateful to President R. L. Marquis of the State Teachers College at Denton. For the coöperation of President H. F. Estill at Huntsville, President J. A. Hill at Canyon, President C. E. Evans at San Marcos, President S. H. Whitley at Commerce, President H. W. Morelock at Alpine, President A. W. Birdwell at Nacogdoches, and their respective staffs sincere thanks are extended. Especially is the writer indebted to his wife, Georgia Phipps Crutsinger, for invaluable and painstaking help in making the necessary tedious tabulations. He is further under obligations of gratitude to Miss Lois Boyles and Miss Louellen Remmy of Teachers College, Columbia University, for most careful work in assisting with statistical operations and for preparing the manuscript.

The author gratefully acknowledges his obligation to the members of his dissertation committee, Professor W. C. Bagley, Professor E. S. Evenden, and Professor Thomas Alexander for their constant inspiration, helpful criticism, and genuine friendly interest. There is a kind of encouragement and inspiration that can be obtained only from personal contact with thoroughly professional and scholarly men.

G. M. C.

CONTENTS

INTRODUCTION

Origin of the Study

The Board of Regents of the Texas State Teachers Colleges, during the academic year 1928-1929, expressed to the Council of Presidents a desire that a study be made of the seven state-supported teacher-training institutions of the state. A committee of the presidents was appointed to collect data and to direct the progress of the study. A very comprehensive and detailed outline of data to be collected was prepared by the staff of the East Texas State Teachers College at Commerce under the leadership of President Whitley, a member of the committee of presidents. In the fall of 1929 the writer was assured by two of the presidents that the Council would probably be willing to turn over to him the prosecution of the study. Upon that assurance, the outline provided by President Whitley was carefully transformed into a series of data sheets, and a tentative plan drafted for the study which would secure as much of the information suggested by the outline as possible, and also provide for the consideration of the problem of a possible state program of teacher training.

Copies of the data sheets and the proposed plan were submitted to the Council of Presidents at a meeting held in Austin, Texas, in February, 1930. After some discussion the Council gave permission for the prosecution of the study and pledged the assistance of each college in collecting data. As soon as possible a sufficient number of copies of the data sheets were prepared and forwarded to each president for use in securing information from his institution. During the latter part of March the writer visited each of the colleges for conferences and for the purpose of collecting the completed data sheets. No financial assistance was available for carrying on the investigation, and it soon became apparent that without aid a complete and detailed survey of teacher training in an area as large as Texas would be impossible; also that study of facilities and procedures for professional preparation of teachers for the state must be a continuous process. No single study of this nature can be considered final.

Purpose

Professional education of teachers as a special undertaking was begun in Texas, as in many other states, by privately conducted normal schools. Public officials have been slow to recognize it as a proper and necessary responsibility of the state. The education of physicians, lawyers, engineers, and agriculturists seems to have been considered of more pressing importance than the professional preparation of workers for the public schools, which has been a comparatively recent development. As the United States Office of Education points out:

> The increased professionalization of teaching and of teacher training is a noteworthy tendency of the past few years; it has been relatively a short time since almost anyone who wished to realize a little money out of a high-school education could secure a job in the schools. Since progress in teacher training is intimately associated with progress in public education as a whole, some tendencies toward the professionalization of public-school teaching are of interest. Such teaching more and more partakes of the nature of the learned professions of medicine, law, and theology.[1]

The purpose of the present study is:

1. To investigate the status of agencies which have been established by the State of Texas for the special purpose of educating teachers.
2. To show enough of their history to explain their present status.
3. To evaluate in terms of the best known standards the professional attainments of these agencies.
4. To work out such suggestions for their progress as may seem warranted.
5. To determine as accurately as possible from data available the magnitude of the task that should be undertaken by the state's teacher-training institutions.
6. To develop certain proposals for the establishment of a definite state program of teacher education which will be adequate for the needs of the public schools.

Scope

Conditions under which the study was carried on forced the setting up of certain limitations which were observed:

[1] Frazier, Benjamin W. *Teacher Training, 1926-28.* United States Bureau of Education, Bulletin 1929, No. 17, pp. 3-4. (Advance sheets from the Biennial Survey of Education in the United States, 1926-28.)

1. The institutions for the training of white teachers and the teacher needs of the schools for white children were considered exclusively. As is shown in Chapter V of the present study, approximately 17 per cent of the children of legal scholastic age in the state are Negroes, and about 12 per cent of the public-school teachers are of that race. Although a separate division of the State Department of Education is entrusted with the supervision of Negro schools, investigation of the problem of preparing Negro teachers seems to be needed as a separate study.

2. The collection of certain data relating to the students in training had to be foregone because of the expense that would have been necessary. The nature of these data is indicated, however, and suggestions are made for the handling of that work by the college staffs.

3. Investigation was limited largely to the state teachers colleges. The evaluation of the teacher-training work done by other state institutions and by other colleges and universities was based on published reports.

4. A thorough study of the state's need of teachers, based on primary data, was found to be beyond the resources available for this study. Materials used were: data found in the State Department of Education, published reports, and studies made in other states.

5. Consideration of the historical development of teacher training in the state has been limited to that necessary to show the background of present conditions.

Sources of Information

In addition to the data sheets which have been referred to, the following general sources of information have been used: (1) a questionnaire to a sampling of superintendents to secure data on the number of inexperienced teachers; (2) auditors' reports; (3) published reports of the State Department of Education, the Board of Regents of the Texas State Teachers Colleges, the United States Office of Education, and the United States Bureau of the Census; (4) the statutes of Texas; (5) catalogues of the colleges; (6) yearbooks of the American Association of Teachers Colleges; (7) published studies and surveys of teacher training; (8) certain unpublished theses and studies.

CHAPTER I

THE STATE OF TEXAS AND THE INSTITUTIONS THAT TRAIN ITS TEACHERS

Texas is unique among the states of the American Union in its enormous size, the wide variety of its physiographic and climatic conditions, the distribution and character of its population, history and traditions, and rapid development. Its varied peculiarities have been, and will continue to be, factors of importance in the building of a system of public education, of which a program of teacher training is necessarily an integral part.[1] It does not fall within the scope of this study to trace in detail the efforts that have been made to give the state a system of educational institutions, or even to discover the vicissitudes through which the present facilities for the training of teachers have developed. Enough of the background will be examined to show present developments in their proper setting. Interesting borrowings from other states are to be seen, as are certain similarities in the gradual and occasionally erratic nature of procedures and methods.[2]

The area of Texas, 265,896 square miles, exceeds by 17,000 square miles the combined area of the following thirteen states: New York, New Jersey, Pennsylvania, Connecticut, Massachusetts, Vermont, New Hampshire, Rhode Island, Maine, Delaware, Maryland, Ohio, and West Virginia.[3] Some significant distances within the state are as follows: from Texarkana on the eastern border to El Paso, nearly 900 miles; from Texline in the extreme northwest to Brownsville at the mouth of the Rio Grande River, about 1,020 miles; from the Oklahoma border north of Denison to Brownsville, 760 miles. The area included in the Panhandle is approximately 175 miles

[1] Eby, Frederick. *Development of Education in Texas.* The Macmillan Company, New York City, 1925. Ledlow, W. F. *Protestant Education in Texas.* Dissertation in the University of Texas, 1926. (Unpublished.)

[2] Interesting comparisons are found in the development of teacher training as presented by: *Bulletin No. 14* of Carnegie Foundation for the Advancement of Teaching, by Steele in Vermont, Myers in Ohio, Donovan in Kentucky, Grant in Arkansas, Mangun in Massachusetts, Meader in Connecticut, Taylor in Pennsylvania, and Hill in Missouri. See bibliography.

[3] *Atlas of the World,* pp. 3-8. Funk & Wagnalls Company, New York City, 1924.

square. The entire state is divided into 254 counties, several of which are larger than the State of Rhode Island.

As to the place of Texas in any grouping of states, McConnell, in his study of *Social Cleavages in Texas*, very aptly points out:

> Owing to wide variations in the characteristics of the different sections of Texas, the State does not conform completely to any of the usual classifications of the States of the Union. It may be considered southern, since only the State of Florida has a lower latitude. It is central in that it belongs to that group which forms the great central strip of the Union. It is a Gulf State because of its long coastline which extends one fourth of the distance around the arc formed by these States. Finally, it is western because of its extensive areas of plains and Cordillera region. From these facts it is readily seen that different divisions of the State may have characteristics which mark them as southern, central, or western.[4]

One who travels extensively over the state is convinced that, from the standpoint of the manners, customs, and traditions of the people, there are more communities showing characteristics of western and central regions than there are exhibiting those usually attributed to the south.

Three of the great physiographic provinces of the North American Continent extend into Texas and prominently affect its topography, climate, and vegetation. They are: the Atlantic and Gulf Coastal Plains, the Great Plains, and the Western Cordilleras. Each of these may be divided into clearly distinguished lesser regions as shown in Chart I. The location of the teachers colleges is shown by this chart, indicating the nature of the physiographic regions in which they are situated. The college at Commerce is in the black prairie region; the one at Denton, in the same region near the edge of the eastern cross timbers; the one at Huntsville, in the east Texas timber region; the one at San Marcos, in the southern extremity of the black prairie region, the one at Canyon, in the Panhandle high plains region; the one at Nacogdoches, in the east Texas farming-timber region; and the one at Alpine, in the trans-Pecos region in the eastern border of the Western Cordilleras.[5]

The climatic features of Texas likewise show a wide variation, greater than that found over the same size area in the eastern or

[4] McConnell, W. J. *Social Cleavages in Texas, A Study of the Proposed Division of the State.* Studies in History, Economics and Public Law, Vol CXIX, No. 2, pp. 15-16, Columbia University, 1925.

[5] Excellent descriptions of the physiographic regions of Texas are to be found in the Economic Survey of Texas made by the Southwestern Bell Telephone Company, St. Louis, 1928.

middle-western portions of the country. Not only are extremes of precipitation and temperature found between widely separated portions of the state, but many localities are subject to such extremes from year to year. It is not the mean annual temperature, for

CHART I

PHYSIOGRAPHIC REGIONS OF TEXAS

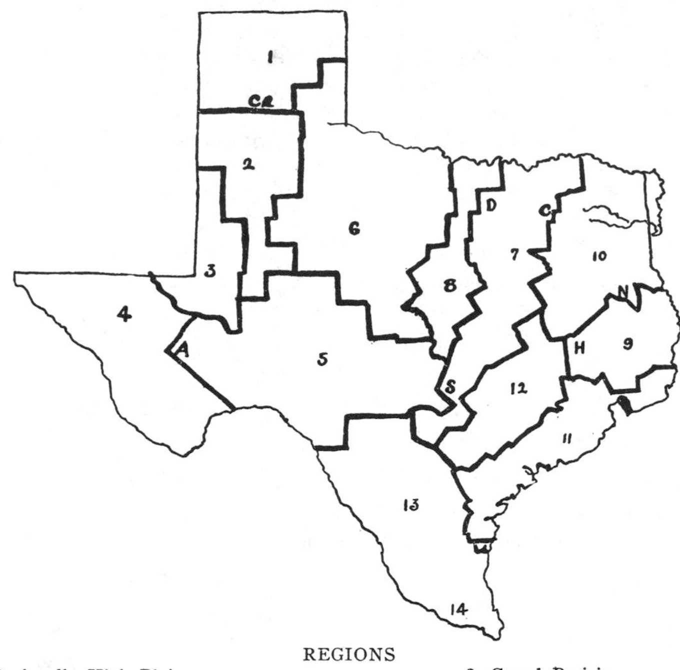

REGIONS

1. Panhandle High Plains
2. South High Plains
3. High Plains Grazing
4. Trans-Pecos
5. Edwards Plateau
6. Low Rolling Plains
7. Black Prairie
8. Grand Prairie
9. East Texas Timber
10. East Texas Farming-Timber
11. Coastal Prairie
12. Prairie-Timber
13. Rio Grande Plain
14. Lower Rio Grande Valley

STATE TEACHERS COLLEGES

A—Sul Ross, at Alpine; C—East Texas, at Commerce; Ca—West Texas, at Canyon; D—North Texas, at Denton; H—Sam Houston, at Huntsville; N—Stephen F. Austin, at Nacogdoches; S—Southwest Texas, at San Marcos.

example, that prevents the commercial production of citrus fruits in many of the counties but rather the occasional brief periods of freezing weather. Similarly, the mean annual rainfall would support profitable farming in many counties were it not for occasional droughts. Generally speaking, the climatic variations are greatest in the western portion and least in the eastern portion of the state. Tables 1 A and 1 B show the mean annual precipitation and the mean

TABLE 1 A

VARIATIONS IN PRECIPITATION, 1911–20*

YEAR	NUMBER OF INCHES West	East
1911	10	60
1912	7	59
1913	7	66
1914	14	70
1915	10	61
1916	6	48
1917	2	37
1918	8	57
1919	10	85
1920	6	63
Average	8	61

* McConnell, W. J. *Op. cit.*, p. 20.

annual temperatures over the state. There is a gradual decrease in the annual rainfall from the eastern portion toward the western portion, the variation being from more than fifty inches to less than ten inches. The difference in mean annual temperature between the

TABLE 1 B

EXTREMES IN MEAN ANNUAL TEMPERATURES, 1911–20*

YEAR	DEGREES, F. Extreme North	Extreme South
1911	55	75
1912	52	73
1913	53	74
1914	56	72
1915	54	73
1916	55	74
1917	54	73
1918	54	74
1919	53	74
1920	54	74
Average	54	74

* McConnell, W. J. *Op. cit.*, p. 22.

northern and southern portions of the state amounts to approximately twenty degrees, Fahrenheit.

The difference between the mean annual temperature in the extreme northern portion and that of the Rio Grande Valley is approximately as great as the difference between mean annual temperature in Chicago and that in New Orleans, or between mean annual temperature in New York City and that in Jacksonville, Florida. Highest summer temperatures recorded range from 110 to 116 degrees, while the lowest temperatures within the state range from 3 to 19 degrees below zero.

The territory now included in the State of Texas has been under the control of six different governments at various periods in its history. During the first half of the sixteenth century the Spaniards first visited this region and for more than a hundred years conducted sporadic expeditions of exploration and conquest, being incited by stories of fabulous wealth possessed by the natives. However, the French government laid claim to the territory by virtue of the explorations de La Salle made during the latter part of the seventeenth century, and the forts and posts established by its explorers and its subjects from Louisiana. In 1762 the region was ceded to Spain, but no extensive program of settlement was undertaken by that nation, and it was not until after the purchase of the Louisiana Territory by the United States in 1803, that settlers from the American states began to appear in Texas. When Mexico achieved independence from Spain in 1824, Texas became a state under the Mexican government. Immediately a program of encouraging settlers from the United States was inaugurated which, under the "empresario system," resulted in rapid colonization. On March 2, 1836, Texas declared its independence of Mexico and set up an independent republic, and, by vanquishing the Mexican army in the battle of San Jacinto on April 21, 1836, made good its claims to independence. The republic lasted until Texas was annexed by the United States through a joint resolution of Congress, March 1, 1845. The president of the Republic of Texas retired in favor of the governor of the State of Texas on February 16, 1846. The fifth government to control Texas was the Confederate States of America. Since a majority of the immigrants who made up the population of Texas had come from the slave-holding states, there was sufficient pro-slavery sentiment to lead to the adoption of Articles of Secession in January, 1861. The sixth change in government occurred in the spring of 1870 when the legislature of Texas ratified the fourteenth and fifteenth amendments and the state was readmitted to the Union. It is significant to note that the terms of annexation allowed Texas to retain its public lands, and that its boundaries were fixed to include portions of territory which now form parts of New Mexico, Oklahoma, Kansas, Colorado, and Wyoming. After the close of the Mexican War, the United States paid to Texas $10,000,000 for its claim to lands now belonging to these states, and the boundaries of the state were fixed as they are at present.

The census of 1930[6] showed that the State of Texas, with a total population of 5,824,715, continued to hold the rank of fifth among the states of the Union. The four states having a larger population were New York, Pennsylvania, Illinois, and Ohio. The numerical increase in population between 1920 and 1930 was the greatest of any decade in the history of the state and amounted to 24.9 per cent. Five states had a higher percentage of increase: California, Florida, Michigan, Arizona, and New Jersey. The per cent of increase during the previous decade, 1910 to 1920, was 19.7 per cent. A notable feature revealed by the 1930 census was the increase in the urban population. Classing as urban those incorporated cities and towns of 2,500 or more, the urban population of Texas was 41 per cent of the total as compared to 32 per cent in 1920. The actual farm population in 1930 was approximately 35 per cent of the total. The percentage of foreign-born and of those of foreign stock is decreasing in Texas. Foreign-born and the children of those born abroad, constituted approximately 15 per cent of the total population. The Negro population was 13 per cent of the total. Aside from the larger cities, the most rapid increase in population was found to be in the Panhandle and South Plains counties and in the lower Rio Grande Valley. Brenholtz,[7] in his study of population as a factor in the need of secondary-school teachers, using the technique of a logistic growth curve, predicted that the population of Texas would not increase so rapidly as it has during the past thirty years, and that the upper asymptote of her population would be reached between 1950 and 1980. The scattering of the population is shown by the density—population per square mile—in the several

[6] Census figures used in this study are preliminary reports taken from *The Texas Almanac*, for 1931, published by *The Dallas News*, Dallas, Tex.

[7] Brenholtz, Harold. *Population as a Potential Factor in the Need for Teachers for Secondary Schools of a State, with Special Application to California and Texas*, Chap. V. Doctor's thesis at the University of California, 1930. (Unpublished.)

counties. For the state as a whole the density was 22.2 persons per square mile, but varied among the counties from 379.3 in Dallas County to less than 1 in several western counties.

Table 2 was prepared to show the distribution of total population and scholastic population in the immediate territory of each

TABLE 2

TOTAL AND SCHOLASTIC POPULATION IN THE IMMEDIATE TERRITORY OF EACH TEACHERS COLLEGE, 1930

Territory of College at	Total Population	Scholastic Population
Alpine	25,050	7,418
Canyon	83,671	19,357
Commerce*	292,338	84,412
Denton*	688,413	161,148
Huntsville	121,350	38,294
Nacogdoches	144,565	43,184
San Marcos	168,840	43,319

* Half the population of Collin County was counted in the territory of the college at Denton, and half in the territory of the college at Commerce.

teachers college. The plan of distributing state funds for the support of public schools requires that a census of children between 6 and 17 years of age be taken annually in March. The scholastic population figures shown are those obtained by the census of 1930. Immediate territory was taken as the county in which each college is situated and counties contiguous to it. Pronounced variation is shown in the distribution of population, and by reference to Table 10 it will be seen that the enrollment at each college is closely proportional to the population of the territory in which it is situated.

The wealth of Texas is increasing more rapidly than the population. The total assessed valuation for state taxation in 1930 was $4,328,212,712, which represented an increase of 27.6 per cent over the valuation for 1920.[8] More than half the total assessed valuation is composed of assessments of real estate. Reports of a census of total actual wealth are available for the years 1890, 1900, 1904, 1912, and 1922 only. Comparison of actual wealth and assessed values for those years shows a conservative ratio of 3 to 1. An increasing divergence between actual and assessed values has been indicated for a number of years. This is caused primarily by the

[8] *The Texas Almanac*, for 1929 and 1931.

fact that county boards of equalization are made the courts of last resort in fixing renditions for both state and county taxation. Furthermore, assessed values count only such property as is subject to ad valorem tax. Taking into consideration all these factors, it has been estimated that the actual wealth of the state is not less than $14,000,000,000.[9] The rate of increase in wealth can be attributed to industrial development, including manufactures, petroleum production and refining, the production of sulphur and other minerals, and the growth of utilities corporations. However, the wealth is very unevenly distributed among counties and sections of the state, as indicated by assessed valuations and Federal income tax returns.

Because of the wide variations in characteristics that have been briefly described, proposals have been made at various times to divide the state into several smaller states, as many as five having been suggested. However, McConnell, reaches this conclusion:

> It has been contended by advocates of division that a great many advantages would accrue to the people of the State were such a step consummated, but thus far an overwhelming majority of the people of Texas refuse to concur, or concurring refuse to admit that these advantages cannot be realized by procedure more compatible with their sense of loyalty to the traditions of the State.[10]

The chances are, therefore, that Texas will never be divided and that the perfecting of a system of public education, including a program of teacher training, will be accomplished on the present state-wide basis, and upon foundations already laid.[11]

Prior to the war between the states there were three groups of persons from which teachers for Texas schools were drawn: a relatively large group of untrained and poorly qualified itinerants who used teaching merely as a stepping stone to more profitable employment; a second and much smaller group of cultured people, educated in the best colleges and universities of the United States and Europe, who were genuinely interested in the profession of teaching; and a third influential group, primarily religious missionaries, who engaged in teaching as the most practical means of accomplishing their major purpose. As early as the first years of the Republic serious concern was felt and expressed regarding the inadequate supply of qualified teachers. Plans were proposed to remedy the situation, and the

[9] The *Dallas Morning News,* December 16, 1929, p. 15.

[10] McConnell, W. J. *Op. cit.,* p. 194.

[11] Smith, J. W. *Survey of Development and Needs of the North Texas State Teachers College,* Chapters III and IV. Master's thesis, Southern Methodist University, Dallas, Tex., 1925. (Unpublished.)

encouragement given to private and denominational schools was prompted, in considerable degree, by the desire to train a corps of efficient teachers for the common schools.[12] However, it was not until 1879, four years after the framing of the present State Constitution, that the first state school for the training of teachers was opened. The Sam Houston Normal Institute at Huntsville began its first session on October 10, 1879 in the former Austin College building that had been given to the state by the citizens of the town. This was four years prior to the opening of the State University. Dates of the opening of other teacher-training schools were as follows: at Denton, 1901; at San Marcos, 1903; at Canyon, 1910; at Commerce, 1917; at Nacogdoches, 1918; and at Alpine, 1919.[13] The South Texas Normal College, which was opened at Kingsville in 1922, was changed to the Texas College of Arts and Industries in 1929, removed from the centrally administered group of teacher-training institutions, and placed under a separate board of regents.[14] The establishment and location of these institutions saw sectional claims and counter claims; the influence of bonuses offered by towns; the acceptance by the state of property formerly belonging to private schools; in fact, most of the factors generally operating in the location of normal schools as found by Humphreys.[15]

As the following census figures show, these colleges are located in small and very gradually growing towns.

Town	Population 1920	Population 1930
Alpine	931*	3,495
Canyon	1,618	2,821
Commerce	3,842	4,267
Denton	7,626	9,587
Huntsville	4,689	5,028
Nacogdoches	3,546	5,687
San Marcos	4,527	5,134

* Not considered complete.

Under acts of the legislature establishing the first four teacher-training schools—at Huntsville, Denton, San Marcos, and Canyon—

[12] Eby, Frederick. *Op. cit.*, pp. 292-97.

[13] *Fourth Biennial Report of the Texas Normal Schools*, Austin, Tex., 1919.

[14] *General and Special Laws Passed by the Regular Session of the 41st Legislature.* Chap. 286, pp. 627-31, 1929.

[15] Humphreys, H. C. *The Factors Operating in the Location of State Normal Schools.* Contributions to Education, No. 142, Bureau of Publications, Teachers College, Columbia University, 1923.

their control was vested in the State Board of Education. At that time this board was an ex-officio body composed of the governor, comptroller, and secretary of state, and through this board the management of minor business affairs of each institution was delegated to a local board of resident citizens. In 1911 at a special session of the 32nd Legislature the Normal School Board of Regents which was composed of the state superintendent of public instruction and four members appointed by the governor, was created. This act abolished the local boards of managers and vested complete control of all normal schools in the Board of Regents. Pursuant to the adoption of a constitutional amendment in 1912, which provided for terms of six years for all members of boards controlling the institutions of higher learning, the legislature in 1913 increased to six the members of the Normal School Board of Regents, and the state superintendent was not included.[16] The terms of members were so arranged that not more than two would retire at the end of each biennial period. In 1929 the number of members of the Board of Regents of the Texas State Teachers Colleges was increased to nine.[17] The 38th Legislature, in 1923, had established the title "Teachers Colleges" to be applied to all institutions formerly known as Normal Schools and Normal Colleges.[18]

Although Texas experimented for some time with the use of local boards in the administration of its teacher-training institutions, for nearly twenty years the state has had the benefit of the centralized control made possible by one board, and has avoided many undesirable and wasteful features which have been found under the multiple-board system.[19] However, a study of the minutes of the Board of Regents and its biennial reports shows that frequent attention has been given to minor executive details. Meetings have been held at irregular intervals and for varying periods of duration, as immediate needs have seemed to demand. No uniform system of reports has been used, and data presented have not been of general significance to teacher training as a homogeneous undertaking of the state. Evidently the administration of the institutions has been undergoing a

[16] *Revised Statutes of Texas* (1925), Chap. 9; and *Fourth Biennial Report of the Texas Normal Schools,* pp. 8-9.

[17] *General and Special Laws Passed by the Regular Session of the 41st Legislature,* Chap. 135, p. 295, 1929.

[18] *General Laws Passed by the Regular Session of the 38th Legislature,* Chap. 160, p. 341, 1923.

[19] A criticism of multiple boards is found in *The Professional Preparation of Teachers for American Public Schools,* Bulletin No. 14, 1920, of the Carnegie Foundation for the Advancement of Teaching, Chap. IV.

steady development, for the more recent reports show an increasing completeness and the later minutes indicate more systematic administrative procedures.

The Board of Regents of the State Teachers Colleges by no means controls the training of teachers within the state. Practically every institution of junior or senior collegiate rank in Texas is a teachers college in the sense that its students may be granted teachers' certifi-

CHART II

LOCATION OF TEXAS COLLEGES

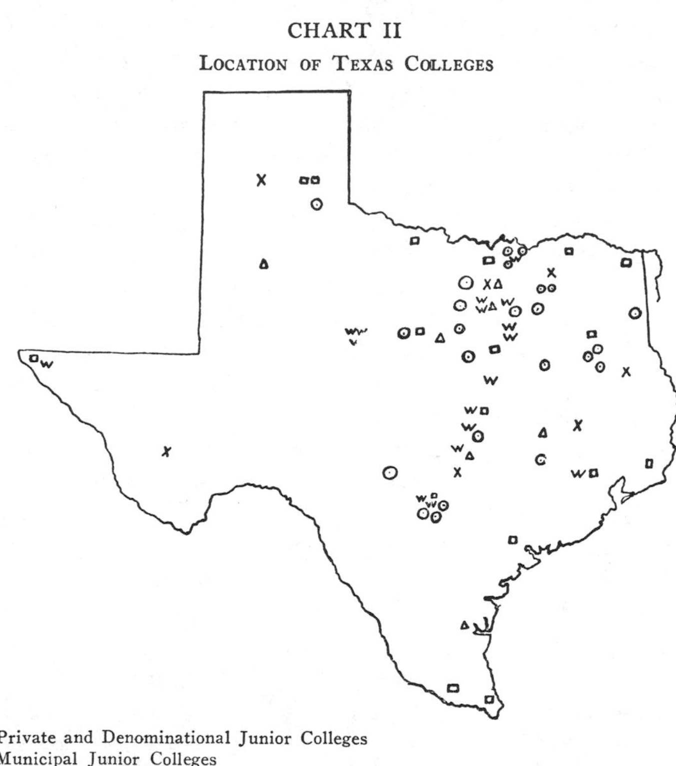

⊙ Private and Denominational Junior Colleges
□ Municipal Junior Colleges
x Teachers Colleges
Δ Other State Colleges
w Independent Senior Colleges

cates upon the basis of college credits earned. Near the close of 1929 reports show that the work of sixty-nine institutions, in addition to the seven teachers colleges, was accredited by the State Department of Education as the basis for certification of white teachers. Thirteen other colleges were accredited for colored students. The location of institutions for white students is shown in Chart II, from which it is

TABLE 3

NUMBER AND PER CENT OF TEACHERS' CERTIFICATES BASED ON CREDITS FROM VARIOUS TYPES OF INSTITUTIONS

Type of Institution	Number of Certificates Issued 1919–1928	Per Cent of Certificates
19 Independent senior colleges	18,053	20.9
8 Teachers colleges*	40,725	47.6
7 Other state-supported institutions	12,368	14.3
25 Independent junior colleges	4,726	5.5
17 Municipal junior colleges	1,763	2.0
13 Colleges for colored	8,340	9.7
Total	85,975	100.0

* The college at Kingsville is counted among teachers colleges in this report.

seen that most of these colleges are situated in a strip that extends from north to south through the middle of the state. There are few in the western part, although the eastern portion seems to be fairly well served. Table 3 shows the number and types of these institutions and the number of certificates issued based on credits earned during the ten-year period, 1919-28.[20]

TABLE 4

SOURCES OF CERTIFICATES FROM 1919 TO 1928

Year	Number of Certificates Based on Examination	Number of Certificates Based on College Credits	Total Number of Certificates Based on Examination and College Credits	Per Cent of Certificates Based on Examination	Per Cent of Certificates Based on College Credits
1919	4,808	4,158	8,966	54	46
1920	5,970	5,642	11,612	51	49
1921	5,534	6,446	11,980	46	54
1922	5,187	7,670	12,857	40	60
1923	6,473	8,377	14,850	44	56
1924	4,395	12,851	17,246	24	76
1925	4,787	9,906	14,691	33	67
1926	1,413	11,526	12,939	11	89
1927	1,125	13,209	14,334	8	92
1928	806	15,432	16,238	5	95*

* Reid, J. R. "The Certificate Pendulum," *Texas Outlook*, p. 35, August, 1929.

[20] Figures from a report of the State Department of Education, published in the *Texas Outlook*, p. 46, December, 1929. List of approved colleges, 1928, is found in the *Twenty-fifth Biennial Report of the State Department of Education*, pp. 116-18.

Five separate boards, in addition to the board for teachers colleges, control state-supported institutions. Each is autonomous in the administration of the institution it serves, and has no connection with the others. Independent and municipal colleges are controlled by their own governing bodies and by city school boards, respectively. By ordering their several institutions to comply with minimum statu-

TABLE 5

VALUATIONS OF PLANT AND EQUIPMENT*

ALPINE		
Grounds and improvements	$ 24,863.40	
Buildings	314,745.86	
Equipment	80,755.00	
Total Valuation		$ 420,364.26
CANYON		
Grounds, improvements, paving .	$ 94,868.56	
Buildings	971,467.49	
Equipment	222,544.78	
Total Valuation		$1,288,880.83
COMMERCE		
Buildings and grounds	$814,734.56	
Equipment	142,417.48	
Total Valuation		$ 957,152.04
DENTON		
Grounds	$214,969.89	
Buildings	684,391.27	
Equipment	505,713.33	
Total Valuation		$1,405,074.49
HUNTSVILLE		
Grounds	$104,376.30	
Buildings	578,430.66	
Equipment	202,861.82	
Total Valuation		$ 885,668.78
NACOGDOCHES		
Grounds	$ 65,796.64	
Buildings	426,836.97	
Equipment	94,242.78	
Total Valuation		$ 586,876.39
SAN MARCOS		
Grounds	$ 68,000.00	
Buildings	461,000.00	
Equipment	107,775.00	
Total Valuation		$ 636,775.00
Grand Total Valuation		$6,180,791.79

* Figures taken from the *Tenth Biennial Report of the Board of Regents,* for the biennium ending August 31, 1930.

tory requirements[21] as to standards and facilities of instruction, these governing boards can make them institutions for teacher training.

The accrediting of colleges offering work upon which teachers' certificates may be based, together with the abolishing in 1925 of all certificates based on examination, except three-year certificates, which are not valid in first- and second-class high schools,[22] has had a pronounced effect upon certification of teachers in Texas. (See Table 4.) This is emphasized by an excerpt from a report of the Chairman of the State Board of Examiners: "Records of certification of teachers in the public schools of Texas are not available for years prior to 1919, but if they were the percentage columns would possibly show about the same results, in reverse order, for the very early years of certification of teachers as those they show for 1928."

Texas is evidently committed to the policy of securing college-trained teachers for the public schools. It is predicted that the next change in the certification laws will abolish examinations as a basis for certification and make college training prerequisite to the issuance of all certificates. The fact that nearly half, 47.6 per cent, of the college certificates issued from 1919 to 1928 were based on credits earned in the teachers colleges indicates the importance of these institutions, among many other colleges, to the public free school system of the state. It is, therefore, considered worth while to examine the investment which the commonwealth has made in the physical equipment of these institutions, and the extent to which it supports them.

TABLE 6

VALUATIONS PER CAPITA OF STUDENTS ENROLLED*

	ENROLLMENT	VALUATION PER CAPITA
Alpine	281	$1,496
Canyon	711	1,728
Commerce	1,158	826
Denton	1,603	876
Huntsville	660	1,311
Nacogdoches	539	1,088
San Marcos	1,030	618
Total	5,982	$1,134 (Average)

* Based on enrollment for the winter term, 1930, as shown in Table 10.

[21] *Revised Statutes of Texas*, Article 2888, 1925.

[22] *Laws, Rules and Regulations Governing State Teachers' Certificates*. Bulletin No. 252, February, 1929, State Department of Education.

The figures presented in Tables 5 and 6 show that the State of Texas has an investment of more than six million dollars in the physical plants of the seven institutions that have been established to prepare teachers for the public schools, an investment of $1,134 per student based on the enrollment for the winter term of 1930. Wide variations are noted in the total valuations and in the per capita valuations as shown. The college at San Marcos has the lowest per-capita valuation, $618, and the college at Denton has third from the lowest, $876, although it has the highest total valuation. The college at Commerce, with a total valuation proportionately little less than that at Canyon, shows a per capita valuation of slightly less than half that at the latter school. Definite data in explanation of variations have not been found, but evidently the state has invested funds for capital outlay on some other basis than student load. However, as shown in subsequent tables, it is the practice at all institutions to use local funds to make investments for capital outlay. Texas compares favorably with other states in the matter of buildings and equipment of the institutions established for the training of white teachers. Figures for the years 1927-1928[23] show only three states, Missouri, Pennsylvania, and Wisconsin, in which larger amounts have been invested in state-owned institutions of that character. The confidence of Texas in professional schools for teachers, as thus expressed, is noteworthy, in view of the fact that many other colleges within the state are engaged in similar work.

The purpose of Table 7 is to show the tendency in regard to the means of financing capital outlays in the Texas teachers colleges. The figures for the year indicated are typical of years when no major appropriations are granted for new buildings. A considerable proportion, ranging from 21 per cent to 77 per cent, of expenditures for ordinary capital outlays is financed from local funds. Each school maintains its own accounting records and organization and none distributes expenditures to the functions used by the United States Office of Education. It is not certain that the amounts shown include all expenditures for capital outlays since uniform headings were not employed in reports from which data were derived. However, the percentages shown to be drawn from local funds are perhaps indicative of the exact situation. Local funds are derived from such sources as gifts from local organizations and individuals, student

[23] *Statistics of Teachers Colleges and Normal Schools, 1927-1928,* United States Bureau of Education Bulletin, 1929, No. 14, p. 13.

TABLE 7

AMOUNTS AND PERCENTAGES FROM LOCAL FUNDS INVESTED IN PERMANENT IMPROVEMENTS AND EQUIPMENT DURING THE YEAR ENDING AUGUST 31, 1929. (Departmental Maintenance not Included.)*

	AMOUNT FROM LOCAL FUNDS	PER CENT LOCAL FUNDS
Alpine	$17,972.04	77
Canyon	12,912.10	25
Commerce	10,327.11	67
Denton	42,978.72	67
Huntsville	12,941.08	41 †
Nacogdoches	2,073.03	52
San Marcos	6,365.88	21

* Data from the *Tenth Biennial Report of the Board of Regents*, and auditors' reports.

† An expenditure of $136,813.67 from a major state appropriation for a new building was omitted in determining this per cent, since no other college had a major building appropriation available that year.

fees, receipts from athletic games and from public entertainments, income from dormitories, cafeterias, bookstores, and textbook rentals, interest on bank deposits, and receipts from publications. Items of capital outlay financed by local funds were found to include: driveways and walks, tennis courts, fences, grandstands and athletic fields, furniture and other equipment, outdoor theaters, minor buildings, trucks and busses, water systems, and remodeling of buildings.

The importance of contributions made by the local funds toward the financing of salaries and departmental maintenance is presented in Table 8. Table 9 shows the percentage of each local fund coming from the matriculation fees of students. Conferences with administrative officials have given the information that matriculation fees are used for the payment of salaries, although reports of the Board of Regents and of auditors do not indicate this fact. First-hand knowledge of practices leads to the opinion that many of the items of expenditure from local funds which are charged in the reports to departmental maintenance are really expenditures for items of capital outlay. Approximately half the total expended for departmental maintenance by all seven institutions, during the biennium for which figures are shown, came from local funds—51 per cent in the first year and 44 per cent in the second. The very great difference in these percentages among the several schools is noticeable and cannot be accounted for on the basis of state policy. The colleges at Denton and at Commerce, leading in enrollment, show the highest

TABLE 8

TOTAL AMOUNTS EXPENDED FOR SALARIES AND DEPARTMENTAL MAINTENANCE DURING 1928–1929 AND 1929–1930; AND PERCENTAGES DRAWN FROM LOCAL FUNDS *

	For Salaries				For Departmental Maintenance			
	1928–1929		1929–1930		1928–1929		1929–1930	
	Total Amount	Per Cent from Local Fund	Total Amount	Per Cent from Local Fund	Total Amount	Per Cent from Local Fund	Total Amount	Per Cent from Local Fund
Alpine	$ 107,735.25	6	$ 100,784.92	7	$ 12,179.09	4	$ 10,569.13	3
Canyon	267,375.31	10	253,576.06	12	23,098.65	42	17,540.47	28
Commerce	279,765.19	13	280,261.34	12	22,806.87	64	23,324.25	60
Denton	418,569.23	6	405,840.58	9	34,641.86	73	19,103.80	71
Huntsville	241,941.91	7	239,819.30	8	34,478.56	46	8,894.85	20
Nacogdoches	193,500.34	7	189,540.15	7	11,509.22	46	16,341.67	54
San Marcos	275,007.02	10	262,837.87	7	20,534.14	44	8,313.62	20
Total	$1,183,894.25	9	$1,732,660.22	9.6	$159,248.39	51	$104,087.79	44

* Figures from the *Tenth Biennial Report* of the Board of Regents.

TABLE 9

AMOUNTS OF MATRICULATION FEES AND THEIR PER CENTS OF TOTAL LOCAL FUND RECEIPTS FOR EACH YEAR OF THE BIENNIUM 1928–1930*

	1928–1929		1929–1930	
	Amount, Matriculation Fees	Per Cent of Total Local Fund	Amount, Matriculation Fees	Per Cent of Total Local Fund
Alpine	$ 15,253.50	20	$ 11,960.00	24
Canyon	37,685.20	18	56,018.58†	20
Commerce	57,710.00	42	55,255.00	41
Denton	83,329.39	50	99,353.15	55
Huntsville	40,379.50	31	87,469.50‡	72
Nacogdoches	32,622.47	43	26,246.00	41
San Marcos	49,475.00	34	48,660.00	31
Total	$316,455.06	34	$384,962.23	43

* Data from the *Tenth Biennial Report* of the Board of Regents.

† Fees, fines, and miscellaneous receipts. ‡ Fees and fines in one sum.

TABLE 10

ENROLLMENT OF STUDENTS OF COLLEGE RANK FOR EACH OF FOUR TYPICAL TERMS *

College	Spring, 1929	Fall, 1929	Winter, 1930	Summer, 1929
Alpine	258	255	281	594
Canyon	720	752	711	1,126
Commerce	1,217	887	1,158	2,165
Denton	1,577	1,387	1,603	3,308
Huntsville	772	674	660	1,525
Nacogdoches	701	526	539	1,070
San Marcos	1,254	891	1,030	2,065
Total	6,499	5,372	5,982	11,853

* Data from direct reports of the registrars.

per cents of departmental maintenance paid from local funds. The smallest college shows 4 per cent and 3 per cent of maintenance expense paid from that source. Approximately 9 per cent of salaries at all institutions were paid from local funds. These salaries as reported include those for operation and maintenance of the plants, as well as those for instruction. Use of local funds for salaries varies from 6 per cent to 13 per cent among the institutions.

It is pertinent to notice here the provisions of a statute generally known as the Pollard Act, which was approved in March, 1927.[24] This statute limits the matriculation fees which may be collected from a student in state institutions of higher education to $30.00 per term of nine months, and to $5.00 per term of six weeks. Laboratory fees are limited to $4.00 per student per course in any year. Optional fees for the support of student activities are, however, permitted. This act appears to be an expression of a state policy to provide higher education largely at public expense. Yet, considering the large proportions of capital outlays, salaries, and departmental maintenance financed by local funds, the policy seems to be nullified. Among the teachers colleges, those having the greatest student load find it necessary to pay the largest proportion of current expenses from local funds. It will be noticed from a study of Tables 9 and 10 that the percentages of local funds coming from matriculation fees tend to be directly proportional to the enrollment.

The situation just described tends to bring about certain undesir-

[24] *General and Special Laws Passed by the Regular Session of the 40th Legislature*, Chap. 237.

able conditions and to lead away from an effective state program. It encourages institutional autonomy by placing the administrative staff of each college in a position to regard an increasing enrollment as necessary to adequate financial support. Requests for state appropriations are likely to be based on enrollment figures, but failing to secure appropriations in the amounts asked for, the institution has recourse to the local fund, as augmented by the increased enrollment. State legislators and executives, in their efforts to promote economy, gradually come to see in local funds a real and valid reason for limiting appropriations. Under a law which limits matriculation fees, a state institution will likely discover a large enrollment to be a fiscal liability rather than an asset. The report of the study of teachers colleges in Missouri has the following to say in regard to financial support:

> There seems no justification for such variation in these matters [collection and use of fees]. Assuming that the State intended its teachers' colleges to provide professional training for teachers, free from tuition, student fees should not be spent for instructional salaries. Likewise it seems unjust to take from the students of any year the money for any items which might be classed as capital outlay, such as additions to buildings, fixed equipment or permanent improvements. Much could be done to remedy this variety of practice by listing specifically the services which are to be provided the students as a result of their student fees or the activities of the college to which student fees may be applied.[25]

However, irregularity of support, with the consequent embarrassment to administration, has obtained in most of the states. Hamilton[26] found that the states almost uniformly established a policy of charging no fees to those preparing to teach; yet is forced to conclude that the state teachers college is a product of evolution in that no state projected a college in planning for training teachers. The result has been that such institutions have been handicapped financially. Frasier and Whitney[27] report that there is a recent tendency to raise student fees in higher educational institutions of all classes and to make students bear a larger proportion of the cost of their

[25] Division of Field Studies, Institute of Educational Research, Teachers College, Columbia University, *Preliminary Report on Publicly Supported Higher Education in the State of Missouri,* p. 396, 1929. (This publication will be referred to hereafter as *Report on Publicly Supported Higher Education.*)

[26] Hamilton, F. R. *Fiscal Support of State Teachers Colleges,* Chap. I. Contributions to Education, No. 165, Bureau of Publications, Teachers College, Columbia University, 1924.

[27] Frasier, George W. and Whitney, Frederick L. *Teachers College Finance,* Chap. IX. Colorado State Teachers College, 1930.

education. State teachers colleges are reflecting this tendency to which is ascribed, as a contributing cause, the unwillingness of state legislatures to provide adequately for rapid increases in student enrollment. These authors protest against a state policy that would place financial barriers in the way of securing ultimately a competent master teacher for every schoolroom.

Additional evidence of the irregularity and uncertainty of the financial support given to the Texas teachers colleges is obtained from a study of the Acts of the Legislature making appropriations. Although each institution prepares and submits to the State Board of Control its budgetary estimates nine or ten months in advance of the date of the biennial sessions of the legislature, appropriations have been delayed until a few weeks before they are actually to be used. The Board of Control is empowered to prepare the budget covering the needs of all state activities, yet its recommendations need not be, and are not in practice, followed by the legislatures. The general appropriations for the biennium of 1927-1929 were not approved until June 17, 1927, about three months before the opening of the next regular session.[28] For the biennium of 1929-1931 appropriations were not finally filed with the Secretary of State until August 9, 1929, four or five weeks before the beginning of the year's work.[29] The colleges were not assured of appropriations for their summer sessions of 1929 until March 23 of that year,[30] and on April 9, 1930 appropriations were approved for the support of the summer sessions of that year.[31] However, as is shown in Table 10, the teachers colleges must care for a student load in the summer sessions that is practically double that of any term of the regular session. In order to complete the payment of salaries for the summer of 1928, an emergency appropriation was made in March, 1929.[32] Funds for the support of the summer sessions of 1931 had not been appropriated up to February 20 of that year, but at that date were still subject to the action of a conference committee of the House and Senate.[33]

[28] *General and Special Laws Passed by the First Called Session of the 40th Legislature,* Chap. 101.

[29] *General Laws Passed by the Second and Third Called Sessions of the 41st Legislature,* Chap. 15.

[30] *General and Special Laws Passed by the Regular Session of the 41st Legislature,* Chap. 228.

[31] *General Laws Passed by the Fourth and Fifth Called Sessions of the 41st Legislature,* Chap. 85.

[32] *Laws Passed by the Regular Session of the 41st Legislature,* Chap. 184.

[33] The *Dallas Morning News,* February 21, 1931, p. 3; *Denton Record-Chronicle* of the same date, p. 1.

Such obvious handicaps to administration are not confined to the teachers colleges. No state educational institution is able to make definite arrangements for an adequate staff or to plan a curricular program far enough in advance to assure its rendering the maximum service. The tendency of the plan used in Texas is to make lobbyists of the administrative officers whose principal tasks should be found on the campuses of their own institutions. Certainly a complete and efficient program of preparation for the proper number of teachers for the public schools of the state is impossible with no systematic financial support. Permanent salary schedules with provisions for promotions and sabbatical leaves for study, generally considered necessary to the building of the highest type of teaching staff, must await a more stable system of support.

The United States Office of Education reports total current expenditures of normal schools and teachers colleges under six main heads or functions, in accordance with what is known as the standard system of accounting in education. The six functions are: (1) administration (or general control), (2) instructional service, (3) operation of the school plant, (4) maintenance of the school plant, (5) auxiliary agencies and sundry activities, (6) fixed charges. Expenditures for capital outlays are not included in current expenditures under that system. The plan of accounting used in the Texas teachers colleges, as shown by auditors' reports and reports of the Board of Regents, does not distribute expenditures under those headings. A typical list of expenditure classifications found in Texas reports is as follows, although they are not uniform in all the colleges: salaries, departmental maintenance, repairs and improvements, new buildings, print shop, cafeteria, dormitories, miscellaneous, student activities, and extension department.

An attempt was made in this study to determine with some accuracy the cost of training teachers in Texas teachers colleges upon some unit basis. It was found, however, that data would not be available for that purpose without prohibitive expense. Data sheets on finance were not completely filled out as official records were found inadequate. That such a situation is not peculiar to Texas, or to teacher-training institutions, is shown by Stevens and Elliott in their study of unit costs in higher education:

A reconnaissance of this particular field of public finance soon revealed the clear but disconcerting fact that any basic survey of support and costs which might have value for the higher institutions of the country as a whole was entirely beyond the resources of the Inquiry. Without excessive labor, but few of our public or private schools are able to furnish, from current records, accurate financial data other than those of gross totals of annual income and expenditures. The United States Bureau of Education had already found it practically impossible to collect, on a country-wide basis, properly classified facts of the expenditures of even the tax-supported institutions of higher education. Published financial reports, by reason of multifarious classifications of accounts, seldom reveal facts serviceable for comparative purposes. In a few instances, institutions keenly aware of the significance of knowing the facts controlling their economic strength, have had the foresight to set up accounting and statistical procedures which will enable their executive officers to guide their operation with wisdom and confidence.[34]

Frasier and Whitney[35] also point out the difficulties encountered in determining unit costs in the field of teacher training; nevertheless they emphasize the importance and value of knowing such facts, and enumerate eight types of bases that have been proposed for use in computing unit costs. Facts relative to such costs are necessary for the establishment of proper standards for appropriations, and are valuable to the internal administration of an institution in justifying the several departments and activities. The authors just mentioned use as the most practical basis the student clock-hour, which means one hour of instruction for one student. The United States Office of Education has used the student unit, based on equivalent enrollment, in its reports. Equivalent enrollment, or the average annual carrying load, is computed as follows: The student census figures for each of the three terms of the thirty-six weeks' session are added, and the sum divided by 3; where the summer quarter is divided into two six weeks' terms, the enrollments for the two terms are added and the sum divided by 6; the sum of the two quotients gives the equivalent enrollment.[36] However, since the reports from the Texas colleges did not show enrollment for the two six-weeks' terms of the summer session separately, the equivalent enrollment, as given in Table 10, was computed on the basis of four typical quarters. Because it was impossible from data available to determine accurately total current expense and equivalent enrollment, the per-student costs, as shown in Table 11, can be considered merely suggestive.

[34] Stevens, E. B. and Elliott, E. C. "Unit Costs of Higher Education." *The Educational Finance Inquiry Reports,* Vol. 13, p. 3. The Macmillan Company, 1925.

[35] Frasier, George W. and Whitney, Frederick L. *Teachers College Finance,* Chap. IV. Colorado State Teachers College, 1930.

[36] Stevens, E. B. and Elliott, E. C. *Op. cit.,* Vol. 13, p. 3.

TABLE 11

ANNUAL PER-STUDENT COSTS ON THE BASIS OF EQUIVALENT ENROLLMENT FOR SALARIES, DEPARTMENTAL MAINTENANCE, AND STUDENT ACTIVITIES

	EQUIVALENT ENROLLMENT	PER-STUDENT COST
Alpine	347	$349
Canyon	827	353
Commerce	1,357	244
Denton	1,963	231
Huntsville	908	305
Nacogdoches	709	315
San Marcos	1,310	223
Average		$289

Enrollments shown in this table are based on figures given in Table 6 and do not include training-school pupils. Three classifications of expenditures as reported were used to represent current expense—salaries, departmental maintenance, and student activities. Other classifications, as shown in the *Tenth Biennial Report* of the Board of Regents, were too uncertain to be employed as items in current expense. In so far as the classifications used are uniform among the several colleges the per-capita costs as shown are comparable. The size of the student body seems to be an important factor in the cost per student. The facts in that respect, as shown here, are in accord with the findings of the United States Office of Education as to per-capita costs in state teachers colleges throughout the nation:[37]

ENROLLMENT	PER-STUDENT COST
Fewer than 400	$439.67
400– 799	355.37
800–1,199	297.74
1,200–1,599	233.51
1,600–1,999	194.80
Seven schools with more than 2,000	263.46

Per-capita costs for current expenses at five Texas teachers colleges are shown in the Office of Education circular just referred to; and while they do not agree with figures arrived at in this study, they

[37] Phillips, Frank M. *Per-Capita Costs in Teacher-training Institutions, 1927-1928.* United States Bureau of Education, Statistical Circular No. 11, January, 1929.

serve to show comparisons among teacher-training institutions of thirty-five states. According to figures there presented the average cost per student for current expense in the five Texas teachers colleges reporting was $184.78. Only seventeen schools of the 117 reporting to the Office showed a lower cost than this average. Five of them were in Oklahoma, two in California, one was in Illinois, one in Maine, two were in Missouri, one was in New York, one in Virginia, one in West Virginia, and three were in Texas.

It is recognized by modern students of educational administration that the physical equipment of an institution sets a very definite limit to the program of educational service it is able to offer, and that well-kept grounds and buildings justify the necessary investment. Texas has invested more than six million dollars in the plants of its teachers colleges (Table 5). It is, therefore, desirable to examine these plants from the standpoint of the functions they are to serve. In recent years the use of score cards has been found valuable in studying the physical plants and equipment of schools. While it is not claimed that these cards are absolutely objective instruments of measurement, they do, with their accompanying standards, represent the consensus of judgments on the part of expert students as to the best now known in regard to physical equipment. Such a score card and standards have been developed for teacher-training institutions.[38] By use of the score card close analysis of each item which composes the entire physical plant can be made and each element evaluated. The total possible score of 1,000 points represents an ideal situation for every item; one which no institution that has existed for a number of years could be expected to attain. Neither would it likely be achieved by a young institution unless liberal appropriations and careful planning had been available in its construction. A score of 800 or more is considered indicative of very efficient equipment for a teachers college, while scores between 600 and 800 show that institutions so rated are well provided for as compared to the average for the country.[39] Any of a number of factors may reduce the score allotted to an institution which has some very excellent features in its physical equipment. Among these are: inaccessibility of the location of the college, which is affected by the number and condition of roads and by general trans-

[38] Evenden, E. S., Strayer, G. D. and Engelhardt, N. L. *Score Card for Physical Plant of Normal Schools and Teachers Colleges.* Bureau of Publications, Teachers College, Columbia University, 1929.

[39] *Report on Publicly Supported Higher Education,* pp. 290-292.

portation facilities. The presence of old, unsuitable, or poorly maintained buildings among others more modern will lower the rating, as will the lack of modern service systems, such as heating and ventilating, cleaning, fire protection, and others. The lack of adequate and properly designed and equipped classrooms, laboratories, and shops, and the presence of inadequate or ill-adapted practice school rooms will detract from the score. A lowered rating will also result if any of the following items are lacking or are not up to standard: administration offices and facilities, library (including reading and seminar rooms), auditoriums and assembly rooms, health and recreation facilities, dormitories, lunchrooms, and student activity and social rooms. According to the weighting scheme used in the Evenden, Strayer, Engelhardt Score Card, relatively great importance is attached to instruction rooms and practice school rooms and the equipment of these units—a total of 400 of the 1,000 points being allotted to these two general items.

In evaluating the physical plants of the Texas teachers colleges an attempt was made to secure two independent scores for each—one made by an administrative officer of the college and the other by the writer. The scores shown in Table 12 represent an average of these. Granting that they may be slightly high, the total scores, ranging from 690 to 805, indicate that these colleges are comparatively well equipped, and that administrators have given consistent attention to this important feature. Improvements definitely provided for or projected will, when realized, result in higher scores for several of the institutions. Certain of them are discounted in the scoring because of the general inaccessibility of the towns in which they are located, or because of the small size or unsuitable character of their campuses. By reference to Table 6 and Table 12 it is noticed that the total scores allotted to these institutions are closely proportional to the valuations of their plants per student.

An attempt to analyze the percentages shown in Table 12 focuses attention on certain features which are deserving of consideration in view of the major function of these institutions. The per cents allotted to the practice school facilities, with one exception, indicate the necessity of improving what is considered by students of teacher training the most important and characteristic part of professional schools. The high score given to the practice school at Canyon is due to the well-planned building completed there just a few years ago, and to the comparatively small number of college students to be

TABLE 12

SCORES ALLOTTED TO THE PHYSICAL PLANTS OF THE TEXAS TEACHERS COLLEGES SHOWING MAXIMUM POSSIBLE SCORES, ALLOTTED SCORES, AND THE PER CENTS ALLOTTED SCORES ARE OF POSSIBLE SCORES

	Total Score		Site		Buildings		Service Systems		Instruction Rooms		Practice School		General Units	
	Allotted Score	Per Cent	Allotted Score	Per Cent	Allotted Score	Per Cent	Allotted Score	Per Cent	Allotted Score	Per Cent	Allotted Score	Per Cent	Allotted Score	Per Cent
Maximum Possible Score	1000		110		155		175		220		180		160	
Alpine	751	75.1	75	68	132	85	137	79	184	84	97	54	121	76
Canyon	805	80.5	98	89	124	80	124	71	182	83	169	94	108	67
Commerce	690	69.0	104	94	97	62	111	63	159	72	129	71	90	56
Denton	723	72.3	100	91	130	80	130	75	177	80	92	51	94	59
Huntsville	726	72.6	87	79	114	73	121	69	181	82	121	67	93	58
Nacogdoches	743	74.3	88	80	142	92	131	74	167	76	128	71	87	54
San Marcos	705	70.5	67	61	114	73	117	67	160	73	146	81	101	63

furnished practice facilities. The college at Alpine, having no practice school on its campus, is compelled to use rooms in the town school building, located a considerable distance from the college. These rooms are not constructed for use as practice units. At Denton the score represents the inadequacy, in proportion to college enrollment, of the practice school facilities, as well as the lack of complete equipment for the high-school division of the school. In general, but to a lesser degree, similar conditions exist at the other institutions.

The scores allotted to general units mentioned above, which serve the institution as a whole, show that the colleges have given less attention to these than to other parts of their plants. The state has made no appropriations for dormitories or dining rooms at the teachers colleges. Where such are found they represent either a heritage from the private school which preceded the state institution, or the investment of private capital. Lack of adequate and suitable buildings and equipment for libraries at certain institutions detracts from the scores. Emphasis seems to be placed on athletic facilities, above provision for health and general recreation by some colleges, and even then the athletic plant does not closely approach the standard in each. Auditoriums and minor assembly rooms are needed at a few colleges as are also student activity rooms. In some instances administrative offices are crowded and not conveniently arranged; adequate fireproof vaults for the storage of important financial and personnel records seem to be a general need.

The American Association of Teachers Colleges, since its organization in 1923, has been interested in library facilities. This interest has stressed the working materials in the library above buildings and furniture, and has constantly been apparent in standards which have been published from year to year. The intensive study of libraries by Rosenlof,[40] authorized by the Association, is another evidence of this interest, and of the importance accorded to such facilities by those actively engaged in teacher training. The standards adopted in 1930 require four-year institutions to have at least 15,000 volumes, exclusive of public documents and bound periodicals. And it is suggested that this minimum be increased to 25,000 by 1940. In computing the number of volumes in any library not more than

[40] Rosenlof, G. W. *Library Facilities of Teacher-Training Institutions.* Contributions to Education, No. 347, Bureau of Publications, Teachers College, Columbia University, 1929.

15 per cent shall be allowed for duplicates. A further requirement states that books should be distributed, according to the Dewey system, approximately as follows:

		Per Cent
000–099.9	General, Library Economy and Bound Periodicals	7.5
100–199.9	Philosophy and Psychology	5.0
200–299.9	Religion and Bible Stories	2.5
300–399.9	Sociology and Education	20.0
400–499.9	Language and Philology	2.5
500–599.9	Sciences	7.5
600–699.9	Useful Arts	7.5
700–799.9	Fine Arts	5.0
800–899.9	Literature	20.0
900–999.9	History and Geography	20.0

Not fewer than 150 appropriate periodicals are required. The recommendations go further than the standards in suggesting training school libraries, size of the library staff, annual expenditures in the budget, and general physical equipment.[41] While he disclaimed any great virtue in considering the number of library books per student, Rosenlof found an average of 18 per student in 63 degree-granting institutions, and a range of from 4 to 68. He concluded that practically no improvement is being made in this particular and that the library is being neglected.[42]

Partial data concerning the libraries of the Texas teachers colleges were obtainable during the progress of this study, but it seems evident that more exact methods are needed in compiling continuously information of this nature at each institution. To render maximum service in a professional institution a library should maintain records of materials available—their nature and extent—of the degree of its usefulness, and of its development in proportion to the growth of the institution. The facts presented in Table 13 show that the libraries of these colleges, with the exception of the two most recently established, have a greater number of volumes than the minimum set by the American Association of Teachers Colleges. The number of periodicals available in three of them exceeds the minimum standard. While no separate item in published reports of disbursements is devoted to expenditures for libraries, the number of volumes added to stock and bound during the year 1928-29 indicates a commendable effort to keep these libraries growing. The reports of

[41] *Ninth Yearbook of the American Association of Teachers Colleges,* pp. 15-17.
[42] *Ibid.,* pp. 23-24.

TABLE 13

DATA CONCERNING LIBRARIES

	ALPINE	COM-MERCE	DENTON	HUNTS-VILLE	NACOG-DOCHES	SAN MARCOS
Total number of volumes	12,362	22,000	29,050	27,000	12,970	29,800
Number of magazines ..	115	123	154	175	112	198
Number of newspapers ..	7	10	10	6	8	8
Capacity reading rooms .	300	200	250	270	250	500
Total circulation for year	32,076	187,593	210,850	—	91,345	250,000
Per-student circulation ..	92	137	102	—	128	190
Volumes added 1928–1929	2,033	1,497	4,449	2,500	950	4,000
Volumes bound 1928–1929	250	60	561	500	90	2,000
Hours library open daily.	9	8½	10	9	—	11

circulation of books might be taken as an index of a library's usefulness, and possibly of teaching methods used in the institution. Based on equivalent enrollment as shown in Table 11, the annual per-student circulation ranged from 92 to 190.

Certain other published studies have made valuable contributions toward the solution of the library problems which are inseparably connected with the development of a program of teacher training. Among them Works's[43] investigation of general college and university libraries presented certain findings and conclusions which are significant and which have value for those administratively responsible for the development and conduct of libraries in teachers colleges. A scarcity of records to show the growth and service of libraries was discovered which rendered direct comparisons between institutions unreliable. Since 1900 the number of volumes in libraries has increased more rapidly than the number of students. Regular enrollment was not considered the most important factor in the growth of a college library. Such growth is affected more directly by the methods of instruction, by the increase in graduate students and courses, and by the very large increase in the size of summer schools. The increasing demand for duplicate copies and the use of reserved books, due to changes from the textbook method of instruction, were found to contribute greatly to the work of the library staff. Colleges included in the study kept their libraries open for an average of 78 hours per week, and devoted from 34 per cent to 72 per cent of total library expenditures to paying the cost of library service. In

[43] Works, George A. *College and University Library Problems*, Chap. 2. American Library Association, 1927.

general it was concluded that inadequate consideration had been given to the status and compensation of the workers in the library. At certain institutions libraries were found to be developing their extension service at a very rapid rate and to be carrying out a policy of inter-library loans. Hamilton[44] found evidence to indicate that the libraries in teachers colleges have been receiving very limited financial support, and that the amounts devoted to that purpose vary greatly among such institutions. He concluded that the development of efficient libraries in teacher-training institutions is primarily a fiscal problem.

The percentages of utilization that are made of teachers college buildings constitute an important type of information for administrators. Efforts to arrive at such percentages present a series of complicated difficulties. No studies of this problem as it affects teachers colleges have been found which are comparable to the thorough study of utilization of high-school buildings made by Morphet.[45] That study developed criteria to bring about uniformity in computing utilization, set up certain techniques to be used in computing percentages of utilization, pointed out the factors most likely to influence the percentage of utilization of a building, suggested, as a result of findings, the probable maximum utilization of each type of room, and proposed steps that should be taken in analyzing specific situations to determine the degree of congestion. For obvious reasons a teachers college presents a situation different from that in a high school, so that findings for the two will have little comparable value. Morphet employed two units in his investigation, namely, room utilization and pupil station utilization.[46] If it were possible to use any building to 100 per cent capacity for both units, it would mean that each room of whatever character was filled to capacity every available hour in the day, six days in the week.

The need of additional buildings can be most accurately shown in terms of the per cent of utilization of those on the campus, provided none of the following is contemplated or expected: (1) significant changes in or additions to the curricula; (2) multiplication of electives; or (3) an unusual increase in the number of students. Also, a reliable check on the efficiency of the schedule and the sectionizing of classes is made possible by the determination of utilization per-

[44] Hamilton, F. R. *Op. cit.*, pp. 29-33, 1924.

[45] Morphet, Edgar L. *The Measurement and Interpretation of School Building Utilization.* Contributions to Education, No. 264. Bureau of Publications, Teachers College, Columbia University, 1927. [46] *Ibid.*, Chaps. IV and V.

centages. Certain varying and interrelated factors are to be considered in finding the room accommodations needed at any institution. Among these are: (1) the number of periods in the day and the number of days in the week used in the schedule; (2) the size of classes; (3) special types of rooms required by the curricula and courses offered; (4) the use of certain rooms for several different purposes; and (5) the changing enrollment from term to term. When such factors have been considered, it has been estimated that a reasonable standard for the utilization of classrooms in teachers colleges is from 50 per cent to 75 per cent of their capacity; and for laboratories (except a few highly specialized ones) not less than 40 per cent.[47]

Investigation of the utilization of rooms in the Texas teachers colleges revealed the fact that data bearing on that problem are not generally available. Once record forms are set up, however, the task of recording for each term rooms in use during each period, the student capacity of each, and the number of students scheduled for each would be comparatively simple. Since such records are not uniformly and completely kept, it is possible to show in Table 14 the facts for only five of the institutions. The percentages are based on the number of periods actually used in the schedule at each. The maximum number per day for both lecture rooms and laboratories at any college was nine, the minimum for lecture rooms five, and for laboratories seven. All institutions reporting used a six-day week. The greater the number of periods in the schedule the higher the room capacity. For example, a school using a six-period day would increase the capacity of its rooms 33 1/3 per cent by adopting an eight-period day. It is obvious also that increasing the capacity lowers the percentage of actual use. The percentages of utilization shown for those colleges having five- and six-period days would be considerably lowered if their room capacity were based on an eight-period day, as is shown in Table 15. It is doubtful whether a college schedule of less than eight periods per day can be successfully defended as an efficient use of buildings. The maximum weekly utilization found for lecture rooms was 78.2 per cent, based on a five-period daily schedule. School No. 2 shows a utilization of 65.5 per cent for lecture rooms and 38.2 per cent for laboratories, both based on a nine-period day schedule. The minimum utilization found was 48 per cent and 25.8 per cent for lecture rooms and labora-

[47] *Report on Publicly Supported Higher Education,* p. 314.

TABLE 14

PERCENTAGES OF ROOM UTILIZATION (LECTURE ROOMS AND LABORATORIES), DAILY AND FOR THE WEEK, IN FIVE COLLEGES. WINTER TERM, 1930

	Monday		Tuesday		Wednesday		Thursday		Friday		Saturday		Weekly Total	
	Per Cent Lecture Room	Per Cent Laboratory	Per Cent Lecture Room	Per Cent Laboratory	Per Cent Lecture Room	Per Cent Laboratory	Per Cent Lecture Room	Per Cent Laboratory	Per Cent Lecture Room	Per Cent Laboratory	Per Cent Lecture Room	Per Cent Laboratory	Per Cent Lecture Room	Per Cent Laboratory
School No. 1 *	53	24.5	62	33.7	56	22	54.5	45.9	53	24.5	48.5	34.7	54.5	30
School No. 2 †	65.5	39	65.5	36	65.5	39	65.5	36	65.5	39	65.5	36	65.5	38
School No. 3 ‡	54.5	26.1	42.6	17.6	55	29.5	42.9	17.8	55	42.2	37.5	10.2	48	25.8
School No. 4 §	73	29	83	45	73	25	83	53	73	20	83	25	78.2	32.6
School No. 5 **	62.7	33	50.7	23	62.7	34	50.7	25	62.7	34	50.7	11	56.6	27.2

* Scheduled six lecture periods and seven laboratory periods per day.
† Scheduled nine lecture periods and nine laboratory periods per day.
‡ Scheduled eight lecture periods and eight laboratory periods per day.
§ Scheduled five lecture periods and seven laboratory periods per day.
** Scheduled nine lecture periods and eight laboratory periods per day.

tories, respectively, in School No. 3. Information gained through visits indicates that there are considerable numbers of small classes conducted in these institutions. If definite figures for size of classes using rooms were available, the utilization percentages would doubtless be lowered. With the exception of School No. 2, these colleges do not appear to be reaching the standard of utilization suggested above. It should be remembered, however, that the student load in the summer is approximately double that of the regular session.

TABLE 15

PERCENTAGE OF TOTAL WEEKLY UTILIZATION OF LECTURE ROOMS AND LABORATORIES, CALCULATED ON THE UNIFORM BASIS OF AN EIGHT-PERIOD DAY

	LECTURE ROOMS PER CENT	LABORATORIES PER CENT
School No. 1	40.9	25.5
School No. 2	76.3	43.0
School No. 3	48.0	25.8
School No. 4	48.9	28.5
School No. 5	63.7	27.2

Calculated on the uniform basis of an eight-period day, the percentage of total weekly utilization was found as shown in Table 15. These percentages can be considered comparable in so far as the data on which they are based are complete and accurate.

SUMMARY

1. The State of Texas, because of its size and peculiar history, and the great variety of its climate, geographical areas, and population distribution presents a situation which is unique among the states. Its varied features are important factors in the development of a system of public education, which must include a program of teacher training. Because of these variations, proposals for a division of the state have been made in the past. There is evidence, however, that division is hardly to be expected and that educational programs will be developed on the present state-wide basis and from beginnings already made.

2. The state maintains seven teachers colleges, six of which were established subsequent to 1900. With one exception all are located in towns of less than 6,000 population. Their general administrative control is vested in one board of nine members appointed by the

governor. The internal administration and management of each institution has been left largely to the president and his staff.

3. The training of teachers has become a prominent function of every institution of collegiate rank within the state. In addition to the state teachers colleges, sixty-nine institutions for whites are accredited to offer work leading to teachers' certificates. The professional work done in these denominational, independent, state, and municipal colleges is very loosely supervised by the State Department of Education. Notwithstanding the number of these colleges, more than 47 per cent of the certificates issued from 1919 to 1928 were based on credits earned in the teachers colleges. Present certificate laws are tending to make college work rather than examinations the basis of certification. This probably is the only indication of a state policy looking toward a program of supplying professionally trained teachers to the public schools. Setting up and administering professional courses have been left largely to the initiative and judgment of each college or university.

4. Texas ranks fourth among the states in the amount invested in its teachers colleges. The total investment of more than six million dollars apparently has been distributed among the institutions on no definite basis of student load or of population to be served. During 1929, a typical year, local funds supplied from 21 per cent to 77 per cent of the amounts invested in permanent improvements by the several colleges. It appears, therefore, that the favorable situation in regard to the value of physical plants is due to the initiative and management of the regents and administrators rather than to the operation of a state policy. Local funds have also figured prominently in financing salaries and in departmental maintenance.

5. Uncertainty and embarrassing delay have characterized appropriations for all state institutions of higher education. The teachers colleges have felt the effects of such procedure especially in their efforts to make adequate provision for the greatly increased enrollment in the summers. The development of salary schedules providing for promotions, retirement, and sabbatical leaves has been impossible under such conditions.

6. Accurate determination of unit costs in these institutions is possible only at great expense, by reason of the lack of uniformity and multifarious classifications of accounts. Costs per student, as calculated from current reports available, show considerable differences among the colleges. These differences are due to the size of

the enrollments and possibly to the nature of the curricula and courses offered. Studies of cost per student, published by the United States Office of Education, show that the Texas teachers colleges rank very low among the teachers colleges of the country.

7. Judgments of the physical plants based on the Evenden, Strayer, Engelhardt Score Card and Standards give the Texas colleges a very satisfactory rating. Total scores allotted range from 690 to 805 out of a possible 1,000. The condition of campuses and buildings is evidence of the careful attention which has been given to them. Scores allotted to rooms and equipment devoted to the practice school reveal deficiencies, and point to the conclusion that the facilities for observation, participation, and student teaching have not been developed uniformly with the more strictly academic types of equipment. Certain features of the physical equipment known as general units were noticeably low in the scoring. Among these were: dormitories and dining rooms, health and physical education equipment, library rooms, assembly and seminar rooms, and fireproof vaults for all records.

8. With two exceptions, the libraries contain volumes and periodicals in excess of the minimum number set by the standards of the American Association of Teachers Colleges. Reports of the number of volumes added and the number bound during one year indicate a commendable effort to keep these libraries growing. Detailed records of the percentage of books of each classification were not available.

9. Complete data on which to base calculations of percentages of room utilization were not obtainable. Such computations as could be made indicate that the Texas teachers colleges, during the terms of the regular session, are not generally showing as high per cent of utilization of lecture rooms and laboratories as has been suggested by other studies. The increased enrollment during the twelve weeks of the summer session has not taxed to the limit the room capacities of most of these institutions.

10. In general the laws of the state and the machinery for administering its program of education have tended to place the teachers colleges in the same category with other institutions of collegiate rank except in the amounts appropriated for salary schedules, maintenance, and equipment. Certain differences in appropriations are shown in other portions of the study. The result has been to retard their development as peculiarly professional institutions, and to place them in competition with the liberal arts colleges.

Proposals

1. The purpose of the following proposals is to suggest some contribution toward the development of a state program by which an optimum number of efficient teachers can be economically trained to serve the public schools. In such a worthy enterprise institutional rivalries can serve no useful purpose. The sole criterion for judging proposals and procedures should be the progress of education in the state.

2. The teachers colleges are, by virtue of their expressed purpose, an integral part of the public free school system of the commonwealth. Among other institutions of higher learning, they especially should serve as guides and leaders of public education and be responsive to the needs of the public schools.

3. A closer integration and coördination of the state's teacher-training institutions are needed. In some states these are accomplished through a state director of teacher training who is a member of the State Department of Education. In Texas they would be facilitated by requiring more detailed and uniform reports to the Board of Regents. The rank and growth of the state in population, and its increasing wealth and industrial development emphasize the necessity of unifying teacher-training procedures.

4. Complete standards concerning facilities and curricula for the professional preparation of teachers should be set up and administered by a centralized authority for the entire state. It is proposed that such authority be vested in the State Board of Education, and that the Board of Regents of the teachers colleges be required to participate in the formulation of the standards. Any institution in the state whose work is accredited toward certification of teachers should be required to meet these standards.

5. A plan should be adopted to give stable and adequate financial support to the teachers colleges, based on their known needs. It is proposed that the State Board of Education be empowered to determine the number of teachers needed annually by the schools of the state. From such figures a close approximation of the numbers to be trained by the teachers colleges could be made. Funds necessary for current expenses should be provided by a stable plan which is suggested in more detail in the last chapter. The plan should be sufficiently flexible to care for unforeseen changes. Efficient administration of each institution depends on fiscal support which is stable

and the amount of which is known well in advance of the period of need.

6. It is proposed that accounting procedures at each teachers college be based on the standard system used by the United States Office of Education. Continuous studies of unit costs in totals and as allocated to departments and curricula are suggested as material contributions to the efficiency and economy of the state's teacher-training program.

7. Administrative officers of each college should make frequent examinations of the physical equipment with reference to recognized standards. The adequacy and suitability of each feature of such equipment can be properly judged only in terms of the peculiar professional purpose of the institution. Data on which to base calculations of room utilization should be continuously available. Adjustments of daily class schedules, and plans for additional capital outlays can be made most efficiently on the basis of present facilities and the use that is being made of them.

8. Equipment for the laboratory schools and facilities for student teaching outside these schools should be enlarged and improved.

9. It is proposed that detailed reports from the library staff of each college be required annually, and that such reports be made the basis of careful studies of library needs. Several of the Texas teachers colleges are in need of more adequate library buildings and equipment in order to render the service that should be expected of libraries in professional institutions. It is also suggested that more careful attention be given to libraries in the budgetary procedures of each college.

CHAPTER II

THE STUDENTS OF THE TEXAS STATE TEACHERS COLLEGES

In a public enterprise carried on by the state at public expense—an enterprise so significant as the preparation of teachers for the public schools—the character, ability, and background of the students in training for service are of major importance. It seems almost axiomatic that the kind of raw material out of which teachers are to be made is of as great significance as are the curricula and procedures used in training them. This has a very practical meaning when one considers that the teachers colleges of the nation are investing annually an average of $236.46 in the training of each of their students.[1] An attempt is made in another section of this study to estimate, from data available, the amount that is being invested annually by the State of Texas in the training of each student in the teachers colleges. On the basis of the figure just shown, a state would have invested in each person taking a four-year program of training practically one thousand dollars, exclusive of legitimate charges for capital outlay for plant and equipment. The producer of cattle in Texas no longer attempts to turn out his product in volume without first learning something about, and making some selection in, the stock with which he starts.

So far as the writer is aware, little or nothing has been done by any agency of the State of Texas toward securing other than the most meager facts concerning the people who are admitted as students to its teachers colleges, and no evidence has been found to indicate that there has been an attempt to select from among applicants for admission those who likely would make useful members of the teaching profession. This is not true of the state's effort to train young people for the medical profession. The College of Medicine of the State University, located at Galveston, has provided means by which information regarding applicants for admission is

[1] *Statistics of Teachers Colleges and Normal Schools, 1927-1928.* United States Bureau of Education Bulletin, 1929, No. 14, p. 6.

very carefully assembled, and selection from among the applicants is made on the basis of this information. An extract from the published requirements for admission reads as follows:

> Candidates must be at least 18 years of age, and each candidate less than 21 years of age must present a written statement from parent or guardian showing permission to matriculate. Applicants must furnish evidence of good moral character and fitness for the profession of medicine. Students coming from other colleges must present letters of honorable dismissal.[2]

The complete statement of admission requirements occupies almost four full pages of the catalogue number of the bulletin. The question naturally arises in the mind of one who pauses to think on this matter: Is the preparation of teachers of less importance to the state than the preparation of physicians, and is the selection among candidates for the former any less important and necessary? In a personnel study of students in training for the teaching profession, Whitney says in regard to the importance of such a study:

> The state must know—and the efficient normal school administrator must find out for the state—what value as teachers the groups found in the teacher training institutions have.[3]

With such considerations in mind, a partial study of the student personnel of the Texas teachers colleges was undertaken as a part of the present investigation. The study was only partial because of the limitations of time and of financial resources. It included the students in residence at the several colleges during the winter term, 1930. This term covered the period from January 1 to March 15. The chief sources of information, aside from the personal knowledge and contacts of the writer, were the published bulletins of the colleges, the reports from the registrars, and the replies made by the students themselves to a series of questions presented to them.[4] According to the reports of the registrars there were 5,982 students in residence at the seven colleges during the winter term, 1930; and of these, 3,640, or 60.8 per cent, sent in replies to the questions. The replies were carefully tabulated and the facts obtained are pre-

[2] For a full statement of admission requirements in the College of Medicine see: *University of Texas Bulletin,* No. 3005, Catalogue of the Medical Branch, pp. 19-22, Feb. 1, 1930.

[3] Whitney, F. L. *The Intelligence, Preparation and Teaching Skill of State Normal School Graduates in the United States,* p. 22. Dissertation in the University of Minnesota, 1922.

[4] Thirty questions regarding nativity and education of parents, location of students' homes, the types of teaching students plan to do, etc.

sented in Tables 16 to 34 and the discussion accompanying them.

For reasons suggested above, a psychological examination of the students in these colleges, together with certain other measures that have been used in similar studies elsewhere, was omitted. The Thurstone psychological examination was administered to the freshmen in the state-supported colleges and all teacher-training institutions in Missouri in the fall of 1929. The general conclusion reached from the results of these tests is that the state teachers colleges enroll the group which is least highly selected from the standpoint of intellectual ability as measured by the examinations given.[5] The report cited further suggests in discussing the lower ranking of teachers college students:

> It would appear, then, that the problem is probably one of selection and elimination instead of any inherent failure on the part of the work of teaching to attract students of superior ability.[6]

Whitney, in his study of the student personnel of normal schools over the entire country[7] used nine measures of traits indicative of fitness for the work of the teaching profession. These were: (1) teaching success during the first semester after graduation; (2) intelligence; (3) secondary-school record; (4) record in academic subjects in normal school; (5) record in professional subjects there; (6) student-teaching success; (7) physique, health, etc.; (8) chronological age; and (9) personality rating. None of these measures are given attention in the present study except the chronological age and the grades made in class work in the teachers colleges. However, other information presented in this chapter regarding the students in training indicates the general nature of the student bodies at the several institutions.

The American Association of Teachers Colleges, in its Standards for Accrediting Teachers Colleges,[8] in addition to requirements regarding health and living conditions, does not make very elaborate demands upon its members with respect to the qualifications of students. These are listed under requirements for admission and limits of registration.

> *Requirements for Admission.* A. The quantitative requirements of admission to a teachers college or normal school accredited by this Association

[5] *Report on Publicly Supported Higher Education,* pp. 378-82.

[6] *Ibid.,* p. 382.

[7] Whitney, F. L. *Op. cit.*

[8] See *Ninth Yearbook of the American Association of Teachers Colleges* for the standards as revised at the annual meeting in Atlantic City, N. J., Feb. 22, 1930.

shall be at least 15 units of secondary-school work, or the equivalent. These units must represent work done in a secondary school approved by the state department of public instruction of the state in which the college is located, and must conform to the definitions of the various units as recommended by the state department of public instruction, or must be evidenced by the result of examinations. Experienced teachers over 21 years of age may be admitted to a teachers college or normal school for such work as they are qualified to take, but before receiving a diploma or a degree, they shall meet the full entrance requirement. If the state department of public instruction maintains no accrediting list of secondary schools or publishes no definitions of secondary-school units, those of a regularly recognized accrediting agency shall be used.

B. Equivalence for entrance or secondary-school work shall be determined only by regularly scheduled written examinations, which shall be of such character as to satisfy the Committee on Admission of the college that the applicant is fully prepared to do college work as hereinafter defined.

C. Experience in teaching shall in no case be accepted for entrance, or credit toward graduation, except supervised teaching in the training school.

Limits of Registration of Students. A. No teachers college shall be placed on the accredited list, or continue on such list for more than one year, unless it has a regular registration of at least 200 students of college grade.

B. A notably small proportion of students of college grade registered in the third and fourth years, continued over a period of several years, shall constitute ground for dropping a teachers college from the accredited list. Fifteen per cent of the enrollment of a teachers college should be in the junior and senior years.

C. A normal school with a two-year curriculum must have an enrollment of at least 150 students of college grade, one-third of whom must be in the second year.

Texas teachers colleges admit men and women on an equal basis and with the same privileges. As will be seen from examination of Table 17 A, one-third or more of the students in each of the institutions are men. Another noteworthy fact is that the percentage of students in the two upper years, junior and senior classes, is well above the minimum set by the American Association of Teachers Colleges referred to above. Table 16 presents these percentages based on enrollment figures for the winter quarter, 1930, as reported by the several registrars. A hasty examination of the records reveals the fact that the percentage of students in the junior and senior years has been gradually increasing during the past few years.

School administrators generally concede that a larger percentage of men than is at present employed in the teaching personnel of public schools is desirable. Many leaders in the profession of education believe there should be more men among the teachers in the elementary

TABLE 16

NUMBER AND PERCENTAGE OF STUDENTS IN JUNIOR AND SENIOR YEARS

College at	Total Enroll-ment	Total Juniors and Seniors	Per cent Juniors and Seniors
Alpine	281	63	22.4
Canyon	711	174	24.4
Commerce	1,158	259	22.3
Denton	1,603	376	23.4
Huntsville	660	168	25.4
Nacogdoches	539	162	30.0
San Marcos	1,030	273	26.5
Total	5,982	1,475	24.6

schools. Yet the forces of tradition and possibly other factors have been so strong that salary schedules generally have not made equal provision for elementary and secondary teachers, notwithstanding the fact that individuals in both groups may have equivalent qualifications as to training, experience, and general fitness. The result has been that the work of teaching in the elementary schools has not attracted men, and in some places it is difficult to secure a sufficient number of qualified men for the junior high schools and general high schools. The writer has observed that the two-year normal schools of New England, most of which attempt to train only elementary teachers, have, in most instances, no men among their students. Tables 17 A and 17 B show that the four-year program of the Texas teachers colleges is attracting a considerable number of young men. As will be seen from another section of this study, these Texas colleges are making an effort to train teachers for all levels of the public-school service. Table 17 A shows that the lowest percentage of men during the winter of 1930 was at Canyon, 27.7; and the highest at Commerce, 43.3. The per cent of men in the combined enrollments of the colleges was 34.9. These figures might mean that the teaching profession is attractive to young men in Texas if it were not for the facts in Table 28 showing the anticipated teaching tenure of the students. It will be seen that the colleges that have a relatively high percentage of men report a correspondingly large proportion of them as planning to enter professions other than teaching. Viewed as professional institutions, therefore, the Texas teachers colleges might be

TABLE 17 A

Enrollment of Men in Texas Teachers Colleges Winter Quarter 1930

Alpine			Canyon			Commerce			Denton			Nacogdoches			San Marcos			Huntsville			Grand Total		
No. Men	Total Enroll-ment	% Men	No. Men	Total Enroll-ment	% Men	No. Men	Total Enroll-ment	% Men	No. Men	Total Enroll-ment	% Men	No. Men	Total Enroll-ment	% Men	No. Men	Total Enroll-ment	% Men	No. Men	Total Enroll-ment	% Men	No. Men	Total Enroll-ment	% Men
115	281	40.9	197	711	27.7	501	1158	43.3	539	1603	33.6	174	539	32.2	328	1030	31.8	239	660	36.25	2093	5982	34.9

TABLE 17 B

Percentage of Men in Senior Classes

Alpine			Canyon			Commerce			Denton			Nacogdoches			San Marcos			Huntsville			Grand Total		
No. Men	Total Seniors	% Men	No. Men	Total Seniors	% Men	No. Men	Total Seniors	% Men	No. Men	Total Seniors	% Men	No. Men	Total Seniors	% Men	No. Men	Total Seniors	% Men	No. Men	Total Seniors	% Men	No. Men	Seniors	% Men
10	27	37.0	22	86	25.5	49	99	49.5	56	146	38.3	21	61	34.4	46	138	33.3	31	72	43.1	235	629	37.4

Note: The percentage of men in the student bodies of the Texas teachers colleges does not differ materially from similar percentages found by the Institute of Educational Research of Teachers College in the five state teachers colleges in Missouri in the fall of 1929, as shown in the *Report on Publicly Supported Higher Education*, p. 369. Percentages of men students are given as follows:

	Per Cent
In the total enrollment of all five colleges	36.9
Warrensburg	32.0
Kirksville	37.7
Maryville	41.1
Cape Girardeau	40.0
Springfield	36.1

criticized for having so many men. Such criticism could be based on the assumption that the presence of a considerable number of students without professional aim lowers the general professional tone of the institution. However, a reassuring fact is presented in Table 17 B, which shows the percentage of men in the senior classes of the several colleges. With two exceptions the percentage of men in the senior class is higher than the percentage in the entire student body. This may mean that a longer period of training tends to fix and stabilize the professional ambitions of young men so that they are led to remain in the teaching profession; or that they use the bachelor's degree obtained at a teachers college merely to satisfy the prerequisites for entrance to some other profession. Unfortunately, no systematic effort has been made by the Texas teachers colleges to keep a record of the careers of their students subsequent to graduation,[9] and it is practically impossible without great expense to determine the number of graduates who remain permanently in the teaching profession.[10] However, the results of studies of the effect of prolonged training on length of tenure indicate that in general a lengthened period of pre-service training results in longer tenure in the teaching profession.

Tables 18 A, 18 B, and 18 C show some interesting facts in regard to age, parentage, and location of homes of students in the Texas teachers colleges, together with facts about ages of students in teacher-training institutions of other states. The tendency in other professions, noticeably law and medicine, seems to be toward setting up prerequisites in the matter of academic training that will make it impossible for very young persons to be admitted to professional schools. For example, the bachelor's degree required of candidates for admission to some of the medical schools, whether designed for that purpose or not, certainly has the effect of raising the ages of students in these colleges. The next result, of course, is that those who are ready to enter the active practice of that profession have reached a mature age. The young man able to qualify for the active practice of medicine before the age of twenty-six is rare. Those in charge of training young people for the important profession of teach-

[9] On the presence of non-professional students, see Hill, C. M.: *A Decade of Progress in Teacher Training*, p. 36. Also on the effect of men students and especially those who do not intend to make teaching a permanent profession, see *Bulletin No. 14* of the Carnegie Foundation for the Advancement of Teaching, pp. 292-95.

[10] For a study of the effect on tenure in the teaching profession exerted by prolonged pre-service training, see Benson, C. E.: *Output of Professional Schools for Teachers*, Chap. VI.

ing might well give some consideration to this matter of the maturity of the people whom they are attempting to train. It seems reasonable to assume that as great a degree of maturity is necessary in a person who undertakes to teach and guide the development of young people as is needed in the person who attempts to cure their physical ills. The figures shown in the table referred to reveal the fact that the median ages of students from the freshman to the senior classes, inclusive, in the seven teachers colleges of Texas range from approximately 19 years to over 24 years. The average median age of freshmen is 19.4, which is at least a year higher than the ages of first-year students in New Jersey. The average median age in all Texas colleges is one year above the median found in Missouri teachers colleges. In view of the fact that the only prerequisite to entrance to the Texas colleges is high-school graduation, the maturity of the college students is commendable. However, the range of ages reported is a matter which might well be given some consideration in the framing of a state program of teacher training. The youngest age reported is 14, and each of the colleges has students who are 15 and 16 years of age. If these institutions were strictly professional schools, the policy of admitting persons so young might justifiably be questioned. It is certain that they would not be admitted to schools that train for some of the other professions. The presence of students who are 35 years of age and more in colleges of undergraduate rank doubtless indicates that each of these colleges is training individuals who have had a number of years of experience in the practice of the profession for which they are getting further training. This is another situation that is not found generally in institutions that train for other professions. From the standpoint of the service rendered by the colleges to the state, such a situation is commendable, but the wisdom of certification laws that would admit persons to the teaching profession with no college training should be seriously questioned. Students of advanced age are found in the freshman and sophomore classes as well as in the junior and senior classes.

It will be seen from Table 18 A that the Texas teachers colleges are training students who are the children of American-born parents, and students who have their homes in Texas. Not less than 94 per cent of the students in any of the colleges are children of American-born parents, and in most colleges the percentages are even higher.[11] Also not less than that percentage in any of the colleges have their homes

[11] The Federal Census of 1920 shows 82.7 per cent of the total population of Texas to be foreign-born and children of foreign-born.

TABLE 18 A

Age and Nativity in Per Cents of Students in Texas Teachers Colleges

	Median Age	Youngest	Oldest	Total Reporting
ALPINE				
Freshman men	20.5	17	26	25
Freshman women	19.0	16	48	47
Sophomore men	20.7	18	29	21
Sophomore women	20.3	17	40	38
Junior men	21.1	18	24	10
Junior women	21.6	17	48	20
Senior men	22.0	20	29	9
Senior women	22.9	18	37	23
Total				193
94 per cent are children of American-born parents 96 per cent have their homes in Texas				
CANYON				
Freshman men	19.9	16	23	55
Freshman women	18.4	16	37	172
Sophomore men	20.6	18	34	35
Sophomore women	19.9	18	39	94
Junior men	21.6	19	35	31
Junior women	21.1	18	39	41
Senior men	24.9	21	48	14
Senior women	22.7	19	51	36
Total				478
98 per cent are children of American-born parents About 94 per cent have their homes in Texas				
COMMERCE				
Freshman men	20.7	16	28	68
Freshman women	19.3	16	44	221
Sophomore men	20.5	17	28	37
Sophomore women	20.1	17	45	94
Junior men	21.6	18	39	26
Junior women	21.6	18	38	33
Senior men	23.9	18	42	16
Senior women	22.1	18	34	27
Total				522
98 per cent are children of American-born parents All but 1 of the 522 reporting have their homes in Texas				
DENTON				
Freshman men	19.6	15	33	187
Freshman women	19.5	14	53	365
Sophomore men	20.3	17	24	100
Sophomore women	19.7	15	50	195
Junior men	22.0	16	42	72
Junior women	20.7	17	44	118

TABLE 18 A—*Continued*

	Median Age	Youngest	Oldest	Total Reporting
DENTON (*Cont'd*)				
Senior men	22.9	17	48	67
Senior women	22.5	17	45	131
Total				1,235
98 per cent of all reporting are children of American-born parents				
97.5 per cent have their homes in Texas				
NACOCDOCHES				
Freshman men	19.3	17	39	27
Freshman women	18.9	15	30	77
Sophomore men	20.6	18	29	24
Sophomore women	19.7	17	29	48
Junior men	21.0	18	31	16
Junior women	20.6	17	25	35
Senior men	22.9	19	27	6
Senior women	21.8	17	43	19
Total				252
All but two of the 252 reporting are children of American-born parents				
All but six of the 252 reporting have their homes in Texas				
HUNTSVILLE				
Freshman men	20.2	16	42	103
Freshman women	19.7	16	37	157
Sophomore men	20.7	15	28	50
Sophomore women	19.9	16	45	94
Junior men	21.7	19	30	31
Junior women	21.2	17	46	50
Senior men	24.7	20	39	26
Senior women	22.2	18	37	37
Total				548
95 per cent are children of American-born parents				
All but three of the 548 reporting have their homes in Texas				
SAN MARCOS				
Freshman men	19.7	16	25	29
Freshman women	18.1	16	54	149
Sophomore men	20.6	17	25	31
Sophomore women	19.8	16	60	84
Junior men	21.2	18	30	12
Junior women	21.9	18	35	27
Senior men	24.5	21	30	15
Senior women	23.7	18	56	29
Total				409

94 per cent are children of American-born parents
99 per cent of all reporting have their homes in Texas
Average median age in all colleges, 21.02

TABLE 18 B

NATIVITY OF THE PARENTS OF STUDENTS IN OTHER STATES

	Born in United States		Foreign	
	Fathers Per Cent	Mothers Per Cent	Fathers Per Cent	Mothers Per Cent
5 New Jersey State Normal Schools	57.9	61.6	42.1	38.4
4 Michigan State Teachers Colleges (1922)	70.5	73.9	29.5	26.1
1 City Teachers College in the Middle West	81.0	84.0	19.0	16.0
13 Pennsylvania State Normal Schools (1922)	87.7	86.9	12.3	13.1
3 Louisiana State Teachers Colleges	96.5	98.4	3.5	1.6
4 Connecticut State Normal Schools	46.5 Both parents native-born		37.1 Both parents foreign-born 16.4 One parent foreign-born	
55 Liberal Arts Colleges (1924)	87.7	90.4	12.3	9.6

TABLE 18 C

GENERAL FACTS IN REGARD TO AGES OF STUDENTS IN TEACHER-TRAINING INSTITUTIONS IN OTHER STATES

In Missouri in 1929*
- Median age for all five state teachers colleges .... 20 years
- Range of middle 50% .... 18 to 22 years
- Entire range .... 18 to 73 years
- In all five colleges:
  - 18 per cent are 18 years of age
  - 20 per cent are 19 years of age
  - 15 per cent are 20 years of age

In New Jersey in 1929†
- Median age of students at entrance:
  - At Montclair .... 17 years 9 months
  - At Newark .... 17 years 8 months
  - At Paterson .... 17 years 9 months
  - At Trenton .... 17 years 9 months

In Missouri in 1915‡
- Median age of all students .... 20 years
- Range of middle 50%.......................... 18 to 22 years
- Entire range.......................... 12 years to over 50 years
  - 11 per cent are less than 19 years of age
  - 23 per cent are less than 20 years of age
  - 15 per cent are 20 years of age
  - 50 per cent are more than 21 years of age

In Missouri in 1926§
- Median age of all students .... 18.6 years

* *Report on Publicly Supported Higher Education*, p. 370.

† Bagley, W. C. *Professional Education of Teachers in New Jersey.* (Unpublished study made in 1928.)

‡ Carnegie Foundation for the Advancement of Teaching, *Bulletin No. 14*, pp. 117, 429.

§ Hill, C. M. *A Decade of Progress in Teacher Training*, p. 15.

in Texas. From the standpoint of educational policy, it is doubtless true that the public-school officials and patrons of America desire that American children be taught by American teachers. This attitude could hardly be interpreted to mean that the administrators and patrons of the public schools favor a strict adherence to a narrow policy of nationalism in American education. Neither is it likely that they would look with favor upon the introduction of a large foreign element into the ranks of the public-school teachers.[12] From the standpoint of the state's financing and administration of teacher training, no doubt those responsible would look with approval upon a situation in which Texas money is spent to educate Texas people. Such an attitude would be in complete accord with American legal sanctions where the control and support of public education have developed as functions and responsibilities of the separate states. While measures to control the age, nationality, and place of residence of students admitted to the state teachers colleges could properly be adopted by the State of Texas, there is nothing in the present conditions that seems to indicate the urgent need of such measures as a part of a state program of teacher training.

The spirit of democratic government as exemplified in America seems to indicate that a state, in its efforts to provide public service of a personal nature, should distinguish clearly between eleemosynary and educational endeavors. On the same principle, a state could hardly justify the establishment and maintenance of educational institutions designed for the special benefit of those of its citizens who chance to be on any particular economic or social level. There is no reason, therefore, to regard the teachers colleges of Texas as designed to serve any class or group of citizens. The justification for their existence is that they perform a distinct service in the state's general program of public education. Nevertheless, admitting the soundness of these principles, it is a responsibility of the administration of public education to ascertain some pertinent facts concerning persons who are being trained in the state's several educational institutions. To discharge in part, at least, that responsibility, the facts in Tables 19 A, 19 B, and 20 are presented. The former table shows a distribution of the family incomes of students in the several colleges, together with comparable data from other states. On the basis of medians, the highest incomes represented among the seven teachers colleges of

[12] For a discussion of the distinction between nationalism and democracy, and their development in France, England, Prussia, and the United States, including their influence on public education, see Reisner, E. H. *Nationalism and Education Since 1789.*

TABLE 19 A

Number and Per Cent of Students Reporting Total Annual Income of Family

	Alpine		Canyon		Commerce		Denton		Nacogdoches		Huntsville		San Marcos	
	No.	%	No.	%	No.	%	No.	%	No.	%	No.	%	No.	%
Less than $1,000 ...	5	5.6	15	4.7	16	3.9	50	6.5	21	10.4	47	13.4	27	13.6
$1,001–2,000	28	31.5	72	22.5	215	53.3	289	37.6	76	37.6	136	38.6	75	37.9
$2,001–3,000	24	26.9	88	27.5	100	24.8	214	27.9	60	29.7	100	28.4	51	25.7
$3,001–4,000	13	14.6	30	9.4	31	7.7	109	14.2	15	7.4	25	7.1	17	8.5
$4,001–5,000	11	12.4	35	10.9	19	4.7	46	5.9	14	6.9	22	6.3	15	7.5
Over $5,000	8	8.9	80	25.0	22	5.5	60	7.8	16	7.9	22	6.2	13	6.6
Median income	$2,730.1		$2,171.4		$1,138.2		$2,790.		$2,934.3		$1,052.4		$1,041.	

Comparable Figures from Other States

	Median Parental Income
5 New Jersey Schools*	$2,768
13 Pennsylvania State Normal Schools (1924)	2,197
9 Massachusetts State Normal Schools (1922)	3,231
3 Louisiana State Teachers Colleges (1923)	2,665
5 Missouri State Teachers Colleges (1925)	2,000
1 Middle-West City Teachers College (1927)	2,834
1 School of Education, Florida State College for Women (1928)	2,927
55 Liberal Arts Colleges and Universities (1924)	3,129
5 Missouri Teachers Colleges (1929)†	2,300
	Q_1 1,493; Q_3 3,038

* Bagley, W. C. *Op. cit.*, p. 21.

† ***Report on Publicly Supported Higher Education***, p. 375, 1929.

TABLE 19 B

NUMBER AND PER CENT OF STUDENTS WHO REPORT THAT OTHER MEMBERS OF THE FAMILY BESIDES FATHER CONTRIBUTE TO FAMILY INCOME

	Alpine		Canyon		Commerce		Denton		Nacogdoches		Huntsville		San Marcos	
	No.	%	No.	%	No.	%	No.	%	No.	%	No.	%	No.	%
Students reporting that others contribute	53	27.7	165	53.9	302	57.8	368	29.7	80	31.7	199	34.8	80	19.5
Total reporting	191		306		522		1,238		252		548		410	

TABLE 20

NUMBER AND PER CENT OF CHILDREN IN FAMILIES FROM WHICH STUDENTS COME

	ALPINE		CANYON		COMMERCE		DENTON		NACOGDOCHES		HUNTSVILLE		SAN MARCOS	
	No.	%	No.	%	No.	%	No.	%	No.	%	No.	%	No.	%
1 child	8	4.4	19	3.9	23	4.3	64	5.4	10	3.7	33	5.9	23	5.7
2 children	27	14.8	44	9.0	55	10.3	163	13.8	36	13.5	71	12.8	59	14.5
3 children	32	17.5	66	13.5	85	15.9	190	16.0	44	16.5	67	12.1	63	15.5
4 children	31	16.9	68	13.9	77	14.4	183	15.5	47	17.6	99	17.8	63	15.5
5 children	22	12.0	80	16.4	78	14.6	160	13.5	35	13.1	75	13.5	44	10.8
Over 5 children	63	34.4	211	43.2	216	40.4	423	35.8	95	35.5	209	37.7	155	38.0
Median number in family		4.2		5.4		5.6		4.5		4.7		5.9		4.7

Comparable Figures from Other States

	Median No. of Children
Glassboro*	3.11
Montclair Normal School	2.66
Montclair College	2.48
Newark	3.23
Paterson	3.12
Trenton	2.95
4 Michigan State Teachers Colleges (1922)	3.14
9 Massachusetts State Normal Schools (1922)	4.6
3 Louisiana State Teachers Colleges (1923)	4.4
55 Liberal Arts	3.7
5 Missouri Teachers Colleges (1929)†	3.0

* Bagley, W. C. *Op. cit.*, p. 24 † *Report on Publicly Supported Higher Education*, p. 374

Texas rank favorably with those represented in teacher-training institutions of New Jersey, Pennsylvania, Louisiana, Missouri, Florida, and mid-western city colleges. With possibly a few exceptions, the Texas institutions are drawing students from about the same economic level as are those of other states. It should be noted, however, that the data for Texas were obtained from the replies of students, and an examination of these replies indicated a considerable degree of approximation and a lack of accurate information on the part of the students who replied. Yet from more than three thousand replies some indication of the actual situation might be expected. Another factor that makes for inaccuracy in these figures is the fact that nearly half the students come from homes of farmers, as shown in Table 22 A. However, after making due allowances for such inaccuracies, it seems evident that the Texas teachers colleges are training students who come mostly from families whose annual income is less than $3,000. This may be true of the other state institutions of collegiate rank; so far as the writer is aware no recent data from them are available. Certainly the state should not deny educational advantages of any kind to capable young people solely because they come from homes with moderate financial incomes. The facts shown in Table 20 shed additional light upon the financial resources of the Texas teachers college students. The range of the median number in the families represented in the several colleges is from 4.2 to 5.9. Texas families are noticeably larger than those represented in the teacher-training institutions of New Jersey, Michigan, Massachusetts, Louisiana, Missouri, and the average of fifty-five liberal arts colleges. A moderate income for a large family means less financial backing for individual members. From the table it will be noticed that in all the Texas teachers colleges, 34 per cent or more of the students come from families of more than five children. From Table 19 B it is learned that many students come from homes where other members as well as the father contribute to the family income. In one college 19.5 per cent of the students report such a situation and in another 57.8 per cent report it. This is additional evidence that these colleges are furnishing educational advantages to young people of moderate financial circumstances. The facts of Table 21 which show the percentages of students who are wholly and partially self-supporting offer additional support to that statement.

From Table 21, it appears that of all the students in all the teachers colleges of Texas nearly one-fifth, 18.6 per cent, are entirely self-supporting, and slightly over 31 per cent are partially so. The original replies indicate that students support themselves in college from their own savings or by working while in school. There is not

TABLE 21

NUMBER AND PER CENT OF STUDENTS AT EACH COLLEGE WHO ARE ENTIRELY SELF-SUPPORTING; DEPENDENT ON PARENTS OR OTHERS; AND PARTIALLY SELF-SUPPORTING

	Entirely Self-Supporting		Entirely Dependent		Partially Self-Supporting	
	No.	%	No.	%	No.	%
Alpine	25	14.1	83	46.9	69	38.9
Canyon	70	16.2	178	41.2	184	42.6
Commerce	87	16.4	259	48.9	183	34.5
Denton	238	20.1	616	52.1	329	27.8
Nacogdoches	40	15.9	144	57.1	68	26.9
Huntsville	109	20.4	288	53.8	138	25.8
San Marcos	88	20.7	208	48.9	129	30.4
Total	657	18.6	1,776	50.3	1,100	31.1

a great variation among the several colleges in this respect, and it is very likely that the size of the town in which the college is located is an important factor in determining the number of self-supporting students, for, in general, the larger the town the more numerous are the opportunities for students to find employment. The percentage of self-supporting students in the Texas colleges is noticeably lower than in the Missouri colleges in 1915 and in 1926. In the former year, one-half the men and nearly one-third the women students were wholly self-supporting;[13] and in 1926, 30 per cent of all students were entirely self-supporting, and 31 per cent were partially so.[14] As Hill suggests,[15] entire or partial support on the part of students is often taken as a sign of an eager interest in getting an education and that students who depend on themselves will make the most of their opportunities. However, as he points out, this is not by any means true in all cases. A full course in college is designed to be a full-time task for the student of average or higher ability. The courses in the best professional colleges are certainly as exacting as this. It seems reasonable to assume, therefore, that the student who is forced to expend part of his time, energy, and thought in earning his living has just that much of a handicap in his main task.

[13] Carnegie Foundation for the Advancement of Teaching, *Bulletin No. 14,* p. 118.

[14] Hill, C. M. *A Decade of Progress in Teacher Training,* p. 20.

[15] *Ibid.,* pp. 21-22.

In addition, such a student is often denied participation in those college activities generally known as extracurricular, which, if properly used, contribute materially to the training of those who plan to serve as teachers in the public schools. The writer has known a few students who seemed to take the position that they should be excused for poor work in their courses because they had to devote from four to six hours a day to the job by which they earned their living. Certainly it is not in accordance with the public welfare to deny college and professional training to young people who are dependent upon themselves financially, but from the standpoint of college administration the amount of college work such students undertake should be closely supervised and limited.

It is evident, therefore, that the State of Texas through its teachers colleges is investing in the training of young people who do not come from the upper economic or social levels, and, in so doing, is exemplifying the American spirit of democracy in education. Texas is not peculiar in this respect; all available studies indicate that the teacher-training institutions in all parts of the country are doing practically the same thing.[16] Published studies indicate that this is true of other colleges.[17] Whatever value, therefore, a college training has in discovering and developing abilities and capabilities in young people is being extended freely to those who come from economic and social levels commonly regarded as being the less favored.

Another indication of the nature of the material from which the state is making teachers, and of the classes of citizens who are taking advantage of the offerings of the teachers colleges, is given by the facts presented in Tables 22 A and 22 B. The occupational groups which students represent are hardly a matter that should be controlled arbitrarily by state authority, yet the information presented in these tables should be of some interest and value to those directly in charge of the teacher-training institutions. This is particularly true when the educational advantages and the cultural background usually found in the different groups are considered, for

[16] Moffett, M'Ledge. *The Social Background and Activities of Teachers College Students,* pp. 13-24. Contributions to Education, No. 375. Teachers College, Columbia University, 1929.

Coffman, L. D. *The Social Composition of the Teaching Population.* Contributions to Education, No. 41. Teachers College, Columbia University, 1911.

Carnegie Foundation for the Advancement of Teaching, *Bulletin No. 14,* pp. 117-22; and studies of teacher training in Louisiana, Michigan, Missouri, (1929), Pennsylvania, Massachusetts, New Jersey, and other states.

[17] Reynolds, O. E. *The Social and Economic Status of College Students.* Contributions to Education, No. 272. Teachers College, Columbia University, 1927.

TABLE 22 A

NUMBER AND PER CENT OF STUDENTS IN TEXAS TEACHERS COLLEGES WHOSE FATHERS OR GUARDIANS ARE IN OCCUPATIONS INDICATED

	Alpine		Canyon		Commerce		Denton		Nacogdoches		Huntsville		San Marcos		Total	
	No.	%	No.	%	No.	%	No.	%	No.	%	No.	%	No.	%	No.	%
Farmer	50	29.2	259	55.2	320	61.0	506	45.9	113	43.7	221	43.6	183	47.5	1652	48.3
Business	33	19.3	63	13.4	62	11.8	200	18.1	42	16.2	62	12.2	46	11.9	508	14.8
Physician	6	3.5	3	.6	9	1.7	24	2.2	4	1.5	13	2.6	5	1.3	64	1.8
Public office holder	7	4.1	5	1.1	14	2.6	39	3.5	7	2.7	19	3.7	9	2.3	100	2.9
Teacher	7	4.1	12	2.6	10	1.9	57	5.2	7	2.7	28	5.5	8	2.1	129	3.7
Mechanic	7	4.1	13	2.7	13	2.4	47	4.4	15	5.8	23	4.5	19	4.5	139	4.1
Profession other than physician or teacher	7	4.1	9	1.9	6	1.1	26	2.4	4	1.5	9	1.8	8	2.0	69	2.0
Laborer	7	4.1	15	3.2	10	1.9	38	3.4	13	5.0	17	3.4	10	2.5	110	3.2
Clerk	2	1.1	8	1.7	8	1.5	31	2.8	2	.8	9	1.8	3	.07	63	1.8
Others	45	26.3	82	17.4	72	13.7	133	12.1	51	19.8	106	20.9	94	24.4	583	17.1

TABLE 22 B

PERCENTAGES OF STUDENTS IN OTHER INSTITUTIONS WHOSE FATHERS ARE IN OCCUPATIONAL GROUPS INDICATED

	UNSKILLED LABOR		SKILLED LABOR	BUSINESS (CLERICAL)		BUSINESS (PROPRIETORS)	FARM	PROFESSION
5 New Jersey Schools	3.5		30.1	11.3		31.7	6.0	8.3
9 Massachusetts State Normal Schools (1922)	11.4		39.8		29.7		7.6	5.7
13 Pennsylvania State Normal Schools (1924)	14.0		33.2		21.3		18.7	9.9
3 Connecticut State Normal Schools (1923)		47.0			27.0		8.0	5.0
4 Michigan State Teachers Colleges							33.5	6.7
1 Middle-West City Teachers College (1927)		23.0		16.0		28.0	9.4	11.1
3 Louisiana State Teachers Colleges (1923)	5.0		10.4		23.4		34.2	6.9
School of Education, Florida State College for Women (1928)		11.2			48.5		19.6	14.1
Teachers College, Univ. of Florida (1928)		11.8			41.7		25.2	12.3
55 Liberal Arts Colleges and Universities—Country as a whole (1923)	.5		6.3		43.4		23.3	18.3
5 Missouri Teachers Colleges (1929)		19.0			20.7		47.2	10.2

it is doubtless true that the curricular offerings of institutions that train for any branch of the public service must be determined in some measure by the equipment of the students admitted. Nearly half of all the students reporting from all the colleges, 48.3 per cent, are children of farmers. The highest percentage from the farming group at any one college is 61 and the lowest, 29.2. The next ranking group is the business group from which 14.8 per cent of all the students come. The large percentage shown in the occupations listed as "others" results from the wide variety of occupations reported by students. A rather surprising fact is that only 3.7 per cent report that their fathers are teachers, while comparatively few, 1.8 per cent, are children of physicians, and only 2 per cent are children of those in professions other than medicine or teaching. The percentages from the homes of mechanics (skilled laborers) and laborers—4.1 per cent and 3.2 per cent, respectively—are noticeably low in comparison with similar percentages in institutions of other states as shown in Table 22 B. From this same table it will be seen that only in the teacher-training institutions of Michigan, Louisiana, and Missouri among the states shown are there as high percentages of students whose fathers are farmers as is the case in Texas institutions. The facts here under consideration are generally in accord with those shown in Tables 19 A and 19 B, and also with those presented in Table 21 which give information as to the incomes of students' families, the number in the family contributing, and the percentage of students who are wholly or partially self-supporting. The occupational groups most largely represented by the Texas students are not those who enjoy the highest incomes.

A matter that is of considerable significance to the state as the provider of public education, and to society in general, is the relationship that may exist between the occupation of fathers and the ability of their children to profit by the educational facilities that are offered them. A state policy offering professional training on the college level, regardless of the ability of students to profit by it, would be unwise and uneconomical. It is generally conceded that the so-called intelligence tests measure the ability of young people to do the usual type of school work successfully and to profit by doing it. Closely connected with paternal occupation is the whole matter of the cultural and social background of children. The correlation that may exist between paternal occupation and family background and the intelligence of children has been the subject of numerous studies.[18] Reynolds in a study of occupations of fathers of students[19] presents the following facts adapted from a table by Dexter[20] together with his own conclusions:

Occupations of Fathers	Median I Q of Children
Proprietors	111
Professional service	117
Managerial service	108
Commercial service	104
Clerical service	103
Agricultural service	94
Artisan proprietors	97
Building trades	98
Machine trades	100
Printing trades	95
Miscellaneous trades	95
Transportation service	97
Public service	94
Personal service	91
Miners, lumber-workers, fishermen	90
Common labor	89

This tabulation, which brings out the relation between occupations of parents and intelligence of children, tends to discredit any striking psychological difference between the various occupational groups. There are some average differences, but they are not significant enough to explain why we find certain occupational groups very well, and others very poorly, represented in college, in proportion to their numbers in the general population. In the main, however, the order is the same and to that extent reflects the social and economic status of the occupation.

Stoke and Lehman[21] in their critical examination of data on this general problem reach the following conclusions:

1. Intelligence test scores correlate rather loosely with social and economic status, the correlation ranging usually from .30 to .40.
2. The great majority of superior children (I. Q. 120-140) and the great

[18] Reynolds, O. E. *The Social and Economic Status of College Students.* Contributions of Education, No. 272, Bureau of Publications, Teachers College, Columbia University, 1927.

Stoke, S. M. and Lehman, H. C. "Intelligence Test Scores of Social and Occupational Groups," *School and Society,* Vol. XXXI, No. 794, pp. 372-77, March 15, 1930.

Haggerty, M. E. and Nash, Harry B. "Mental Capacity and Parental Occupation." *Journal of Educational Psychology,* Vol. XV, No. 9, pp. 559-72, December, 1924.

[19] Reynolds, O. E. *Op. cit.,* Part II, Chap. 3, pp. 20, 21.

[20] Dexter, Emily S. "The Relationship Between Occupation of Parents and the Intelligence of Children, *School and Society,* June 2, 1923.

[21] Stoke, S. M. and Lehman, H. C. *Op. cit.,* pp. 372-77.

majority of gifted children (I. Q. 140 or above) come from the non-professional classes.

3. In the United States the great majority of gifted children come from families that receive rather modest incomes.

An attitude toward this problem that differs from the one just presented, in that it sees distinct intelligence levels among occupational groups, is shown by Haggerty and Nash:[22]

> If we may be allowed to use the word "intelligence" as designating the differential capacities of pupils of the same chronological age to make scores in the Haggerty Intelligence Examination Delta 2, it is obvious that there are clear-cut intelligence levels in the occupational groups listed in Table 4. Not only do the medians of the first 12 groups exceed the medians of the last seven, but almost 75 per cent of the first 12 groups, which include nearly 400 children, exceed all but 25 per cent of the last seven groups, which include nearly four thousand children. In other words, but little more than one-fourth of the children of miners, masons, stoneworkers, laborers, farmers, bakers, and blacksmiths appear to be as able to profit by the work of the elementary school as that school is now organized as are three-fourths of the children of druggists, brokers, officials, insurance men, lawyers, teachers, office workers, doctors, dentists, accountants, bankers, and merchants.[23] Such differences as these have great significance for education if they should be substantiated by extensive investigation. They go beyond the results of the Army examinations which showed that the men actually pursuing an occupation were characterized by a definite intelligence status. The present data show that this intelligence level also characterizes the children of such parents. The father's occupation appears to afford a rough index of the child's intelligence or its capacity to profit by schooling, and possibly of the type of school most serviceable to its needs.

A partial summary of a study of foster children and siblings made by Freeman, Holzinger, and Mitchell presents the following conclusions relative to the point under consideration:

> 1. These facts appear to indicate that an improvement in environment produces a gain in intelligence. 2. That a part of the resemblance between siblings reared together is due to the influence of a single environment. 3. The superior intelligence of the siblings in the better homes appears, therefore, to give evidence that the character of the home affects the child's intelligence to a marked degree.[24]

[22] Haggerty, M. E., and Nash, Harry B. "Mental Capacity of Children and Parental Occupation," *Journal of Educational Psychology*, Vol. XV, No. 9, p. 563, December, 1924.

[23] "The authors have no desire to generalize facts beyond their implicit meaning. It is conceivable that change in home environment or changed school conditions during early years might alter somewhat the relative position of the several groups. The present data neither support nor negate such a possibility."

[24] Freeman, F. N., Holzinger, K. J., and Mitchell, B. C. "The Influence of Environment on the Intelligence, School Achievement, and Conduct of Foster Children." *Twenty-seventh Yearbook of the National Society for the Study of Education*, Part 1, pp. 103-217.

Conclusions reached by Barbara Stoddard Burks in her study[25] indicate that home environment contributes about 17 per cent of the variance in I. Q.; that parental intelligence alone accounts for about 33 per cent; and that the total contribution of heredity is about 75 per cent or 80 per cent.

The foregoing discussion indicates the indefinite nature of present knowledge concerning the relation of parental occupation to the intelligence of children. Facts presented, however, are sufficient to render indefensible an attempt to use occupational status as a factor in any basis employed for the selection of students for admisssion to teachers colleges. It also must be granted that the state needs for its public service the best abilities its population affords regardless of the occupational or economic levels from which they come.

The figures in Table 23 contribute additional evidence as to the economic status of the students who are being trained in the state teachers colleges of Texas; and also make possible some estimate of the financial investment that is being made by those preparing to enter the profession of teaching. The data that are summarized in Table 23 came from the replies of students. These replies indicated rather loose methods of accounting for personal expenses, and to that extent the correctness of the figures may be questioned. Yet if the number of replies from each college as shown in the table is indicative of conditions, some insignificant facts are revealed. That approximately one-fifth of the students in several of the colleges state that their annual expenses are around $100 means, if that figure is correct, that a considerable proportion of them are making a very small investment in their professional equipment as compared to that required for attendance at schools that train for other professions. However, the facts presented in Table 24 show that approximately one-fourth of the students in the Texas colleges have their homes in the county in which the college is located. This may account, in a measure at least, for the low annual expense of attendance. Between thirty and forty-six per cent of the students report the annual expense of college training to be not more than $200. The median annual expense at the several colleges ranges from $261 to $350, with an average annual median cost in all of them of $291. 90. On that basis a student who takes a four-year course of training has a financial investment in his professional equipment that amounts to about $1,200. It is evident, from the percentage of those

[25] Burks, Barbara Stoddard. "The Relative Influence of Nature and Nurture upon Mental Development," *Ibid.* pp. 219-316.

TABLE 23

NUMBER AND PER CENT OF STUDENTS WHO SPEND VARIOUS AMOUNTS IN TEXAS TEACHERS COLLEGES

	Alpine		Canyon		Commerce		Denton		Nacogdoches		Huntsville		San Marcos	
	No.	%	No.	%	No.	%	No.	%	No.	%	No.	%	No.	%
Less than $100	30	20.4	62	13.4	40	8.1	146	13.7	45	18.4	77	17.0	60	18.1
$101–150	18	12.3	70	15.3	68	13.8	144	13.6	24	9.8	59	13.1	56	16.9
151–200	12	7.5	38	8.3	75	15.2	64	6.0	19	7.6	24	5.3	21	6.3
201–250	9	6.2	38	8.3	40	8.1	58	5.5	18	7.3	19	4.2	13	3.9
251–300	5	3.4	26	5.6	89	18.0	118	11.1	24	9.8	37	8.2	36	10.9
301–350	8	5.5	29	6.3	43	8.7	101	9.5	18	7.3	46	10.2	31	9.3
351–400	12	7.5	50	11.0	81	16.4	132	12.4	32	13.1	72	15.9	43	12.9
401–450	10	6.8	18	3.9	28	5.6	84	7.9	15	6.1	45	9.9	23	6.9
451–500	15	10.2	48	10.4	15	3.0	116	10.9	19	7.6	30	6.6	22	6.6
501–550	3	2.0	9	1.9	2	.4	18	1.7	7	2.9	12	2.7	1	.03
551–600	9	9.2	31	6.7	2	.4	34	3.2	14	5.7	18	3.9	9	.3
Over 600	15	10.2	41	9.0	10	2.0	47	4.4	10	4.1	13	2.9	16	4.8
Median Cost	$261		$258.6		$287.7		$350.5		$266.6		$340.1		$279.4	

Average Median Cost for All Colleges—$291.9

who admit spending more than $600, that each college has a small group of students who enjoy exceptionally liberal financial support. In the study of higher education in Missouri made in 1929 the median cost per student of attending the teachers colleges was found to be higher than the figure just shown for the Texas colleges. The median cost as shown in that state is $333, with a total range of from $100 to $2,400. The highest median cost shown for any one college there is $376.[26]

> The effect of the school itself in determining the choices of students is difficult to measure. Like most educational institutions, its influence saturates its immediate vicinity, and weakens rapidly with increasing distance. Accessibility, too, plays an important rôle. The local county supplies about one-fourth of all the students in the normal schools, including 18 per cent who come from the local town. Six or seven contiguous counties furnish another fourth; the remaining twelve or fifteen counties in the district contribute a third, while one-seventh come from other portions of the state.[27]

Such was the situation found in Missouri in 1915. In the same state in 1926 Hill[28] found that 30 per cent of the students resided in the same county in which the college was located, while 91 per cent came from the district in which the college was located. The investigation made in the same state in 1929[29] showed that 36.9 per cent resided in the same town, and 8 per cent within the same county but outside the town in which the college was located. Judging by these figures it seems that the tendency is for the teachers colleges in Missouri to draw increasingly greater percentages of students from the immediate vicinity. Table 24 shows similar facts concerning the Texas teachers colleges, and it will be seen that the percentages are fairly comparable to those shown for Missouri. Fully one-fourth of all the students in the seven Texas teachers colleges reside in the county where the college is situated; almost two-thirds have their homes within one hundred miles of the college they attend; and in two of these colleges almost three-fourths of the students come from within a radius of 100 miles. The Texas schools seem to draw larger percentages of students from greater distances than do those in Missouri, but this may be accounted for by the much greater area embraced within the State of Texas. It seems that the building of

[26] *Report on Publicly Supported Higher Education*, p. 378.

[27] Carnegie Foundation for the Advancement of Teaching, *Bulletin No. 14*, pp. 118, 119.

[28] Hill, C. M. *A Decade of Progress in Teacher Training*, p. 22. Contributions to Education, No. 233, Bureau of Publications, Teachers College, Columbia University, 1927.

[29] *Report on Publicly Supported Higher Education*, p. 371.

TABLE 24

NUMBER AND PER CENT OF STUDENTS WHOSE HOMES ARE IN COUNTY WHERE COLLEGE IS LOCATED AND WITHIN 100 MILES OF THE TEACHERS COLLEGE

	TOTAL REPLIES	FROM COUNTY WHERE COLLEGE IS		WITHIN 100 MILES	
		No.	%	No.	%
Alpine	193	51	26.4	71	63.8
Canyon	477	116	24.3	323	67.7
Commerce	522	127	24.3	370	70.8
Denton	238	379	30.6	768	62.0
Nacogdoches	1,252	75	29.8	191	75.7
Huntsville	548	124	22.6	341	62.2
San Marcos	410	55	13.4	219	53.4
Total	3,640	927	25.5	2,283	62.7

roads and the general improvement of transportation facilities tend to widen the area from which colleges draw their students, although this does not appear to have been true in Missouri during the past fifteen years. However, definite data on this point are lacking, but would be valuable to a State Board of Education that attempted to control the work of all state colleges and prescribe the character of work that each institution would be expected to do. From Table 25, the second column, it will be seen that there is a noticeable similarity between the percentages of students who reside in the town where the college is situated and those who live in that county.

Table 25 also shows in each of the colleges the percentage of students whose homes are situated in different types of communities, together with some comparable information from a few other states. Unlike the students in the schools of the eastern states, the modal number in the Texas institutions come from farm homes, fully 33 per cent. If to this per cent are added the percentages of those whose homes are in communities of less than 5,000 population, it is seen that practically two-thirds of the students in the Texas colleges come from the open country or from small communities. The per cent from farm homes among the seven colleges ranges from 18.4 to 49.2, but within these extremes the percentages are fairly uniform. Not more than 6 per cent at any school come from homes located in cities of more than 25,000 population. The generally known fact that many rural and smaller communities of Texas still have rather poor and inadequate school facilities, especially on the secondary

TABLE 25

NUMBER AND PER CENT OF STUDENTS IN EACH TEXAS COLLEGE WHO COME FROM EACH TYPE OF COMMUNITY

	The College Town		Farm		Village Less Than 1000		Town 1000–2500		Town 2500–5000		Town 5000–25,000		Town More Than 25,000	
	No.	%	No.	%	No.	%	No.	%	No.	%	No.	%	No.	%
Alpine	48	25.9	34	18.4	24	12.9	19	10.3	35	18.9	13	7.0	12	6.5
Canyon	116	25.2	172	37.4	36	7.8	36	7.8	44	9.6	34	7.4	22	4.7
Commerce	72	14.5	245	49.2	70	14.0	45	9.0	26	5.2	35	7.0	5	1.0
Denton	245	22.6	310	28.4	163	14.9	128	11.7	83	7.6	108	9.8	54	4.9
Nacogdoches	63	25.0	96	38.1	31	12.3	20	7.9	15	5.9	22	8.7	5	1.9
Huntsville	120	22.5	153	28.7	93	17.5	57	10.7	51	9.6	32	6.0	26	4.8
San Marcos	57	14.1	142	35.1	45	11.1	53	13.1	38	9.4	47	11.6	23	5.6
Total	723	21.1	1152	33.6	462	13.5	358	10.5	292	8.5	291	8.4	147	4.3

TYPE OF COMMUNITY FROM WHICH STUDENTS COME IN OTHER STATES*

	Farm	Less than 1000	1000–5000	5000–25,000	Over 25,000
	Per Cent	Per Cent	Per Cent	Per Cent	Per Cent
New Jersey	5.2	6.9	21.2	24.3	42.2
Connecticut	8.0	3.0	13.0	20.0	56.0
Massachusetts	9.3		19.0	32.0	39.0
Louisiana	40.0	14.0	31.4	13.3	

* Bagley, W. C. *Professional Education of Teachers in New Jersey.* (Unpublished study made in 1928.)

TABLE 26

HOW STUDENTS ENTERED THE COLLEGE WHERE THEY ARE

	Total Reporting	A From Affiliated H. S.		B From Unaffiliated H. S.		C By Entrance Exam.		D From Sub-College		E On Individual Approval		F From Other Colleges	
		No.	%	No.	%	No.	%	No.	%	No.	%	No.	%
Alpine	187	105	56.1	7	3.7	6	3.2	30	16.0	15	8.0	24	12.8
Canyon	497	353	71.0	24	4.8	27	5.4	21	4.2	29	5.8	49	9.8
Commerce	533	260	48.7	32	6.0	22	4.1	111	20.8	47	9.0	61	11.4
Denton	1,199	794	66.4	28	3.1	61	5.1	72	6.0	57	4.7	174	14.5
Nacogdoches	258	160	62.0	7	2.7	9	3.5	43	16.6	12	4.6	27	10.4
Huntsville	558	275	49.2	21	3.7	41	7.3	119	21.3	33	5.9	69	12.3
San Marcos	415	259	62.4	16	3.8	16	3.8	37	9.0	36	8.7	51	12.3

level, gives to the above facts some significance in relation to a state program of teacher training.

The facts presented in Table 26 were derived from the replies of students to the definite question, "How did you enter the college where you are now a student?" The statement at the conclusion of the paragraph just above seems to have some meaning when it is noticed that an average of only about 60 per cent of the students in all colleges entered from fully affiliated high schools. The range of such per cents among the colleges is from 48.7 to 71. The rather large percentages that enter from the sub-college classes is another indication that there are a number of students who come from communities in which affiliated high schools are not accessible. This seems to mean that the state is not only providing the facilities for professional training but is also furnishing secondary schooling that is necessary as a prerequisite for entrance upon professional work on the college level. The figures in the last column which show the percentage of students who say that they transferred from some other college are rather high in some cases, and unfortunately no data are available to explain them. Whether the professional training offered by the teachers colleges is of such a high order as to attract considerable numbers from other colleges is not evident from the facts available. Neither is information available to show the kinds of colleges from which these transfers come, and whether there is much transferring among the teachers colleges. Collection of data on these

TABLE 27

NUMBER AND PER CENT OF STUDENTS TAKING PRE-PROFESSIONAL TRAINING FOR OTHER THAN TEACHING*

	TOTAL REPORTING	TOTAL PRE-PROFESSIONAL		MEDICINE	LAW	ENGINEERING	JOURNALISM	OTHERS
		No.	%	%	%	%	%	%
Alpine	193	42	21.7	12.0	7.2	14.4	14.4	38.0
Canyon	477	111	23.3	8.1	9.0	9.0	10.8	62.1
Commerce	522	77	14.7	10.4	9.0	18.2	6.5	55.9
Denton	1,238	258	20.8	12.7	11.6	20.3	13.5	40.8
Nacogdoches	252	59	23.4	15.3	23.6	10.2	1.4	49.5
Huntsville	548	77	14.1	15.6	9.1	14.3	5.2	54.6
San Marcos	410	60	14.6	10.2	11.8	28.3	8.5	40.7

* Table reads: Of total number of students reporting from Alpine, 21.7 per cent say they are preparing for other professions than teaching. Of the number so preparing, 12 per cent say they are preparing for medicine, etc. Replies to this question were incomplete.

Note: In all colleges, and in almost all the classes there are more men than women who are doing pre-professional work.

points, together with investigation as to whether the Texas teachers colleges are meeting fully the entrance requirements set up by the accrediting bodies to which they belong, is a problem for the internal administration of each of these colleges.

The facts shown in Table 27 also were obtained by tabulating the answers given by students, and have considerable meaning in connection with the formulation of a state program of teacher training. From the third column of this table it will be seen that from 14.1 per cent to 23.4 per cent of the students in the several colleges say that they are definitely planning to use the training obtained to satisfy the prerequisites for entering some profession other than teaching. Among four of the established professions, those of medicine and engineering seem to be the most generally preferred. A similar situation was found in the teachers colleges of Missouri by a study made during the fall and winter of 1929, as evidenced by the following excerpt from the published report:

> In each of the state teachers colleges a wide variety of vocations and professions is listed, and within the entire group of state teachers colleges 30 per cent of all students are interested in some other occupation than that of teaching.
>
> The state teachers colleges have been given the power to confer the A.B. degree and have definitely entered upon the course of offering work in the field of liberal arts colleges as well as work of professional nature for other professions. The presence within these student groups of a fairly large number of students (from 20 per cent to 35 per cent) who are preparing to work in a very wide range of fields means that in terms of student load these institutions are fulfilling their primary function of teacher training with from 65 per cent to 80 per cent of their students and that attention is directed to other ends with the remaining 20 per cent to 35 per cent. These institutions, established as institutions for the training of teachers, should restrict their several student bodies to those individuals whose definite objective is preparation for the teaching profession.[30]

From the standpoint of educational policy and the most economical use of the state's funds, Texas has the problem of determining what shall be the specific purpose and function of each of its institutions of higher learning in terms of the needs of the commonwealth. If such needs should seem to indicate that about one-fifth of the students in each of the teachers colleges should be given training for some vocation or profession other than teaching, and if the financial resources of the state should be found to be adequate to support such a pro-

[30] *Report on Publicly Supported Higher Education,* p. 376.

gram, it should then be made a definite state policy by a constituted authority set up within the state. By the same reasoning, if the needs of the state demand and if the financial resources permit that each of the state's higher institutions other than teachers colleges devote part of its time and energy to training teachers, then such a program should also be a part of the general policy. However, the effect of the presence of a number of students who do not plan to teach upon the strictly professional work and atmosphere of the teachers colleges deserves some consideration. The writer knows of no objective studies on this point, but the matter is discussed in the Carnegie Foundation report[31] and by Dr. Hill. The latter says:

It would be of interest to know to what extent the presence of these men in the teachers colleges diverts the colleges from a really professional attitude toward their work. These men are often leaders in student activities and undoubtedly exert a large influence in framing student opinion and in creating "atmosphere." Should the teachers colleges refuse admission to all students who are not definitely preparing for teaching? No college in Missouri now requires students to pledge themselves to teach. At no time when such a pledge was taken was there any effort to follow up students to see whether they taught as they had agreed to do when they accepted training in the normal schools in Missouri. There has never been legal provision for collecting tuition from graduates of Missouri normal schools who failed to teach after having taken their preparation at the expense of the state. Will the upgrading of the normal schools of the country, together with the distinct tendency on the part of the state universities to devote their energies to senior college and graduate study, make junior arts colleges of the normal schools? Would such an arrangement of the state's program of higher education seriously interfere with teacher training?

Another problem which is suggested by the Missouri study grows out of the fact that many men are still using the teaching profession as a stepping stone to professions which pay bigger returns in money and social standing. It would be desirable to know, before condemning the practice utterly, the total influence of these men on the teaching profession. It is not a question of whether it would be better to have these men in the profession permanently or for only a short time. To that question there is only one answer. Does the teaching profession gain or does it lose by having these men for even a short time? Would the teaching profession be better off if these men did not teach at all? What quality of teaching is done by these men while they are teaching? How do these men compare with men who remain permanently in the teaching profession in general intelligence, outlook upon life, and general culture? These are the questions which have not been answered, and upon their answers depends the determination of the policy of the teachers colleges regarding the admission of these men students.[32]

[31] Carnegie Foundation for the Advancement of Teaching, *Bulletin No. 14,* pp. 124, 293. [32] Hill, C. M. *Op. cit.,* pp. 33-35.

TABLE 28

TEACHING TENURE THAT STUDENTS EXPECT

	Total Reporting	None %	1 Yr. %	2 Yrs. %	3–5 Yrs. %	6–10 Yrs. %	Indefinite %
			ALPINE				
Freshman men	15	53.0	.0	6.0	6.0	12.0	18.0
Freshman women ...	37	30.0	2.7	10.8	27.0	16.2	13.5
Sophomore men	14	42.6	.0	7.1	28.4	14.2	7.1
Sophomore women ..	39	32.9	5.0	10.0	31.0	5.0	15.5
Junior men	10	30.0	.0	.0	10.0	10.0	20.0
Junior women	20	20.0	.0	20.0	20.0	10.0	30.0
Senior men	8	12.5	.0	12.5	25.0	12.5	37.5
Senior women	23	13.0	.0	4.3	34.4	8.6	38.7
			CANYON				
Freshman men	46	70.4	.0	4.4	19.8	4.4	2.2
Freshman women ...	162	19.0	4.4	17.9	42.2	7.9	7.9
Sophomore men	35	4.0	14.2	14.2	11.4	8.6	11.4
Sophomore women ..	92	84.7	8.8	19.8	41.8	8.8	3.3
Junior men	31	38.4	9.6	9.6	19.2	9.6	12.8
Junior women	39	27.5	5.1	10.1	27.6	17.6	10.1
Senior men	12	24.9	8.3	33.2	24.9	.0	8.3
Senior women	38	15.6	2.6	15.6	46.8	10.4	7.8
			COMMERCE				
Freshman men	65	16.5	1.5	7.5	57.0	7.5	7.5
Freshman women ...	213	.8	1.4	7.5	84.0	4.2	1.8
Sophomore men	37	5.2	.0	15.6	59.8	5.2	11.4
Sophomore women ..	92	4.4	.0	12.1	73.7	6.6	2.2
Junior men	25	4.0	.0	12.0	60.0	16.0	8.0
Junior women	35	8.4	2.8	19.6	65.7	.0	2.8
Senior men	15	19.8	.0	.0	46.2	13.2	19.8
Senior women	29	3.4	3.4	10.2	72.4	6.8	3.4
			DENTON				
Freshman men	151	41.0	1.3	10.0	25.1	8.0	13.9
Freshman women ...	347	13.0	4.3	12.7	42.3	14.4	13.5
Sophomore men	100	35.0	2.0	13.0	30.0	10.0	10.0
Sophomore women ..	189	8.0	1.0	10.5	49.2	19.5	20.6
Junior men	51	25.4	.0	27.4	27.4	9.8	11.7
Junior women	101	6.9	3.9	12.8	37.6	14.8	23.7
Senior men	62	11.3	1.6	6.4	25.0	16.0	40.2
Senior women	91	12.0	7.7	16.4	15.4	29.6	18.6
			NACOGDOCHES				
Freshman men	26	41.8	7.6	7.6	19.1	15.2	7.6
Freshman women ...	81	12.1	3.7	7.2	45.6	22.9	6.1
Sophomore men	24	36.9	.0	4.1	24.6	12.3	20.5
Sophomore women ..	48	10.0	2.0	14.0	42.0	20.0	10.5
Junior men	15	52.8	6.6	13.2	19.8	6.6	.0
Junior women	33	27.2	.0	9.0	36.3	27.2	.0
Senior men	5	20.0	20.0	.0	60.0	.0	.0
Senior women	18	5.5	5.5	22.2	38.8	22.2	5.5

TABLE 28—*Continued*

	Total Reporting	None %	1 Yr. %	2 Yrs. %	3–5 Yrs. %	6–10 Yrs. %	Indefinite %
HUNTSVILLE							
Freshman men	59	20.3	1.7	15.3	32.3	22.1	8.5
Freshman women	122	13.1	1.6	13.9	50.8	14.4	13.9
Sophomore men	37	24.3	.0	10.8	21.6	16.2	27.0
Sophomore women	100	9.0	2.0	16.0	35.0	13.0	25.0
Junior men	26	15.3	.0	7.6	7.6	11.4	57.0
Junior women	62	6.4	1.6	8.0	36.8	35.2	11.2
Senior men	28	14.3	3.6	3.6	25.0	21.0	32.2
Senior women	35	22.8	.0	5.7	34.2	17.1	19.9
SAN MARCOS							
Freshman men	51	17.6	1.9	15.2	34.2	13.3	15.2
Freshman women	154	20.1	1.3	7.7	50.0	14.9	5.1
Sophomore men	31	25.6	3.2	9.6	16.0	19.2	25.6
Sophomore women	78	16.7	3.8	7.6	47.4	10.3	14.1
Junior men	13	15.2	7.6	15.2	88.0	7.6	15.2
Junior women	26	26.6	3.8	7.6	26.6	15.2	19.0
Senior men	14	30.0	.0	.0	7.5	7.5	55.0
Senior women	28	.0	7.0	3.5	49.0	3.5	35.0

Note: Those reporting "undecided" are regarded as not planning to teach.

The facts presented in Tables 27 and 28 make it plain that the situation and problems in Texas are very similar to those discovered in Missouri, and that much remains to be done in both states if the training of teachers is to be put on the same professional plane as the training of physicians, dentists, engineers, and others. The percentages given in Table 28 are based on the replies of students to the request, "Indicate how many years you expect to teach." While due consideration must be given to the fact that many young people are not able to state with any definiteness what their plans for the future are, yet the very high percentages of those in all the colleges who say that they do not expect to teach at all is rather surprising if these institutions are to be considered professional institutions. Such replies would not be expected from students in medical, dental, law, or engineering schools. In Table 28 several general and significant facts are apparent. In practically all classes there is a higher percentage of men than women who do not expect to teach, and in general there is a higher percentage of lower-class (freshman and sophomore) students who say they do not plan to teach—also a lower percentage of these same classes who expect to make teaching a life work than is found in the upper classes. However, there are very noticeable proportions of students in the senior classes who say that they do not expect to enter the teaching profession even temporarily. The proportion runs as high as 30 per cent in one instance. Yet, except in two colleges, the percentage of senior men who expect to teach indefinitely exceeds that for most of the other classes. This may indicate that a lengthened period of training for men results in a longer teaching tenure. This is in accord with one of the findings of Benson,[33] to the effect that graduates of professional schools have a much longer tenure of service than that of the general teaching population. However, the percentage of senior women who expect life tenure in teaching is noticeably lower than that of the men. From an examination of columns 3, 4, and 5, Table 28, it appears that teaching tenure of two to five years is most commonly looked forward to by students in all the colleges. The situation that is indicated by the facts in this table suggests certain lines of investigation that could properly be carried on by the internal administration of the several colleges.

TABLE 29

NUMBER AND PER CENT OF STUDENTS WHOSE FATHERS AND MOTHERS ARE HIGH-SCHOOL, COLLEGE, OR TECHNICAL-SCHOOL GRADUATES

	Total Reporting	High-School Graduates				College Graduates				Technical-School Graduates			
		Fathers		Mothers		Fathers		Mothers		Fathers		Mothers	
		No.	%	No.	%	No.	%	No.	%	No.	%	No.	%
Alpine	193	73	37.8	67	34.7	16	8.2	7	3.6	7	3.6	0	
Canyon	477	179	37.5	170	35.6	33	6.9	39	8.1	18	3.7	8	1.6
Commerce	522	103	19.7	94	18.0	40	7.6	20	3.8	30	5.7	13	2.4
Denton	1,188	434	36.5	440	36.9	133	11.1	82	6.9	35	2.9	23	1.9
Nacogdoches ..	252	67	26.5	62	24.6	20	7.9	13	5.1	10	4.2	2	.7
Huntsville	548	153	27.9	164	29.9	60	10.9	30	5.4	23	4.1	18	3.2
San Marcos ...	410	109	26.5	113	27.5	25	6.1	21	5.1	16	3.9	6	1.4
Total	3,590	1,118	31.1	1,110	30.9	327	9.1	212	5.9	139	3.8	70	1.9

Table 29 shows the percentage of high-school, college, and technical-school graduates among the parents of 3,590 students of the seven teachers colleges. Slightly more than 9 per cent of the students have fathers who are college graduates, while only 5.9 per cent of the students have mothers who have had training to the extent of a

[33] Benson, C. E. *The Output of Professional Schools for Teachers,* Chaps. 3 and 8, Warwick & York, Inc., Baltimore, 1922.

college degree. In no college do these per cents exceed 11.1 for fathers and 8.1 for mothers. Less than one-third of all the students have parents who are high-school graduates; and the per cent of students in any college whose parents are high-school graduates does not exceed 37.8 per cent. These facts are not surprising when considered with others that have been presented above, and they add confirmation to the statement made heretofore; namely, that the majority of students in the teachers colleges come from families that are not the most highly favored from the standpoint of economic, occupational, and cultural status.

TABLE 30

NUMBER AND PER CENT OF STUDENTS WHO TAUGHT BEFORE THEY ENTERED NORMAL SCHOOL OR TEACHERS COLLEGE (EITHER BEFORE OR AFTER FINISHING HIGH SCHOOL), THE NUMBER AND PER CENT WHO COME FROM THE HIGH SCHOOL OF THE TOWN WHERE THE COLLEGE THEY ATTEND IS LOCATED, AND THE NUMBER AND PER CENT WHO PARTICIPATE IN EXTRACURRICULAR ACTIVITIES

	Total Reporting	Those Who Taught		From Town High Schools		Extracurricular Activities	
		No.	%	No.	%	No.	%
Alpine	193	19	9.9	24	12.4	101	52.3
Canyon	477	23	4.8	73	15.3	282	59.1
Commerce	522	33	6.3	45	8.6	190	36.3
Denton	1,188	73	6.1	204	17.1	585	47.2
Nacogdoches	252	12	4.7	54	21.4	130	51.5
Huntsville	548	32	5.8	69	12.5	289	52.7
San Marcos	410	19	4.6	44	10.7	138	33.6

The figures shown in Table 30 relative to the students who taught before entering teachers college, to those who came from the local town high school, and to those who took some part in extracurricular activities are based on the replies of the students themselves. An examination of the original replies indicates no reason to question the correctness of the figures presented. From the first part of the table it appears that by far the greater proportion of students now in attendance at the Texas teachers colleges during the regular session has had no experience as teachers. In all the colleges combined an average of 6 per cent reported that they had held teaching positions before entering college, and in no college does that percentage run over 9.9 per cent while in three colleges it goes below 5 per cent. It is evident from the original replies that those who have taught are those who are above the average age of the student body, and have been impelled to attend a teachers college either to keep their certificates in force or by the advancing requirements of the schools in which they teach. This situation is of more than minor importance to the internal administration of the colleges because it should largely influence the content of the curricula and the methods of teaching. Ten years' experience in one of these institutions convinces the writer that a very different situation obtains during the twelve weeks' summer session, and that as a result different teaching methods and materials must be employed during the summer. The percentages of the students in the five state teachers colleges of Missouri who taught before entering college were found in 1929 to be noticeably higher than that just shown for the Texas teachers colleges. They are reported[34] as follows: 7 per cent, 14 per cent, 15 per cent, 18 per cent, and 22 per cent. Earlier studies in the same state show high percentages of experienced teachers among the students. In 1915, 50 per cent of the women and men had held teaching positions before entering normal school, and in 1926, 18 per cent of the women and 13 per cent of the men had taught before college entrance.[35] Table 30 also shows that a considerable proportion of the students at each of the colleges comes from the local town high school, the per cents ranging from 8.6 to 21.4. The percentage of students who participate in extracurricular activities, as shown by this table, is not so large as might be expected in institutions that train for teaching positions where the direction of work of that nature will likely become part of regular duties. Less than 60 per cent in any of the colleges say that they take part in activities of that sort; and the percentage of non-participants runs as low as 33.6 per cent in one college.

Many of the facts presented in the foregoing pages indicate that the teachers colleges of Texas are non-selective institutions in the matter of admitting students. The non-selective character of the teacher-training institutions of Missouri in 1915 is discussed in the report of the Carnegie Foundation as follows:

This lack of a compelling environment is nevertheless only the opportunity for the existing condition and not by any means its cause. The normal schools, as at present conducted, do not desire to be selective institutions. Their tradition is to "do something for the needy student who is struggling

[34] *Report on Publicly Supported Higher Education,* p. 377, 1929.
[35] Hill, C. M. *Op. cit.,* pp. 32-33.

for education," and not to select and prepare fit agents for the public service. It has been to their interest to welcome and retain as long as possible every applicant, strong or weak; large enrollments, the spectacle of doing everything for the community, and "harmony" at all hazards have been the real objectives. Such aims do not accord with a selective function or permit of it. It is obvious from its table of failures alone that the Harris Teachers College is endeavoring to use its diploma in a discriminating way to guarantee the city of St. Louis superior teachers, and it is just as obvious that the state schools are almost completely indifferent to the way in which they mark their product.

This attitude on the part of the state normal schools is needless and injurious, and ought to be changed. State support and control in professional education ought to imply a guarantee of good and trustworthy standards consistently enforced. The state's brand on a teacher should mark a properly selected and thoroughly prepared and tested instructor, fit to teach in the finest schools of the state. As it is, the best developed school systems avoid the state's label and are compelled to ask for state funds with which to prepare teachers of their own. It is doubtful whether a change can be brought about in this respect except under a centralized system, where the competition for size ceases to dominate each move, and where a uniformly stable and effective educational policy can be formulated and enforced.[36]

General observation leads one to believe that the influences which determine the occupational choices of young people are uncertain and

TABLE 31

NUMBER AND PER CENT OF STUDENTS FROM FAMILIES IN WHICH THERE ARE OTHER TEACHERS

	Brothers or Sisters Who Taught		Fathers or Mothers Who Taught	
	No.	%	No.	%
Alpine	52	27	41	21
Canyon	181	38	122	25
Commerce ...	179	34	100	19
Denton	451	38	267	23
Nacogdoches .	99	39	63	25
Huntsville ...	182	33	97	18
San Marcos ..	131	32	86	21

fortuitous; and that the system of public education has been ineffective in providing guidance in this important matter. Those who select teaching appear to be influenced by the same haphazard influences, both as to the choice of that profession and the grade or

[36] Carnegie Foundation for the Advancement of Teaching. *Bulletin No. 14*, p. 326.

branch of the service that they enter. Tables 31 and 32 show some facts on this point regarding the students of the Texas teachers colleges. The former table makes it plain that the influence of other members of the student's family have considerable weight in his choice. Among the several colleges, from 27 per cent to 39 per cent of the students report that they have brothers or sisters who have taught—the average for all the colleges being 34.4 per cent. From the same table it is seen that from 18 per cent to 25 per cent of these students report that their fathers or mothers have been teachers. Discussing this matter the Carnegie Foundation for the Advancement of Teaching says:

> The student's selection of teaching as an occupation appears to have been largely due to the fact that some other member of the family had taught. This possibility appears at least in the cases of over three-fifths of the students; one-seventh of them all belong to families having three or more other teachers.[37]

An effort was made to ascertain what grade or branch of the teaching service the students at each college are preparing to enter; and the results are shown in Table 32. No evidence has been discovered anywhere in this study to indicate that the distribution of those preparing for the various branches of the public-school service has been determined either by the known fitness of students for any branch, or by the known demands of the public schools. The outstanding fact shown by the table is that a large proportion of students in each college are preparing for high-school teaching. Averaging the percentages of those planning to enter that branch of teaching, for all the colleges, indicates that more than 51 per cent of the men and nearly 30 per cent of the women plan to become senior-high-school teachers, but noticeably smaller percentages are preparing for junior high school work. Since, as is shown in the chapter on the demand for teachers in Texas, there are fewer teaching positions in high schools than in elementary, and since present certificate laws of the state permit a teacher who holds a high-school certificate to teach in any of the lower grades, it is likely that the large number preparing for high-school work results from the fact that salaries in high schools are higher than they are in the grades below the high school. Yet those who fail to secure positions in high schools are not prevented by the certification laws from accepting places in the elementary schools, and frequently do so. The rather low percentages who are

[37] Carnegie Foundation for the Advancement of Teaching. *Bulletin No. 14*, p. 118.

TABLE 32

TYPES OF SERVICE FOR WHICH STUDENTS ARE PREPARING*

	ALPINE				CANYON				COMMERCE			
	MEN		WOMEN		MEN		WOMEN		MEN		WOMEN	
	No.	%	No.	%	No.	%	No.	%	No.	%	No.	%
Total Reporting		143				266				490		
Kindergarten-Primary ...	0	.0	23	20.1	0	.0	60	20.4	0	.0	85	23.2
Intermediate grades	0	.0	32	28.0	3	4.2	81	27.5	0	.0	117	31.5
Junior high school	3	10.2	10	8.7	9	12.6	21	7.2	18	14.4	24	6.5
Senior high school	20	68.0	43	38.5	39	54.6	93	31.6	67	53.0	70	19.1
Administration	5	17.0	2	1.6	11	15.4	0	.0	22	17.4	1	.3
Supervisor	1	3.4	2	1.6	2	2.8	6	1.8	0	.0	5	1.0
Rural schools	0	.0	2	1.6	7	9.8	33	11.2	19	15.2	63	17.2

	DENTON				NACOGDOCHES				HUNTSVILLE			
	MEN		WOMEN		MEN		WOMEN		MEN		WOMEN	
	No.	%	No.	%	No.	%	No.	%	No.	%	No.	%
Total reporting		1012				209				450		
Kindergarten-Primary ...	0	.0	124	16.7	0	.0	36	21.8	0	.0	27	8.4
Intermediate grades	7	2.5	176	23.7	3	6.6	37	22.4	4	3.1	109	33.9
Junior high school	23	8.4	93	12.8	4	8.8	22	13.3	11	8.5	49	15.2
Senior high school	175	64.5	278	37.5	12	27.2	47	28.4	57	44.1	100	31.1
Administration	39	14.3	0	.0	16	36.3	1	.6	35	27.1	5	1.5
Supervisor	10	3.6	8	1.1	0	.0	1	.6	6	4.6	2	.6
Rural schools	17	6.2	60	8.1	9	20.4	21	12.7	16	12.4	29	9.0

	SAN MARCOS			
	MEN		WOMEN	
	No.	%	No.	%
Total reporting		401		
Kindergarten-Primary ...	0	.0	38	12.8
Intermediate grades	2	1.9	137	46.2
Junior high school	7	6.6	21	7.1
Senior high school	53	50.4	62	20.8
Administration	35	33.3	0	.0
Supervisor	3	2.8	5	1.6
Rural schools	5	4.7	23	7.7

* Table reads: Of total men and women answering this question (at Alpine), 18.9 per cent plan to be junior high school teachers, and so on.

preparing for teaching in the kindergarten-primary grades, ranging from 8.4 per cent to 23.2 per cent, can probably be explained by the fact that kindergartens have not been given a place in the public-school program of most Texas communities, and probably by the further fact that many school boards do not recognize the necessity for special training on the part of those who teach the very young children. The percentage of those preparing for teaching in rural schools is noticeably low in several of the colleges, especially in view of the fact, as is shown in another section of this study, that a large proportion of the former students of all the colleges are working in rural and small village schools. The percentage distributions shown in the table under discussion will be referred to again in the chapter on curricula.

In considering the selective function of any institution due regard must be given to its objective or objectives. Any school that is to any degree selective has the obligation not only of choosing from among those who offer themselves as prospective students, but of eliminating from its student body those who through lack of ability, which is discovered during the training period, or through lack of sufficient interest, show themselves unworthy of the definite position or work for which they are being trained.

The modern American junior high school is not regarded as selective in this sense, since its object is to assist all the children of the community to find their several interests, abilities, and aptitudes, and to offer such training as will develop these to their fullest capacity within the limits of the scope of the school's program.[38] A teachers college, on the contrary, should naturally be as selective as any other professional school, provided it confines its efforts to the objective for which it was established, and should, therefore, have the duty of eliminating incompetent individuals both from the numbers of those who apply for entrance and from the students in training. In other words, its purpose should not be to provide some sort of training for everybody.

It has already been pointed out that the Texas teachers colleges employ no selective measures in admitting students except the requirement of high-school graduation. In an effort to determine what selective function is performed by the several courses in the various departments, reports were obtained from the several registrars as to the grades made by students in attendance during the winter term of 1930. The number of students in each of the four college classes who made A's, B's, C's, E's and F's, Q's and W's, and X's were

[38] For a presentation of the functions of the junior high school see: Briggs, T. H. *The Junior High School,* pp. 65-72 and Chap. V. Houghton Mifflin Co., Boston, 1920. *The Classroom Teacher,* Vol. 10, Chap. IV. The Classroom Teacher, Inc., Chicago, 1927.

TABLE 33

AVERAGE PER CENTS OF GRADES (A'S, B'S, ETC.) REPORTED AT EACH COLLEGE

	A	B	C	D	E and F	Q and W	X
	Average Grade %	Average Grade %	Average Grade %	Average Grade %	Average Grade %	Average Grade %	Average Grade %
Alpine (18 departments)	16.5	25.8	23.6	8.7	12.2	7.1	4.3
Canyon (20 departments) ...	15.2	31.2	29.1	10.1	9.1	3.3	2.3
Commerce (19 departments) .	15.1	34.9	32.2	7.1	3.3	5.9	1.9
Denton (20 departments)	10.2	26.1	33.1	13.7	10.7	4.6	1.5
Huntsville (20 departments) .	14.5	30.1	37.2	11.5	2.8	.0	4.0
Nacogdoches (18 departments)	15.9	30.7	34.5	12.3	4.5	1.8	.0
San Marcos (20 departments)	10.3	25.5	38.5	13.7	8.1	2.7	.7

reported by departments. The percentages shown in Tables 33 and 34 were calculated from these numbers. The mark "Q" means that the student dropped the course before the end of the term, while

TABLE 34

PER CENTS OF GRADES REPORTED BY EACH DEPARTMENT, AVERAGE FOR ALL COLLEGES, WINTER TERM, 1930

	A	B	C	D	E AND F
	Per Cent	Per Cent	Per Cent	Per Cent	Per Cent
Art	10.9	28.6	43.6	8.5	1.3
Biology	8.2	21.6	38.2	16.3	6.2
Business Administration	15.4	28.5	25.6	9.9	8.2
Chemistry	11.4	21.3	31.2	17.4	8.0
Education	9.8	29.5	38.6	12.1	5.3
Economics & Sociology	11.2	29.0	34.2	12.3	5.3
English	9.5	25.2	33.5	14.0	12.7
Geography	7.5	26.4	38.7	16.5	6.3
Government	11.9	28.8	33.6	9.4	10.2
History	12.7	30.6	30.4	13.9	7.4
Home Economics	13.0	34.8	32.7	11.7	4.3
Industrial Education	12.8	39.5	33.9	4.6	4.4
Latin	33.5	36.7	16.7	5.8	1.7
Mathematics	19.5	24.0	23.0	10.6	11.1
Modern Languages	14.7	26.0	28.8	14.7	8.2
Music	13.1	31.3	36.7	9.0	4.5
Physical Education	17.6	31.0	34.9	5.7	3.6
Physics	15.3	27.2	25.4	13.0	6.6
Speech Arts	11.0	30.5	42.5	6.0	2.4

the mark "W" means that the student withdrew from school. The mark "X" means that the student failed to complete all the requirements of the course, such as required papers, a quiz or piece of laboratory work. Students who receive such a mark are allowed to satisfy the requirements after the close of the term, and receive the proper grade. While fairly complete uniformity in the grading plan is found among the several institutions, very considerable variations are apparent in the percentages of each grade reported, both by colleges and by departments within the same college. It is evident that most of the grades a student receives are made in academic departments, and these could not be taken as a complete measure of his professional fitness for the practice of his profession. No evidence has been found to indicate that any of the colleges administer a comprehensive examination designed to test professional knowledge and ability. It seems evident from the data here presented that the matter of grading students in an institution whose courses lead to a license to practice a profession constitutes a problem to be constantly worked at by some officer in charge of the internal administration of the school.

Table 33 shows the average percentages of each grade reported by each of the colleges. This average is the arithmetic mean of the percentages of each grade reported by all departments of each institution. The percentages of A's are noticeably high in all but two of the colleges, ranging from 10.2 per cent to 16.5 per cent. The sum of the percentages of A's and B's in five schools exceeds 42 per cent, and in one reaches 50 per cent. It is also noticed that the institutions, with one exception, which show low percentages of unsatisfactory grades, E's and F's, report high percentages of A's and B's. In general it is evident that there is a liberal attitude toward grading students in the teachers colleges of Texas, and it can hardly be said that such an attitude is in accord with the idea of using the grading procedure toward selective ends. Judging from personal reports of the registrars and the knowledge the writer possesses concerning conditions, it may be said that the grades of Q and W do not represent an elimination of students by the college except in rather rare cases. Occasionally students drop a course because they realize they will not be able to secure credit, but such students can usually manage to make up the equivalent hours of credit in some other course without serious loss of total time in school. The average percentages of unsatisfactory grades, E's and F's, range from 2.8 per cent to 12.2 per cent. *Bulletin No. 14* of the Carnegie Foundation for the Advancement of Teaching[39] reports such percentages at two different institutions ranging from 5.5 per cent to 10.8 per cent, with failures in specific subjects ranging from 10.6 per cent to 28.8 per cent. A distribution of grades made at the University of Minnesota in five academic courses shows percentages of A's ranging from 3.77 to 8.51; of A's plus B's from 19.8 to 24; and of E's plus F's from 4.79 to 26.75, with most included between 8 per cent and 10 per cent.[40] In comparison with these figures the percentages of unsatisfactory grades reported by at least four of the Texas teachers colleges are not especially low, but it is evident that the percentages of A's and A's plus B's in the Texas schools are strikingly high. No data are available to indicate what proportion of students whose grades are unsatisfactory are asked to withdraw from the Texas colleges. Catalogues of all but one college state in substance that students who fail to make satisfactory grades are placed on probation and may be asked to withdraw.[41] One of the institutions holds that a student who is doing work below the quality required for passing presents an important problem to the administration and to the teachers; and that the chief duty of the college is to save every student possible.[42] In an institution whose efforts are directed toward strictly professional ends, selection among members of the student body can be made only by dropping those who show themselves unable or unwilling to do the quality of work demanded by proper standards. However, to the extent that the Texas teachers colleges are attempting to accomplish other objectives than the professional training of teachers, such a strict conception of selection would hardly hold.

The percentage distribution of grades by departments shown in Table 34 presents some interesting and significant information. The per cent of A's in Education is 9.8; and only three other departments show a lower percentage—English, biology, and geography. The sum of the percentages of A's and B's is unusually high in most of the departments, while those of the unsatisfactory grades are not noticeably high in any, and are comparatively low in several. There has evidently been little or no concerted effort on the part of the seven teachers colleges to work out basic grading procedures that

[39] P. 323.

[40] Hudelson, Earl. *Class Size at the College Level,* p. 58. The University of Minnesota Press, 1928.

[41] Catalogue numbers of the bulletins are as follows: San Marcos, 1929-30, p. 23; Commerce, 1928-29, p. 23; Huntsville, 1928-29, p. 33; Nacogdoches, 1929-30, p. 23; Alpine, 1929-30, p. 46; Denton, June, 1929, p. 59.

[42] *Bulletin No. 53* of the College at Canyon, Catalogue Number for 1928-1929, p. 61.

will tend to some degree of uniformity. The most striking variations are found in the original reports in the grading among the departments of the same institution. For example, in one college the chemistry department ranked 26 per cent of the students as of A grade, while the economics and business administration departments gave only 7 per cent and 3 per cent, respectively, that grade. The history department of the same institution reported 21 per cent A's and the education department 23 per cent, with 4 per cent of unsatisfactory grades in the one and .6 per cent in the other. Another college reports 8.2 per cent A's in history, 4.5 per cent in education, with 13 per cent of unsatisfactory grades in the former and 10.6 per cent in the latter. In still another college 7 per cent of the students in the education department were ranked A and 5 per cent F, while in the same school 13 per cent in the English department were given A's and only 3 per cent F's. These are only a few of a large number of examples of seeming inconsistencies and of wide variances in assigning grades that can be found in the original reports. Three possible causes of this condition and of the high percentages of A's and B's and the low percentages of failing grades in professional institutions of collegiate rank may be: first, low academic and professional standards on the part of the members of the teaching staff; second, absence of any attempt to study grading as a problem in teaching, with a view to placing it on a more objective basis; and third, the possible attempt on the part of administrative officers to influence the grades that are assigned so that they will be pleasing and satisfactory to the students.

Summary and Proposals

The students of the Texas teachers colleges are typically Texan; are children of American-born parents who are farmers or small business men; are twenty to twenty-one years old; and (the majority) are graduates of affiliated high schools. The typical family from which students come has five children, with an annual income of about $2,000 to which two or more members contribute. Almost one-fifth of these students are entirely dependent upon their own resources in their efforts to secure an education, while nearly one-half of them are partially self-supporting. It costs the typical student a little less than $300 to attend college for one academic year, and he plans to devote from five to ten years of his life to teaching. Approximately one-third of all the students are men, and only about

6 per cent of all have taught before they entered a teachers college. However, about one-third have brothers or sisters who have been teachers.

The facts brought out by this study of student personnel suggest some proposals that might profitably be given serious attention during the next few years:

1. The state, through a constituted authority which would probably best be the State Board of Education, should determine the specific function of the teachers colleges. If the educational needs of the state demand that the professional training of teachers be concentrated in these institutions, and their work confined to that objective, such a program should be established and adequately supported. If, on the other hand, it appears that the best interests of the commonwealth can be served by providing for a general collegiate training in these colleges, along with professional education, then the amount and kind of support should be adjusted accordingly. In the past these colleges have been attempting to render a full measure of service without the guidance of any general state policy.

2. Under either policy, machinery should be set up at each institution for the selection and guidance of those who are to prepare themselves for the teaching profession. The selective and guiding program might well be started in the secondary schools and with their coöperation.

3. Each college should place in the hands of some internal administrative officer the responsibility of checking continuously on the ability and achievements of students in training for the profession to the end that the training program might function as a selective agency. Part of the responsibility of this officer would be the promotion of greater uniformity and integration of the grading done by the several departments.

4. Other tests of students' fitness for membership in the profession should be set up and emphasized in addition to grades made in college courses. These tests might include comprehensive examinations, definite personality ratings, grading on health and general physical efficiency, and ratings of ability to succeed with children in actual teaching situations.

5. Research work by each college should secure the professional records of its ex-students as a check upon the effectiveness of its own training, and should determine as accurately as possible the success

and the effect on the teaching profession of those who teach temporarily.

6. A minimum age limit for entrance upon a definite program of professional training should be established. The age of eighteen is suggested. A person who is not at least approaching his legal majority is too young to command general respect as a member of a profession.

CHAPTER III

PERSONNEL OF THE TEACHING STAFFS

Education of young people for practice of any profession requires teachers who are well trained, energetic, progressive, experienced, and thoroughly professional in their relationships and attitudes. No objective proof of such a statement is necessary, and even a hasty examination of the qualifications of the teachers in the best schools which train physicians, lawyers, engineers, and clergymen constitutes sufficient evidence that such institutions accept the truth of that statement. Unfortunately the institutions for the training of teachers have lagged behind other professional schools of the country in this regard.[1] A review of teacher training for the biennium 1926-28, by Frazier, makes the following summary of the situation and tendencies as to the faculties of teachers colleges and normal schools:

> In the teachers colleges and normal schools a distinct effort is made to raise standards of training for staff members. . . . Much room for improvement still exists in the training of the staffs of the normal schools and teachers colleges. The typical teacher-training institution has less than 10 per cent of its faculty with the doctor's degree, and less than one-half of the typical staff have the master's or doctor's degree. . . . The low scholastic standard, however, for training supervisors and demonstration teachers, one-fourth of whom do not hold the bachelor's degree, has been a cause for constant dissatisfaction.[2]

While it must be conceded that degrees do not teach, and that not all qualifications of useful members of a teachers college staff can be objectively measured, nevertheless the duty of applying such measures as are possible devolves upon one who would propose a program of teacher training. The state teachers colleges are, without doubt, an integral part of the state's system of public schools, and the members of their teaching forces belong to the great army of public-school teachers of the commonwealth. The conduct of public education in America may justly be criticized for having invested

[1] The Carnegie Foundation for the Advancement of Teaching, *Bulletin No. 14*, Chap. VI.

[2] Frazier, Benjamin W. *Teacher Training, 1926-1928*, United States Bureau of Education, Bulletin, 1929, No. 17, p. 13.

energy and funds primarily in buildings and physical equipment, and only secondarily in teachers and the training of teachers.[3]

The data for this chapter, which is an effort to make the first general investigation of the facts regarding the teaching staffs of the Texas teachers colleges, were derived principally from the replies to a questionnaire[4] which was circulated in all the colleges with the coöperation of the presidents. Practically every teacher returned a reply, the exceptions being those who were temporarily absent during the week in the winter term of 1930 in which the questionnaires were circulated. The data from the questionnaires were supplemented by references to the college catalogues and by an examination of the official personnel records in the offices of the presidents. Only regular employees of the colleges who did classroom teaching were considered in this part of the study. The tables incorporated in this chapter are based on complete and usable replies to the questions.

The State of Texas employs some 460 teachers in the seven teachers colleges. Accurate data on the marital status of 438 were secured, 48 per cent of whom are men. Of the men an average of 89.6 per cent, in all the colleges, are married, compared to 12.9 per cent of the women. The details as to numbers of men and women reporting and their marital status for each institution are presented in Table 35. There seems to have been a purpose on the part of the

TABLE 35

Number and Per Cent of Married Men and Women in Texas Teachers Colleges—College and Critic Teachers Combined

	Total Reporting	Men				Women				Total		
		Married		Single		Married		Single		Total Men	Total Women	% Men
		No.	%	No.	%	No.	%	No.	%			
Alpine	26	10	83.3	2	16.6	1	7.2	13	92.8	12	14	46.2
Canyon	47	19	95.0	1	5.0	5	18.5	22	81.5	20	27	42.6
Commerce	73	32	88.8	4	11.2	5	13.5	32	86.5	36	37	46.2
Denton	103	41	83.7	8	16.3	11	20.4	43	79.6	49	54	47.6
Huntsville	66	31	96.9	1	3.1	5	14.7	29	85.3	32	34	48.5
Nacogdoches ...	55	22	88.0	3	12.0	2	6.7	28	93.3	25	30	45.5
San Marcos	68	34	91.9	3	8.1	3	9.7	28	90.3	37	31	54.4
Total	438	189		22		32		195		211	227	48.1

[3] For a critical analysis of public education in America, see Counts, George S. *The American Road to Culture,* especially Chap. IX. The John Day Company, Inc., New York, 1930.

[4] See footnote 4, p. 43.

administration of each of the colleges to maintain teaching staffs composed of about one half men and one half women, and in at least three of the schools there seems to have been a preference for married men as teachers.

Ages of faculty members in a professional school are of some significance in determining qualifications. Teachers of teachers should be mature people, and yet a large proportion of teachers of advanced age would not be a favorable indication in a growing institution that laid claim to being progressive. The age distribution for all the Texas teachers colleges presented in Table 36 shows a very commendable situation in comparison with other states. In the Texas schools about 3 per cent more are under twenty-six years of age and about 1 per cent more are over sixty than were found in Missouri colleges in 1926,[5] while the average median age of the Texas teachers, 38.7, is only one year above that for those in Missouri and a year below the average median age of teachers in the Pennsylvania institutions.[6] From the facts collected in this study the women appear to be generally younger than the men, since the table shows that 17.9 per cent of the men and 22 per cent of the women are under 31, and 28.3 per cent of the men and 46.2 per cent of the women are between the ages of 31 and 40. Only three colleges report teachers over 65, with small per cents of that age. This is a rather remarkable fact when it is remembered that none of the Texas colleges has made provision for a retirement fund.

The faculty members of the state teacher-training institutions in Texas are largely native Texans, and one-fifth to one-fourth of their parents were born in Texas. Fully half of them have fathers who are farmers or tradesmen, and slightly more than three-fourths come from families in which there are other teachers. The facts for each college are presented in Tables 37, 38, and 39. Percentages are based on the number of replies to each specific question. There is some variation among the different institutions as to the number of native Texans employed, but the percentage among the teachers does not fall below 44.6 per cent at any college, and in no place does the percentage of teachers whose fathers and mothers were born in Texas fall below 12.5 per cent and 20.8 per cent, respectively. Other than Texans, natives of southern states have the best repre-

[5] Hill, C. M. *A Decade of Progress in Teacher Training*, p. 51.

[6] Wagner, Jonas E. "Professional Status of Faculty Members in Pennsylvania Teacher-Training Institutions." *Educational Administration and Supervision*, Vol. XV, No. 3, p. 209, March, 1929.

TABLE 36

AGES OF MEMBERS OF TEACHING STAFFS: COLLEGE AND TRAINING SCHOOL TEACHERS TOGETHER; MEN AND WOMEN SEPARATE; NUMBER AND PER CENT IN EACH AGE INTERVAL IN EACH COLLEGE

		21–25		26–30		31–35		36–40		41–45		46–50		51–55		56–60		61–65		66–70		Over 70					
	Total Replies	No.	%	No.	%	No.	%	No.	%	No.	%	No.	%	No.	%	No.	%	No.	%	No.	%	No.	%	Medians	Q1	Q3	Range
Alpine																											
Men	12	1	8.3	3	24.6	2	16.6	1	8.3	1	8.3	4	33.2	—	—	—	—	—	—	—	—	—	—	35.0	29.3	47.3	24–48
Women	14	1	7.1	1	7.1	4	28.4	5	35.5	2	14.2	1	7.1	—	—	—	—	—	—	—	—	—	—	36.2	31.8	40.5	22–48
Canyon																											
Men	20	1	5.0	1	5.0	3	15.0	3	15.0	4	20.0	5	25.0	1	5.0	1	5.0	—	—	1	5.0	—	—	43.5	44.0	49.0	23–66
Women	27	3	11.1	4	14.8	6	22.2	4	14.8	4	14.8	1	3.7	3	11.1	1	3.7	—	—	1	3.7	—	—	36.6	30.5	45.1	23–66
Commerce																											
Men	36	2	5.4	4	10.8	5	13.5	5	13.5	8	21.6	5	13.5	3	8.1	3	8.1	1	2.7	—	—	—	—	42.2	34.0	49.0	24–64
Women	37	3	8.1	10	27.0	3	8.1	13	35.1	7	18.9	1	2.7	—	—	—	—	—	—	—	—	—	—	36.9	29.1	40.5	23–47
Denton																											
Men	49	5	10.0	4	8.0	5	10.0	5	10.0	8	16.0	8	16.0	5	10.0	4	8.0	4	8.0	—	—	1	2.0	44.4	34.0	52.8	24–74
Women	54	4	7.2	3	5.4	14	25.2	15	27.0	9	16.2	2	3.6	5	9.0	2	3.6	—	—	—	—	—	—	38.0	33.3	43.5	23–60
Huntsville																											
Men	32	1	3.1	5	15.5	5	15.5	4	12.4	9	27.9	2	6.2	4	12.4	1	3.1	—	—	—	—	1	3.1	41.5	33.0	45.0	25–72
Women	34	1	2.9	5	14.5	6	17.4	6	17.4	5	14.5	4	11.6	3	8.7	1	2.9	3	8.7	—	—	—	—	40.0	33.0	49.1	23–62
Nacogdoches																											
Men	25	2	8.0	2	8.0	7	28.0	4	16.0	9	36.0	1	4.0	—	—	—	—	—	—	—	—	—	—	37.5	32.5	43.1	25–49
Women	30	4	13.2	6	19.8	11	36.3	6	19.8	1	3.3	—	—	2	6.6	—	—	—	—	—	—	—	—	33.0	28.0	37.3	23–54
San Marcos																											
Men	37	1	2.7	6	16.2	5	13.5	6	16.2	8	21.6	2	5.4	3	8.1	5	13.5	1	2.7	—	—	—	—	41.3	33.0	50.4	24–62
Women	31	—	—	6	19.2	9	28.8	3	9.6	7	22.4	3	9.6	—	—	3	9.6	—	—	—	—	—	—	36.5	31.9	44.9	26–59
Totals																											
Men	211	13	6.1	25	11.8	32	15.1	28	13.2	47	22.2	27	12.7	16	7.5	14	6.6	6	2.8	1	.04	2	.09	Average Median			
Women	227	14	6.6	35	15.4	53	23.3	52	22.9	35	15.4	12	5.2	13	5.7	7	3.1	3	1.3	1	.04	—	—	Age: 38.7			

Average median age for other states:

All (5) New Jersey Schools (1929)	38.8	9 Massachusetts State Normal Schools (1922)	43.3
5 Missouri State Teachers Colleges (1926)	37.7	3 Louisiana State Teachers Colleges (1923)	38.0
5 Missouri State Teachers Colleges (1929)	41.0	4 Michigan State Teachers Colleges (1923)	41.5

sentation on these teaching staffs, while those of northern and eastern states come next in rank. Less than 1 per cent of all the teachers were born in foreign countries, and only five countries—Mexico,

TABLE 37

BIRTHPLACES OF TEACHERS AND THEIR PARENTS

	Texas		Southern States		North and East		Mid-West and West		Foreign Countries	
	No.	%	No.	%	No.	%	No.	%	No.	%
					ALPINE					
Teachers ..	11	45.8	5	20.8	1	4.1	7	29.1	0	.0
Fathers ...	3	12.5	13	54.1	3	12.5	4	16.6	1	4.1
Mothers ..	5	20.8	12	50.0	1	4.1	6	25.0	0	.0
					CANYON					
Teachers ..	21	44.6	17	36.1	7	14.8	1	2.1	1	2.1
Fathers ...	6	12.7	31	65.9	7	14.8	0	.0	3	6.3
Mothers ..	10	21.2	27	57.4	8	17.0	1	2.1	1	2.1
					COMMERCE					
Teachers ..	45	61.6	22	30.1	5	6.8	0	.0	1	1.3
Fathers ...	12	16.4	49	67.1	8	10.9	0	.0	3	3.9
Mothers ..	20	27.4	42	57.5	8	10.9	0	.0	2	2.7
					DENTON					
Teachers ..	55	57.2	18	18.7	13	13.5	9	9.3	1	1.0
Fathers ...	14	14.5	50	52.0	19	19.7	5	5.2	8	8.3
Mothers ..	25	26.0	44	45.8	16	16.6	7	7.3	4	4.1
					HUNTSVILLE					
Teachers ..	38	58.4	15	23.1	8	12.3	3	4.6	1	1.5
Fathers ...	16	24.6	33	50.7	7	10.7	3	4.6	6	9.2
Mothers ..	19	29.2	33	50.7	7	10.7	2	3.1	3	4.6
					NACOGDOCHES					
Teachers ..	37	67.2	14	25.5	1	1.8	3	5.4	0	.0
Fathers ...	15	27.2	30	54.5	3	5.4	4	7.2	3	5.4
Mothers ..	24	43.6	22	40.0	3	9.0	3	5.4	1	1.8
					SAN MARCOS					
Teachers ..	38	55.8	24	35.2	1	1.4	5	7.3	0	.0
Fathers ...	14	20.5	46	67.6	3	4.4	3	4.4	2	2.9
Mothers ..	19	27.9	41	60.2	3	4.4	5	7.3	0	.0
					TOTAL					
Teachers ..	245	57.2	115	26.8	36	8.4	28	6.5	4	.9
Fathers ...	80	18.7	252	59.0	50	11.7	19	4.4	26	6.1
Mothers ..	122	28.6	221	51.8	46	11.3	24	5.6	11	2.6

TABLE 38

DISTRIBUTION OF TEXAS FACULTY MEMBERS ON BASIS OF PARENTAL OCCUPATIONS—MEN AND WOMEN, COLLEGE AND CRITIC TEACHERS COMBINED

	AGRICULTURE		TRADES		PROFESSIONS		BUSINESS		OTHERS	
	No.	%	No.	%	No.	%	No.	%	No.	%
Alpine	11	45.8	2	8.3	7	29.1	4	16.6	0	.0
Canyon	23	47.9	1	2.1	16	33.3	5	10.4	3	6.3
Commerce	27	36.9	6	8.2	10	13.6	14	19.1	16	21.9
Denton	37	43.5	12	14.1	22	25.8	14	16.4	0	.0
Huntsville	22	33.8	2	3.1	16	24.6	12	18.4	13	20.0
Nacogdoches ..	25	45.4	5	9.1	10	18.1	9	16.3	6	10.9
San Marcos....	37	54.4	3	4.4	9	13.2	12	17.6	7	10.2
Total	182	43.5	31	7.4	90	21.5	70	16.7	45	10.7

COMPARABLE DATA FROM OTHER STATES

	LABOR (SKILLED)	BUSINESS (CLERICAL)	BUSINESS (PROPRIETORS)	FARMERS	PROFESSIONS
	%	%	%	%	%
Teachers in all 5 New Jersey Institutions*	9.7	7.3	32.3	16.4	25.6
In 9 Massachusetts Normal Schools, 1921*	11.0	23.0		20.0	14.0
In 3 Louisiana State Teachers Colleges, 1926*	8.0	34.4		36.3	16.8
In 5 Missouri State Teachers Colleges, 1926*	10.0	15.0		47.0	15.0
In a Mid-Western City Teachers College, 1927	3.7	37.0		22.2	25.9
In 5 Missouri Teachers Colleges, 1929†	15.0	19.8		50.0	14.8

* Bagley, W. C. *Professional Education of Teachers in New Jersey.* (Unpublished study made in 1928.)

† *Report on Publicly Supported Higher Education*, p. 352.

Scotland, Sweden, Canada, and Germany—are represented. Slightly more than 6 per cent of the fathers of these teachers were born in foreign countries, while less than 3 per cent of their mothers were born abroad. Countries from which foreign-born parents came are: France, Scotland, Germany, Mexico, England, Switzerland, Sweden, Norway, and Ireland. Studies made in Missouri by Hill in 1926[7] and by others in 1929[8] show that more than half the teachers

[7] Hill, C. M. *A Decade of Progress in Teacher Training*, p. 53, Table XXII.

[8] *Report on Publicly Supported Higher Education*, pp. 350-51, 1929.

there are native Missourians, but there is a slightly higher proportion of those who are of foreign-born parentage. In the New Jersey normal schools, however, from 14 per cent to 17 per cent of fathers and mothers of teachers were found to be natives of foreign countries.[9] From comparable figures shown in Table 38 it is seen that the distribution of faculty members on the basis of parental occupations is very similar in all the states listed, except those that are highly industrial. Agricultural and small-business groups supply a large proportion of teachers of teachers.

TABLE 39

NUMBER AND PER CENT OF TEACHERS IN WHOSE IMMEDIATE FAMILIES OTHER MEMBERS (ONE TO FIVE) HAVE BEEN TEACHERS

(COLLEGE AND CRITIC TEACHERS*)

	NUMBER	PER CENT
Alpine	16	66.6
Canyon	38	80.8
Commerce	55	75.3
Denton	72	73.5
Huntsville	50	75.7
Nacogdoches	40	72.7
San Marcos	59	86.7
Total	330	76.7

* Table reads: At Alpine, of the total number of teachers reporting, 16, or 66.6%, come from families in which there are or have been from one to five other teachers.

In Tables 40 and 41, which follow, are some facts which throw interesting side lights on the personnel of the teaching profession. The former presents a percentage distribution of the faculty members of the Texas teachers colleges based on the age at which they began teaching, and the latter shows a summary of the replies obtained to the question, "If you had an opportunity to choose a vocation now, would you choose teaching?" Of the men who reported the age at which they began teaching, 38 per cent started the practice of their profession before they reached the age of twenty-one, while 69.1 per cent of the women began before they reached that age. Such a situation must be regarded as peculiar to the teaching profession since it is practically impossible for a person to qualify for the practice of other professions before he reaches his legal majority. The raising

[9] Bagley, W. C. *Op. cit.*, p. 40.

TABLE 40

AGE OF FACULTY MEMBERS WHEN THEY BEGAN TEACHING (COLLEGE AND CRITIC TEACHERS)

	Total Reporting	Less than 16		16		17		18		19		20		21		22		23		24		25		26		27		Over 27	
		No.	%	No.	%	No.	%	No.	%	No.	%	No.	%	No.	%	No.	%	No.	%	No.	%	No.	%	No.	%	No.	%	No.	%
Alpine	24																												
Men		—	—	—	—	—	—	1	10.0	2	20.0	1	10.0	1	10.0	1	10.0	2	20.0	—	—	1	10.0	—	—	—	—	1	10.0
Women		—	—	2	14.2	—	—	2	14.2	2	14.2	3	21.4	1	7.1	1	7.1	1	7.1	1	7.1	—	—	—	—	1	7.1	—	—
Canyon	48																												
Men		—	—	—	—	—	—	3	15.0	3	15.0	3	15.0	4	20.0	1	5.0	3	15.0	2	10.0	—	—	1	5.0	—	—	—	—
Women		—	—	4	14.2	3	10.7	5	17.8	5	17.8	3	10.7	2	7.1	2	7.1	3	10.7	1	3.5	—	—	—	—	—	—	—	—
Commerce	67																												
Men		—	—	1	3.3	3	9.9	2	6.6	6	20.0	6	20.0	4	13.3	1	3.3	2	6.6	3	9.9	1	3.3	1	3.3	—	—	—	—
Women		—	—	2	5.4	2	5.4	7	18.9	7	18.9	5	13.5	7	18.9	2	5.4	4	10.8	—	—	—	—	—	—	—	—	1	2.7
Denton	95																												
Men		—	—	1	2.2	—	—	5	11.1	7	15.5	9	20.0	4	8.8	5	11.1	3	6.6	3	6.6	6	13.3	1	2.2	—	—	1	2.2
Women		—	—	5	10.0	5	10.0	14	28.0	9	18.0	4	8.0	3	6.0	4	8.0	3	6.0	—	—	—	—	1	2.0	1	2.0	1	2.0
Huntsville	65																												
Men		—	—	—	—	1	3.1	5	15.6	4	12.5	3	9.3	6	18.6	2	6.3	2	6.3	1	3.1	4	12.5	2	6.3	—	—	2	6.3
Women		—	—	2	6.1	7	21.2	5	15.1	7	21.2	5	15.1	3	9.1	1	3.0	2	6.0	—	—	1	3.0	—	—	—	—	—	—
Nacogdoches ...	55																												
Men		—	—	—	—	1	4.0	4	16.0	2	8.0	5	20.0	5	20.0	2	8.0	2	8.0	—	—	—	—	—	—	3	12.0	1	4.0
Women		—	—	1	3.3	2	6.6	8	26.6	5	16.6	3	9.9	2	6.6	7	23.3	—	—	—	—	1	3.3	—	—	1	3.3	—	—
San Marcos	69																												
Men		—	—	1	2.6	4	10.5	4	10.5	2	5.2	7	18.4	7	18.4	3	7.8	5	13.1	1	2.6	2	5.2	—	—	—	—	2	5.2
Women		1	3.2	2	6.4	5	16.1	8	25.8	3	9.6	1	3.2	3	9.6	3	9.6	3	9.6	—	—	1	3.2	—	—	—	—	1	3.2
Total of Men ...		—	—	3	1.5	9	4.5	24	12.0	26	13.0	34	17.0	31	15.5	15	7.5	19	9.5	10	5.0	14	7.0	5	2.5	3	1.5	7	3.5
Total of Women		1	.4	18	8.1	24	10.8	49	21.9	38	17.1	24	10.8	21	9.4	20	8.9	16	7.1	2	.8	3	1.3	1	.4	3	1.3	3	1.3

of standards and requirements for teachers' certificates that has been in progress for the past few years will automatically increase the minimum age at which one may begin teaching.[10] It is interesting to note from Table 40 that in practically every college a higher percentage of women than of men began teaching at an early age. From Table 41 it will be seen that slightly more than one-fifth of all the faculty members indicate that they probably would not choose teaching as a profession if they were free to choose at this time. This could hardly be taken as evidence of lack of success or interest in the profession, for it would likely be found by a careful investigation that among those who thus expressed themselves are some of the most capable and energetic members of the profession. Some typical reasons given for not choosing teaching as a profession follow. "Opportunities for more adequate financial returns are better in other professions if the necessary expenditure for training is considered. Adequate income is necessary for self-respect in any profession." "Advancement in salary is too limited for women." "Teaching offers a small chance of accumulation of funds for old age." "Advancement in salary does not seem to depend very directly upon ability, and amount and quality of work done in teaching." The evidence based on the two tables under consideration seems to indicate that a considerable number of the teachers of teachers find

TABLE 41

NUMBER AND PER CENT OF FACULTY MEMBERS WHO WOULD ENTER TEACHING AND NUMBER AND PER CENT WHO WOULD NOT IF CHOOSING A PROFESSION NOW (COLLEGE AND CRITIC TEACHERS)

	Those Who Would		Those Who Would Not	
	No.	%	No.	%
Alpine	18	75.0	6	25.0
Canyon	36	75.0	12	25.0
Commerce	56	81.1	13	18.8
Denton	79	81.4	18	18.5
Huntsville	53	85.4	9	14.5
Nacogdoches	39	70.9	16	29.1
San Marcos	49	72.1	19	27.9
Total	330	78.0	93	21.9

[10] For a summary of the advancing requirements for certification see: *Bureau of Education Bulletin, 1929, No. 17*, pp. 16-17. Also, *Bulletin, 1927, No. 19:* Cook, Katherine M. "State Laws and Regulations Governing Teachers' Certificates."

themselves in the profession more or less accidentally and not as the result of deliberate and well-planned choice. This conclusion is in harmony with the results of a study of present-day teachers-college students made by E. V. Hollis.[11]

Do teachers in the Texas teachers colleges have others dependent upon them; and are the men heads of families with the financial and social obligations such a position entails? In an attempt to answer such a question, the data used in constructing Table 42 were collected. The facts on this point have considerable significance, indicating whether these teachers, on the salaries they receive, are in positions of economic comfort or strain, and whether or not they might be expected to be able to finance the cost of self-improvement such as: graduate study, personal research, educative travel, active membership in professional organizations, and the accumulation of professional libraries. No data are available to show the number of dependents of Texas residents in other occupations, but there is no apparent reason for thinking that teachers would be different from others in this respect. Teachers, however, do have the obligation to themselves and to their profession for continuous study and professional growth. Table 42 shows the number and percentage of teachers in the teachers colleges who report the number of persons (men and women separately) who are wholly dependent and partially dependent upon them for support. There is an overlapping of these two classes of dependents since the same teacher may contribute to the support of both classes. Therefore, the sum of the per cents of both would be meaningless. The proportion of men who have two or more dependents is very much greater than that of the women. However, only small per cents of the men and none of the women have as many as five or more dependents. The proportion of women who have no partial dependents is less than that for the men, and in general those requiring partial support from these teachers seem to be rather equally distributed among the men and women. It seems that the members of this group of more than four hundred people have as many responsibilities for the care of others as might be expected from an equal number of people selected at random from the general population.

The time, work, and money that a teacher spends in securing his training constitute his capital investment. Contrary to the popular

[11] Hollis, E. V. "Why They Teach," *Educational Administration and Supervision*, Vol. XV, No. 9, pp. 678-84, December, 1929.

TABLE 42

Distribution of Teachers According to Number of Their Dependents

	No Dependents				One Dependent				Two Dependents				Three Dependents				Four Dependents				Five Dependents				Six Dependents				More Than Six			
	Wholly No.	%	Partially No.	%	Wholly No.	%	Partially No.	%	Wholly No.	%	Partially No.	%	Wholly No.	%	Partially No.	%	Wholly No.	%	Partially No.	%	Wholly No.	%	Partially No.	%	Wholly No.	%	Partially No.	%	Wholly No.	%	Partially No.	%
Alpine																																
Men	4	33.3	9	75.0	3	25.0	2	16.6	2	16.6	0	0	0	0	0	0	1	8.3	0	0	2	16.6	1	8.3	0	0	0	0	0	0	0	0
Women	12	85.7	0	0	2	14.2	6	75.0	0	0	2	25.0	0	0	0	0	0	0	0	0	0	0	0	0	0	0	0	0	0	0	0	0
Canyon																																
Men	2	10.0	10	50.0	6	30.0	5	25.0	3	15.0	4	20.0	7	35.0	1	5.0	1	5.0	0	0	1	5.0	0	0	0	0	0	0	0	0	0	0
Women	25	92.6	16	59.3	1	3.7	2	7.4	0	0	2	7.4	0	0	2	7.4	1	3.7	2	7.4	0	0	2	7.4	0	0	1	3.7	0	0	0	0
Commerce																																
Men	4	12.9	17	47.2	3	9.6	10	27.7	9	29.0	5	13.8	8	25.8	3	8.3	6	19.3	0	0	1	3.2	1	2.7	0	0	0	0	0	0	0	0
Women	32	56.1	20	57.1	25	43.8	9	25.7	0	0	6	17.1	0	0	0	0	0	0	0	0	0	0	0	0	0	0	0	0	0	0	0	0
Denton																																
Men	6	13.3	0	0	10	22.2	7	41.1	9	20.0	7	41.1	11	24.4	1	5.8	6	13.3	1	5.8	1	2.2	1	5.3	2	4.4	0	0	0	0	0	0
Women	26	74.2	0	0	6	17.1	9	40.9	3	8.5	8	36.3	0	0	5	22.7	0	0	0	0	0	0	0	0	0	0	0	0	0	0	0	0
Huntsville																																
Men	5	15.5	18	50.0	6	18.6	8	25.0	7	21.8	4	12.5	7	21.8	1	3.1	5	15.6	3	9.3	1	3.1	0	0	0	0	0	0	1	3.1	0	0
Women	27	81.8	15	45.4	4	12.1	10	30.3	1	3.0	3	9.0	0	0	3	9.0	1	3.0	2	6.0	0	0	0	0	0	0	0	0	0	0	0	0
Nacogdoches																																
Men	1	4.0	14	56.0	4	16.0	3	12.0	13	52.0	5	20.0	4	16.0	2	8.0	1	4.0	1	4.0	2	8.0	0	0	0	0	0	0	0	0	0	0
Women	7	70.0	29	72.5	1	10.0	5	12.5	2	20.0	4	10.0	0	0	1	2.5	0	0	1	2.5	0	0	0	0	0	0	0	0	0	0	0	0
San Marcos																																
Men	3	7.8	26	68.4	11	29.0	7	18.4	10	26.3	1	2.6	7	18.4	1	2.6	3	7.8	3	7.8	3	7.8	0	0	1	2.6	0	0	0	0	0	0
Women	25	83.3	17	56.6	5	16.6	5	16.6	0	0	6	20.0	0	0	1	3.3	0	0	1	3.3	0	0	0	0	0	0	0	0	0	0	0	0
Total																																
Men	25	12.3	94	51.6	43	21.1	42	23.0	53	26.1	26	14.2	44	21.2	9	4.9	23	11.3	8	4.4	11	5.4	3	1.6	3	1.4	0	0	1	.4	0	0
Women	154	74.7	97	49.7	44	21.3	46	23.6	6	2.9	31	15.9	0	0	12	6.1	2	.97	6	3.0	0	0	2	1.0	0	.02	1	.5	0	0	0	0

The table reads: 33.3 per cent of the men at Alpine, and 85.7 per cent of the women report that they have no one entirely dependent upon them; while 75 per cent of the men and none of the women report no one partially dependent. Practically one-eighth of all the men and three-fourths of the women have nobody who is wholly dependent upon them; while slightly more than one-fifth of each say that they have one person to support.

idea, which holds that a person having an education has it once and for all and that it cannot be taken from him, the capital investment of an efficient teacher must be well chosen and constantly added to. The results of a study of the nature and extent of the training possessed by the faculties of the Texas teachers colleges are presented in the tables and discussion which follow immediately. Table 43 shows a percentage distribution of the college and critic teachers separately, on the basis of the sequence of training they have taken. Eleven possible sequences are used, together with a distribution showing the percentage of both classes of teachers who are former students of the college in which they teach. The largest per cent, 36.7, of all the college teachers passed through secondary school, liberal arts college, and the graduate school of a university. This is the traditional academic educational sequence. The next ranking per cent, 24.6, of this group passed successively through secondary school, normal school or teachers college, and the graduate school. The third ranking group, 18.4 per cent, attended a liberal arts college after leaving a normal school or teachers college and before entering a graduate school. The other sequences, as shown by the reports received, are represented by approximately uniform percentages of the entire number of college teachers. The sequence followed by the largest proportion of critic teachers, 27.8 per cent, is the one that ranked second with the college teachers, namely, secondary school, teachers college, and graduate school. The second ranking percentage of critic teachers, 23.3, attended a secondary school, then a normal school or teachers college, while the third group in the order of ranking, composed of 20 per cent, passed successively through a secondary school, normal school, and liberal arts college. Only 10 per cent of the critic teachers followed the traditional academic sequence.

If there is a best order of training for either group of teachers, it has not been determined. The literature on teacher training, however, strongly supports the position that teachers of teachers should be given specific professional education to fit them for their responsibilities, and that training in subject matter exclusively is not sufficient. It is of interest to note that slightly more than one-fifth of the teaching force of all the institutions, college and critic teachers combined, are former students of the college in which they teach. In Missouri teachers colleges in 1929 slightly more than one-third of the teachers had received their undergraduate training in the

TABLE 43

Percentage Distribution of Teachers Based on Combination (or Sequence) of Training

Kinds of Training in Their Sequence	Type of Teacher	Alpine		Canyon		Commerce		Denton		Huntsville		Nacogdoches		San Marcos		Total	
		No.	%	No.	%	No.	%	No.	%	No.	%	No.	%	No.	%	No.	%
Secondary school only	College																
	Critic																
Normal or teachers college only	College			1	2.6											1	.2
	Critic	2	33.4					1	5.8							3	3.3
Other college only	College			1	2.6											1	.2
	Critic																
Normal, college and graduate	College							1	1.3							1	.2
	Critic																
Secondary and normal or teachers college	College	1	5.5	4	10.5	2	3.8	4	5.0	1	2.0	4	8.8	3	5.2	19	5.6
	Critic			5	50.0	3	15.0	4	23.6	4	25.0	3	30.0	2	18.2	21	23.3
Secondary, normal and other college	College					4	7.7			6	12.2	5	11.1	6	10.4	21	6.2
	Critic			2	20.0	9	45.0			5	31.3	1	10.0	1	9.1	18	20.0
Secondary, normal, college and graduate	College	5	27.8	3	7.9	6	11.6	21	26.2	9	18.4	5	11.1	13	22.9	62	18.4
	Critic			1	10.0			1	5.8			1	10.0	1	9.1	4	4.4
Secondary and college	College	2	11.1	2	5.3	2	3.8	11	13.7	3	6.1	4	8.9	3	5.2	27	7.9
	Critic	3	50.0			3	15.0	1	5.8	1	6.2	1	10.0			9	10.0
Secondary, college and graduate	College	7	38.8	16	42.2	17	32.7	23	28.8	21	42.8	19	42.3	21	36.9	24	36.7
	Critic	1	16.6	2	20.0	2	10.0	1	5.9	1	6.2	1	10.0	1	9.1	9	10.0
Secondary, normal or teachers college and graduate	College	3	16.6	11	28.9	21	40.4	20	25.0	9	18.4	8	17.8	11	19.4	83	24.6
	Critic					3	15.0	8	47.2	5	31.3	3	30.0	6	54.5	25	27.8
Normal, teachers college and graduate	College																
	Critic							1	5.8								
Ex-students of college where teaching	College	2	8.3	10	20.8	13	18.1	30	30.9	13	20.0	7	12.7	18	26.5	93	21.7
	Critic																
Total College Teachers		18		38		52		80		49		45		57		339	
Total Critic Teachers		6		10		20		17		16		10		11		90	
Total Both Teachers		24		48		72		97		65		55		68		429	

college in which they were teaching.[12] The recommendations in the Missouri report suggest that careful consideration be given to the problem of academic inbreeding.[13] The variations in these per cents among the several colleges will probably be of interest to the respective administrative officers who are charged with the responsibility of recommending and selecting members for the teaching staffs.

It is to be regretted that no objective standards for measuring the preparation of teachers for teachers colleges have been developed except the possession of collegiate degrees. It is not difficult to demonstrate, by selecting isolated cases, that the accumulation of college and university degrees does not insure capable teachers. However, practically no other standards are set up by the recognized accrediting agencies, although it is generally admitted by students of teacher training that the holding of a series of standard degrees including the doctorate may not give an individual the slightest professional training for the specific task of preparing teachers for the public schools. "Professional training in education is rapidly achieving the power to make the tyro in teaching appear quite as much of a bungler as is the novice in medicine."[14] That statement was written fifteen years ago, and, in view of progress that has been made since that time, must be true to a larger degree at present. Modern standards, indeed, are requiring teachers colleges to be staffed with degree-holding teachers, and there are no convincing arguments to refute the claim that degrees do represent study and training. The present standards for accrediting teachers colleges, published by the American Association of Teachers Colleges, to which the Texas institutions belong, make definite requirements on this point. Section V, on the preparation of the faculty,[15] sets up in substance the following minimum standards: Six years from the date of the adoption of these standards are allowed certain teachers in which to meet the minimum provided. Teachers in the college department are expected to be graduates of a college of recognized standing, and to have done a year's study in a graduate school which will presumably confer the master's degree. Teachers in the training school are required by these standards to have a bachelor's degree or equivalent training, and six years after the adoption of these standards the minimum amount of preparation for them will be the same as for teachers in the college department.

[12] *Report on Publicly Supported Higher Education*, p. 358. [13] *Ibid.*, p. 368.

[14] Carnegie Foundation for the Advancement of Teaching. *Bulletin, No. 14*, p. 104.

[15] *Ninth Yearbook of the American Association of Teachers Colleges*, pp. 11-13, 1930.

In addition to the combinations of training shown in Table 43 that have been pursued by the faculty members in Texas, this study attempts to investigate the degrees held by these teachers, together with the sources of the graduate degrees. Table 44 shows the result of the investigation of degrees in the form of a percentage distribution on the basis of the highest degree held. The percentages of men in the college department, of women there, and of men and women in training school were determined separately for each institution. The percentages of all college teachers and of all training school teachers holding each degree are presented in the columns at the right in Table 44. Four hundred sixty teachers were included in this part of the study, and the facts were taken from their replies when such were sufficiently complete and usable. In other cases data were obtained from the catalogues and from official personnel records. Administrative officers, part-time assistants, and secretaries were not included in the tabulations. It will be seen that two-thirds of all teachers in college departments possess the master's degree as their highest degree, and 7.2 per cent are holders of the doctor's degree. Stated differently, nearly three-fourths of all the college teachers possess graduate degrees. However, slightly more than one-fifth, 22 per cent, of these teachers have no degree higher than the bachelor's, while 3.6 per cent have no recognized college degree. The last figures mean that fully one-fourth of all teachers in the college departments have not met the minimum standards as to preparation adopted by the American Association of Teachers Colleges at its meeting in February, 1930. Of all the training-school teachers, 39 per cent hold the master's degree, and 52 per cent hold the bachelor's as the highest degree. Only 9 per cent have no degree, thereby failing to meet the present minimum standards of the Association. The situation as shown for each college will doubtless be of interest to those who are responsible in any way for the work and development of those particular institutions.

In order to show how the teachers in the Texas teachers colleges compare with teachers in the teacher-training institutions of other states as to degrees held, Table 45 was constructed. It will be noticed that the figures from some of the states are several years old, but it is evident that the institutions in the states listed have not met in full the requirements outlined above, and that Texas institutions have made as much progress as have those in the states shown.

The highest per cent of doctor's degrees found in any of the

TABLE 44

Percentage Distribution of Faculties on Basis of Highest Degree Held

	Type of Teacher	Alpine			Canyon			Commerce			Denton			Huntsville			Nacogdoches			San Marcos			All Colleges		
		Men	Women	Both	Men	Women	Both	Men	Women	Both	Men	Women	Both	Men	Women	Both	Men	Women	Both	Men	Women	Both	Men	Women	Both
		%	%	%	%	%	%	%	%	%	%	%	%	%	%	%	%	%	%	%	%	%	%	%	%
No degree	College	10.0	10.0	10.0	6.9	5.3	6.0	3.3	0	1.9	0	0	0	6.9	0	4.0	0	4.3	2.2	2.8	14.2	7.1	3.5	3.7	3.6
	Critic	0	25.0	16.6	0	19.9	17.6	0	6.6	4.5	20.0	8.3	11.7	0	15.4	12.5	0	0	0	0	0	0	3.7	10.9	9.0
Bachelor's degree	College	20.0	10.0	15.0	20.7	23.3	22.0	13.3	18.1	15.4	16.5	23.2	20.0	23.9	20.0	22.4	14.3	34.2	25.0	14.2	28.5	19.6	20.6	24.2	22.2
	Critic	100.0	50.0	66.6	100.0	35.7	47.0	57.1	73.3	68.1	20.0	33.3	29.4	100.	53.8	62.5	50.0	50.0	50.0	50.0	22.2	27.2	59.2	49.3	52.0
Master's degree	College	70.0	80.0	75.0	58.6	71.4	64.0	73.3	81.8	76.9	59.5	72.1	65.8	57.9	80.0	67.3	76.1	60.8	68.1	77.7	57.1	69.6	64.5	70.1	66.9
	Critic	0	25.0	16.6	0	44.4	35.3	42.8	20.0	27.2	60.0	58.3	58.8	0	30.6	25.0	50.0	50.0	50.0	50.0	77.8	72.7	37.0	39.7	39.0
Doctor's degree	College	0	0	0	13.8	0	5.9	10.0	0	5.7	23.8	4.6	14.1	10.3	0	6.1	9.5	0	4.5	5.4	0	3.5	12.1	1.2	7.2
	Critic	0	0	0	0	0	0	0	0	0	0	0	0	0	0	0	0	0	0	0	0	0	0	0	0

The table reads: Ten per cent of the men teachers of college classes at Alpine and ten per cent of the women teachers of college classes have no standard collegiate degrees, while none of the men critic teachers, and 25 per cent of the women critic teachers report no degrees. Of all the college teachers in that institution, both men and women, 10 per cent have no degree; and 16.6 per cent of all critic teachers are without degrees.

Missouri colleges in 1929 was 11.5; and the lowest 5.0. The percentage of those holding only the bachelor's degree ranged from 17.5 to 43.4; and of those with the master's as the highest degree the range was from 45.6 to 70.1. It is suggested in the Missouri report that the low salary schedules, particularly the low maximum salaries, make it very difficult for the institutions in that state to compete with other institutions for teachers who hold the doctor's

TABLE 45

PER CENT OF DEGREES HELD BY FACULTY MEMBERS IN THE TEACHER-TRAINING INSTITUTIONS OF OTHER STATES

	Per Cent with No Degree	Per Cent with Bachelor's	Per Cent with Master's	Per Cent with Doctor's
5 New Jersey schools*	22.8	32.6	40.2	3.8
3 Louisiana state teachers colleges (1923)	27.0	50.0	20.0	3.0
9 Massachusetts state normal schools (1922)	51.0	30.0	18.0	1.0
5 Missouri state teachers colleges (1926)†	11.0	33.0	51.0	5.0
5 Missouri colleges in 1929‡	5.0	27.5	59.7	7.0
All Pennsylvania teacher training institutions, 1928–1929§	5.3	42.8	46.0	5.8

* Bagley, W. C. *Op. cit.*

† Hill, C. M. *A Decade of Progress in Teacher Training*, p. 57.

‡ *Report on Publicly Supported Higher Education*, p. 357.

§ Wagner, Jonas E. "Professional Status of Faculty Members in Pennsylvania Teacher-training Institutions," *Educational Administration and Supervision*, Vol. XV, No. 3, pp. 203, 205.

degree.[16] That this same sort of situation exists in the Texas teachers colleges is revealed in the tables giving the salary distributions.

It will be interesting in this connection to note the progress in the matter of degree qualifications of their faculties that has been made by the Texas teachers colleges since 1919, which was the first year that the bachelor's degree was awarded. The facts shown in per cents of the faculties holding the various degrees, are presented at two- and three-year intervals in Table 46. The percentages for college teachers and training school teachers are shown separately in this table, the data for which were taken from the catalogue files of the several institutions. It is shown that the percentages of teachers with no degree have steadily been reduced as have also the percentages of

[16] *Op. cit.*, p. 357.

TABLE 46

PERCENTAGE DISTRIBUTION OF TEACHERS ON BASIS OF DEGREES HELD FROM 1919 TO 1929. COLLEGES SHOWN SEPARATELY

Location of College	Academic Year	Per Cent with No Degree		Per Cent with Bachelor's		Per Cent with Master's		Per Cent with Doctor's	
		College Teachers	Critic Teachers	College Teachers	Critic Teachers	College Teachers	Critic Teachers	College Teachers	Critic Teachers
Alpine	1918–19	—	—	—	—	—	—	—	—
	1922–23	6.2	20.0	56.2	80.0	37.5	.0	.0	.0
	1925–26	.0	40.0	41.1	40.0	58.8	20.0	.0	.0
	1928–29	10.0	16.6	20.0	50.0	70.0	33.3	.0	.0
Canyon	1918–19	44.4	87.5	37.5	12.5	18.7	.0	.0	.0
	1922–23	22.8	52.4	31.4	38.0	42.8	9.5	2.8	.0
	1925–26	10.5	29.4	39.4	58.8	44.7	11.8	5.2	.0
	1928–29	6.1	13.3	34.7	66.6	51.9	33.0	8.1	.0
Commerce	1918–19	9.0	—	69.7	—	21.2	—	.0	.0
	1922–23	2.7	.0	67.5	80.0	29.7	20.0	.0	.0
	1925–26	3.0	15.7	27.2	61.5	69.7	23.0	.0	.0
	1928–29	.0	.0	12.5	71.5	78.8	30.8	9.0	.0
Denton	1918–19	20.0	85.7	47.2	14.3	30.9	.0	1.8	.0
	1922–23	12.5	37.5	40.6	62.5	45.3	6.0	1.5	.0
	1925–26	5.3	15.8	20.0	57.9	69.3	26.3	5.3	.0
	1928–29	.0	10.0	22.8	50.0	68.7	40.0	8.3	.0
Huntsville	1918–19	33.3	63.6	48.5	27.2	15.1	9.0	3.0	.0
	1922–23	11.4	36.2	47.7	45.4	40.9	18.1	.0	.0
	1925–26	8.7	18.1	39.1	36.3	50.0	45.0	2.2	.0
	1928–29	6.2	6.2	31.2	56.2	60.4	37.5	2.0	.0
Nacogdoches	College established in 1923–24								
	1925–26	5.5	20.0	44.4	80.0	50.0	.0	.0	.0
	1928–29	2.6	.0	26.3	20.0	68.4	80.0	2.6	.0
San Marcos	1918–19	16.6	100.0	50.0	.0	33.3	.0	.0	.0
	1922–23	6.3	27.3	51.2	63.6	40.4	9.0	2.1	.0
	1925–26	4.5	20.0	22.7	70.0	70.7	10.0	2.2	.0
	1928–29	3.7	.0	24.0	38.4	68.5	61.6	3.5	.0

those holding only the bachelor's degree, while the proportion of those with graduate degrees has steadily increased.

Table 47 shows the institutions from which most of the graduate degrees were obtained. The source of 306 such degrees was ascertained and used in calculating the percentages shown in Table 44. The University of Texas ranks first as the source of master's and doctor's degrees, with Columbia University ranking second. Fifty per

TABLE 47

UNIVERSITIES AND COLLEGES THAT HAVE GRANTED THE GRADUATE DEGREES HELD BY TEACHERS IN TEXAS TEACHERS COLLEGES

University or College Granting Degree	No. Graduate Degrees	The Texas Teachers College That has Greatest Number of Graduate Degrees from Each Institution of the First Eight Named
University of Texas	72	San Marcos with 22 reported
Columbia University	65	Denton with 20 reported
Peabody	33	Commerce with 7 reported
University of Chicago	27	Commerce and Denton each reported 6
Southern Methodist University	20	Denton with 11 reported
University of Missouri	14	San Marcos with 5 reported
University of Colorado	7	Nacogdoches and Denton, 2 each
Iowa State College	7	Huntsville with 4 reported

Among other institutions represented with fewer than 7 graduate degrees are:

University of California	University of Wisconsin
Harvard University	Texas A and M College
Leland Stanford	Vanderbilt University
University of Michigan	University of Iowa
Colorado State Teachers College	University of Denver
Clark University	University of Southern California

Baylor University

cent of all the graduate degrees were obtained from the six highest ranking out-of-state institutions shown in this table: Columbia, Peabody, Chicago, Missouri, Colorado, and Iowa. The optimum training for faculty members of a teacher-training institution should include academic work of the highest standard plus an intensive study of professional problems involved in the training of teachers. The institutions in the list just referred to possess the best-known professional schools in America, and the fact that so large a proportion of the holders of graduate degrees in the Texas teachers colleges is trained in them argues well for the professional development of these colleges.

On the assumption that preparation for the most efficient work on the part of those who train teachers for the public schools involves, in addition to education in subject-matter, specific training for the task to be accomplished, an effort was made to determine the per cent of the faculty members who had taken courses dealing with the professional training of teachers. Also, since the professional vigor and activity of teaching staffs is indicated to a considerable degree by the numbers who are continuing formal study, through correspondence courses, extension courses, or by actual residence at universities on leaves of absence, such information was sought from the teachers in the Texas teachers colleges. The results of the investigation are shown in per cents in Table 48. The replies of teachers as to courses taken which dealt with the professional training of teachers proved to be generally ambiguous, and revealed a lack of understanding on the part of many as to the exact nature of such courses. Some regarded all courses in education as giving training for the specific work of teacher training, while others reported having had courses of that nature from institutions in which work of that sort is not offered. The figures are presented as suggestive of the situation in the Texas institutions. The figures shown in column C were

TABLE 48

A. Per Cent of Teachers Who Report Having Taken Courses in the Professional Training of Teachers; B. Per Cent Taking Extension and Correspondence Courses; C. Per Cent on Leave of Absence for Study During Winter Term, 1930

	A	B	C
	Per Cent Who Have Taken Professional Courses	Per Cent Taking Extension Courses	Per Cent on Leave During Winter Term, 1930
Alpine	42.3	15.3	3.8
Canyon	20.8	8.3	12.5
Commerce	41.1	24.7	1.3
Denton	30.4	13.7	14.7
Huntsville	37.9	12.1	10.7
Nacogdoches	34.5	12.7	9.2
San Marcos	22.1	23.5	1.5
Total	31.7	15.8	8.5

based on numbers reported by the presidents or deans of the several schools. Replies of teachers indicate that 43.4 per cent of the total teaching staffs have been granted leaves of absence for study during their experience with the colleges they now serve. Nearly a third of all teachers reported having taken professional courses dealing with the training of teachers; 15.8 per cent said that they were studying by some form of extension work; and 8.5 per cent were reported to be on leave of absence for study during the winter of 1930.

After formal training, the most important element in fitness to train teachers is likely to be the duration and character of a preliminary experience. It is reasonable to assume that each type of professional training has a type of experience best suited to insure its highest efficiency. In the preparation of teachers this would appear obvious enough: a person can scarcely hope to qualify as a guide for teachers of children in the public schools without first-hand and continuous experience with the conditions and problems which he is fitting his students to face.[17]

The teachers in the Texas teachers colleges have had experience, as is shown by the figures presented in Tables 49 and 50 below. The average median length of public school experience of teachers in the college departments is 6.15 years, and in the training schools it is 4.77 years. The ranges of such experience indicate that some teachers in each of the two groups have come into the work of teacher training without public school experience, but data at hand give assurance that not more than about five per cent lack experience of this kind. That the faculty experience has covered practically all levels and phases of public school work is clear from the numerical distribution given in Table 50, and from the percentages of each type of experience that are shown at the end of the table. These numbers and percentages overlap, since individuals frequently reported two or more varieties of public school experience. The number of reports received indicates that more than one-fifth of all teachers have taught in rural schools, one-fourth in other elementary schools, and nearly one-half have served as high-school teachers. A noticeable fact is that only about seven per cent have had experience in other teacher-training institutions; 23 per cent have been teachers in liberal arts colleges; and nearly ten per cent have done teaching in universities. The conditions surrounding this study, however, have not permitted the assembling of detailed data showing the relationship

TABLE 49

MEDIAN NUMBER OF YEARS OF PUBLIC SCHOOL EXPERIENCE

Location of College	College Teachers	Critic Teachers	Range for College Teachers	Range for Critic Teachers
Alpine	5.0	10.0	0–18	0–19
Canyon	5.33	4.0	0–26	0–20
Commerce	9.25	3.5	1–23	0–17
Denton	5.86	3.5	0–27	1–23
Huntsville	6.9	4.33	0–21	0–24
Nacogdoches	5.5	3.0	0–20	0– 3
San Marcos	5.25	5.1	0–22	0–16
Average Median	6.15	4.77		

[17] Carnegie Foundation for the Advancement of Teaching. *Bulletin No. 14*, p. 105.

between character of experience and nature of work being done in their present teaching positions. Evidently, no specific amount of indiscriminate public school experience necessarily increases the professional efficiency of those who train teachers.[18] The study of this relationship in individual cases constitutes a very proper problem for the attention of those responsible for the selection of teachers at each college.

The following facts were ascertained as to the length of time the staff members have served their respective institutions. The median length of service for college teachers is 7.07 years, for critic teachers 4.22, while Q_1 for the former is 4.09 and for the latter, 2.55. The third quartile point for teachers in the college department is 11.44 and for critic teachers, 7.75.

The United States Office of Education says regarding qualifications of teachers in teacher-training institutions:

> The standards of the American Association of Teachers Colleges are not fixed, but are constantly rising. As a result, the steady pressure exerted upon the training institutions to raise the amount of training of their faculties has evoked much discussion. Most objections offered to the increasing quantitative requirements for training are based on the fact that it is difficult to secure really superior teachers who possess the doctor's degree for the salaries most training institutions can afford to pay. No one can intelligently question the value to a college instructor of ample scholarship of the right sort.
>
> The objections raised to the nature of the training which the teachers college faculty member secures in the universities should receive a sympathetic hearing by the large graduate schools and colleges. The average staff member in the teachers college is given little or no opportunity to use the elaborate research techniques which he so laboriously acquired in his graduate training. He is called upon in the teachers college to instruct young people in superior classroom teaching, but he is given no training in such work in the university, nor is he given any particular encouragement to acquire the art for himself. He should know a great deal about elementary education, but the supply of doctors of philosophy adequately equipped with a knowledge in this field is entirely insufficient for the needs of the training institutions.[19]

The salaries received by teachers in the Texas teachers colleges, and the general financial status of teachers, were investigated as a part of this study, with the purpose in mind of determining the power of these institutions to attract and hold teachers of superior

[18] *Ibid.*, pp. 106-7.

[19] Frazier, Benjamin W. *Teacher Training 1926-28*, United States Bureau of Education, Bulletin, 1929, No. 17, p. 14.

TABLE 50

NUMERICAL DISTRIBUTION OF FACULTY MEMBERS ON THE BASIS OF KINDS OF EXPERIENCE BEFORE THEY ENTERED THE COLLEGE WHERE THEY NOW TEACH *

Type of Teacher	Teacher in						Principal of High School	Principal of Elementary School	Supervisor	City Superintendent	County Superintendent	State Superintendent
	Rural School	Graded School	High School	Normal School	College	University						
ALPINE												
College	4	5	12	2	8	2	4	2	2	3	0	0
Critic	0	3	3	1	1	0	0	0	0	0	0	0
CANYON												
College	13	12	19	4	16	6	9	9	0	5	1	0
Critic	2	6	4	1	0	1	0	2	1	0	1	0
COMMERCE												
College	8	11	15	1	5	4	4	5	7	2	1	0
Critic	6	8	11	0	3	0	6	3	1	2	0	0
DENTON												
College	21	25	50	9	30	12	16	14	10	14	1	0
Critic	2	7	6	0	5	0	6	4	0	1	0	0
HUNTSVILLE												
College	14	12	29	2	13	9	15	5	7	6	1	0
Critic	5	5	9	1	1	1	0	0	2	0	0	0
NACOGDOCHES												
College	10	10	25	5	8	4	13	6	8	7	1	1
Critic	1	4	3	2	0	0	1	1	1	1	0	0
SAN MARCOS												
College	15	16	29	3	15	6	11	9	4	12	1	0
Critic	3	4	5	0	1	0	4	0	0	2	0	0
Total College and Critic	104	128	220	33	106	45	89	60	43	56	7	1
Per Cent of All Teachers	22.6	26.0	47.8	7.1	23.0	9.7	21.5	13.0	9.3	12.1	1.0	.2

* Groups overlap.

training and ability. Data were obtained from the replies of teachers to several questions, and from the statutes of the state which made the appropriations to state institutions for the collegiate years of 1929-30 and 1930-31. It seems evident that the problem of salaries in the colleges which train teachers will need careful study as efforts are continued toward raising the standards of training and general qualifications of teachers. It will be seen from figures presented that the Texas teachers colleges are at the disadvantage of competing with institutions for teachers in other states; also with other state-supported colleges of undergraduate rank in their own state.

There is a very definite tendency toward the raising of salary standards for those who train teachers. This is done apparently as an incentive toward advanced training of the type required, and in the attempt to dignify the work of teacher training on the collegiate level to a degree comparable with that of other kinds of college training. The report of the United States Office of Education for the years 1926-28 shows that:

> Salaries for professors in the teachers colleges and normal schools which have a system of academic ranking have increased during the biennium about 11 per cent; the salaries of faculty members with less than the rank of professor, 10 per cent. The increase in the salaries of all teachers in the smaller institutions in which a system of academic ranking is not usually established was 7 per cent. The increase in the salaries of training supervisors in both types of institutions was only 4 per cent in the two years.[20]

No permanent salary schedules for the Texas teachers colleges have been established. The amounts paid have been determined each two years by itemized appropriations of the legislature. Faculty members are ranked as follows: professor and director, professor, associate professor, assistant professor, and instructor. Some associate professorships have other than teaching responsibilities combined with them, for instance: dean of men or of women, director of debating, registrar, or supervisor. Such additional duties usually cause the salaries of associate professors to equal the salaries of professors.[21] Annual salaries as itemized in the appropriations are for the regular session of thirty-six weeks, or three terms. Each of the colleges maintains a summer session of twelve weeks, which is supported by separate appropriations. Because of the unusually heavy enrollments in the summer, regular staff members are asked to remain at their posts during that time, and most of them do so. The annual salary of teachers who teach during the entire summer amounts to their regular session salary plus one-third of that salary. Stated differently, they draw three-fourths of their annual salary during the regular session and one-fourth during the summer. Table 51 shows

[20] Frazier, Benjamin W. *Op. cit.*

[21] *General Laws Passed by the 41st Legislature, Second and Third Called Sessions,* Chap. 15. Published at Austin, Tex.

a distribution of the regular session salaries of faculty members at each college based on the number of usable reports received from the teachers themselves, together with medians and first and third quartile points. A total of 338 such reports was received from college teachers and 90 from training teachers. It is seen that the median salary for all teachers in college departments is $2,343.50, and that Q_1 and Q_3 are $2,066.85 and $2,826.42, respectively, while for training teachers the median is $1,896.65, and the quartile points are at $1,831.43 and $1,961.87. There is evidently little differentiation among salaries paid to the latter group of teachers; and the median salary is $446.85 less than that received by college teachers. Excluding the median salary for the college at Canyon, from which only 38 usable reports from approximately 54 college teachers were received, the median salaries for college teachers are reasonably uniform, the difference between the highest and the lowest being $98.70. The same degree of uniformity, however, is not seen in the medians for training or critic teachers, for a difference of about $114 appears between the highest and lowest of these medians. By reference to Table 44 it will be seen that in the teachers college at Denton 58.8 per cent of the training teachers hold master's degrees, and since this college pays the highest median salary to its training teachers, it may indicate an effort to base salaries of such teachers somewhat upon qualifications as measured by degrees. The college at San Marcos, which has the highest percentage of master's degrees among its training teachers pays a median salary of $40.00 less, while the third quartile point there is slightly higher than for training teachers at any of the other colleges. The range between Q_1 and Q_3 for college teachers' salaries in all the institutions is $779.57; and among the several schools varies from $482.15 at Alpine to $884.72 at Nacogdoches. This range for the other schools is: Denton, $823.15; San Marcos, $791.92; Commerce, $758.33; Canyon, $647.22; and Huntsville, $581.26.

Table 52 shows a distribution of salaries for the summer session as reported. A total of 289 reports from college teachers, and 47 from critic teachers was tabulated. The median summer salary for all teachers in the college departments is $739.13, and for critic teachers, $618.70. The first and third quartile points for the salaries of the former group fall at $575 and $976, respectively, and for the salaries of the latter at $382.25 and $668.70. If the median salary for the summer session is added to the median salary for the

TABLE 51

Distribution of Salaries for Regular Session, Thirty-six Weeks, College and Critic Teachers Separate

	Less Than $1800	$1801–2000	$2001–2200	$2201–2400	$2401–2600	$2601–2800	$2801–3000	$3001–3200	$3201–3400	$3401–3600	Median Salary	Q1	Q3
Alpine													
College	1	1	1	7	1	4	2		1		$2,372.42	$2,243.85	$2,726.00
Critic	3	3									1,800.50	1,700.00	1,901.00
Canyon													
College		5	4	9	2	5	12			1	2,501.00	2,212.11	2,859.33
Critic	4	5			1						1,841.00	1,706.25	1,941.00
Commerce													
College	1	11	6	14	2	6	9	2	1	1	2,322.42	2,034.33	2,792.66
Critic	1	17	1	1							1,906.85	1,848.06	1,953.94
Denton													
College	4	13	15	11	9	2	19		1	6	2,346.45	2,041.00	2,864.15
Critic		15		2							1,914.33	1,857.66	1,970.00
Huntsville													
College	1	9		17	3	5	7		4	1	2,359.82	2,226.82	2,808.14
Critic	1	15									1,894.33	1,841.00	1,947.66
Nacogdoches													
College	7	7	4	11	4	3	1		7		2,273.72	1,915.28	2,800.00
Critic	3	5		2							1,881.00	1,633.34	1,981.00
San Marcos													
College	1	10	11	11	3	5	9	1	4	3	2,346.45	2,064.63	2,856.55
Critic		9	2								1,874.33	1,862.11	1,984.33
Median for All Colleges													
College											$2,343.50	$2,066.85	$2,826.42
Critic											1,896.65	1,831.43	1,961.87

TABLE 52

DISTRIBUTION OF SUMMER SALARIES, COLLEGE AND CRITIC TEACHERS SEPARATE

	Less Than $300	$301–400	$401–500	$501–600	$601–700	$701–800	$801–900	$901–1000	$1001–1100	$1101–1200	Median Salary	Q1	Q3
Alpine													
College				2	2	7	5	2	1		$779.57	$711.71	$866.00
Critic	2			3	1						534.33	225.00	550.00
Canyon													
College			1	6	2	4	3	12		1	851.00	613.50	948.71
Critic		1		2	11	1					576.00	426.00	676.00
Commerce													
College		1		7	11	11	5	8	2	1	737.36	632.81	891.00
Critic		6			6	2	1				526.00	363.49	571.83
Denton													
College	1	1	4	11	7	16	4	14	1	5	776.00	591.99	929.57
Critic		1		1	5	1					661.00	600.00	681.00
Huntsville													
College	1	4	4	5	2	9	5	6	4	1	751.00	526.00	913.50
Critic			1	7	2						558.15	522.45	593.85
Nacogdoches													
College	1	1	3	8	7	9	5	1	5		701.00	563.50	821.00
Critic		1		4		1		1			563.50	519.75	582.25
San Marcos													
College	1	10	4	8	7	3	5	7	2	3	528.57	438.50	891.00
Critic		3	1	1	3						501.00	326.00	533.33
Median for All Colleges													
College											$739.13	$575.00	$976.00
Critic											618.70	382.25	668.70

regular session, the sum will represent very accurately the median salary for the twelve months. Thus calculated, the median twelve-months' salary for college teachers is $3,082.63 and for critic teachers, $2,515.35. There is a difference, then, in the total annual salary of the two groups of $567.28. Determined in the same manner, Q_1 for salaries of college teachers for twelve months is $2,641.85; and Q_3 is $3,802.42. For training teachers the respective quartile points are $2,213.68 and $2,630.57. Between the two groups of teachers there is a difference of $428.17 in the lower quartile, and of $1,171.85 in the upper.

Comparing salaries in the Texas colleges with figures shown in Table 53 A, it is seen that they exceed those in the five Missouri state colleges, but are noticeably less than those in the city training institutions, especially Harris Teachers College. Table 53 B shows that salaries in the New Jersey state normal schools exceed those in Texas. The median salary in the Texas schools is greater by about $143 than that of Missouri colleges, but it is nearly $600 below the median for the New Jersey state institutions, and more than $2,000 less than the median salary at Harris Teachers College in St. Louis. The median for the twelve months in the Texas colleges is nearly $400 less than the national median, covering the same period, for salaries of professors, but exceeds national medians by $482 and $302, respectively, for instructors and salaries in institutions that

TABLE 53 A

COMPARABLE SALARIES IN OTHER STATES

REGULAR SESSION SALARIES	MEDIAN	Q_1	Q_3
Five Missouri State Teachers Colleges, 1929	$2,200.00	$1,838.00	$2,649.00
Harris Teachers College, St. Louis, 1929	4,483.00	3,200.00	4,969.00
Kansas City Teachers College, 1929	2,450.00	2,163.00	3,067.00
St. Joseph Teachers College, 1929 *	2,463.00	2,263.00	3,544.00
Five New Jersey Normal Schools, 1929 †	2,924.00		
TWELVE MONTHS' SALARIES, UNITED STATES MEDIANS GIVEN IN THE MISSOURI REPORTS‡			
For Professors	$3,450.00		$4,225.00
For Instructors	2,600.00		3,000.00
For Non-ranked Teachers	2,780.00		3,367.00

* Figures of Missouri institutions taken from *Report on Publicly Supported Higher Education*, p. 353.
† Bagley, W. C. *Op. cit.*, p. 49.
‡ *Report on Publicly Supported Higher Education*, p. 355.

TABLE 53 B

NORMAL SCHOOL SALARY SCHEDULES, NEW JERSEY, 1929–30 *

Group	Minimum Training for Future Appointees at Entrance	Minimum Salary	Maximum Salary
Instructor	Bachelor's degree	$2200	$3500—Bachelor's degree 3750—½ year of graduate work 4000—1 year of graduate work
Assistant professor ..	Bachelor's degree plus 1 year of graduate work		4600
Associate professor ..	Bachelor's degree plus 1 year of graduate work		5300
Professor	Bachelor's degree plus 2 years of graduate work, or 1 year of graduate work and research or authorship		6000
Training school teachers †		1800	2700

* Bagley, W. C. *Op. cit.*, p. 50.

† Will be put on schedule of instructor when same qualifications are reached.

do not rank staff members. The salary schedule that was put into effect in the New Jersey schools in 1929-30, summarized in Table 53 B, clearly offers better compensation to teachers than is offered by the Texas colleges. The maximum salaries of New Jersey teachers are: for instructors, $4,000; for assistant professors, $4,600; for associate professors, $5,300; and for professors, $6,000. The maximum for training school teachers is $2,700, with provision for a raise to the rank of instructor when qualifications justify it. A commendable feature of the New Jersey schedule is that it very definitely provides a reward for additional training and successful professional work. An examination of the General Laws of Texas[22] in which appropriations for the biennium ending August 31, 1931, are made, shows that the maximum salary for teaching positions in the teachers colleges is $3,600 for the regular session, and that there are only eleven positions of this rank, including deanships, in the colleges. There seems to be no strict uniformity in the amounts appropriated for corresponding positions in the several colleges. From the appropriations it appears that the maximum salaries provided for professors' positions, not including deans, in other state colleges of undergraduate rank are as follows: the University of

[22] *Op. cit.*, Chap. 15.

Texas, $4,500 and $4,000; A & M College, $4,000 and $3,750; Technological College, $4,500 and $3,750; College of Industrial Arts, $3,750 and $3,600; and for the Medical Branch of the University, $5,500, $5,000, and $4,500.

The teachers in the Texas teachers colleges do not augment their salaries to any great extent by work other than their regular teaching. About 12 per cent report extra salary from extension teaching, with amounts ranging from $50 to $600. The average extra income reported from that source is approximately $200. About 23 per cent report additional income from the following activities: magazine writing, dairying, truck gardening, concerts, lecturing, officiating at athletic contests, small royalties, and rents. The median amounts from such sources range between $200 and $300. The reports as to annual savings were incomplete. Only 243, or 52 per cent, reported on this point. Of these, 179 reported yearly savings, including insurance premiums, of slightly less than $200. The amount of savings ranges from less than $100 to $1,000, while in several cases indebtedness incurred in graduate study was reported. It is evident that the members of the teaching staffs depend largely upon the income derived from their salaries for living expenses and for the financing of additional study and educative travel. A similar situation was found by the study of the Missouri teachers colleges, which was made in 1929, and in the report the following conclusion is expressed:

> The fact that these faculties are in great measure dependent upon salaries received for their total income indicates even more clearly the necessity for providing adequate salary ranges with higher maxima in the salary schedules.[23]

The work of teaching in a teacher-training institution is an exacting and time-consuming occupation, carrying with it responsibilities other than those directly connected with the classroom. It is doubtful whether many teachers can successfully do such work and at the same time devote much of their energy and time to other interests and activities. A salary schedule that forces or prompts teachers to scatter their energies is inadequate and unwise.

Information obtained as to the professional activity and vigor of members of the teaching staffs as represented by work outside of classrooms is difficult to portray with economy of space. A teacher

[23] Figures of Missouri institutions taken from *Report on Publicly Supported Higher Education*, p. 356.

in a professional college for teachers is obligated to make contributions to the work of public education in addition to those he makes in his scheduled class periods. These contributions may take the form of professional books, research work, whether published or not, articles for professional journals, textbooks and teaching materials of various kinds, addresses before teachers' institutes and professional associations, and field studies of problems connected with the work of public schools. That the teachers in the Texas teachers colleges are undertaking to discharge in some measure responsibilities of this nature is indicated by reports made by them. Graduate study among teachers will doubtless increase such contributions. The time devoted to preparation for classes varies rather widely according to the reports; 83 per cent indicate that they spend from one to three hours or more in preparation for each class. Almost two-thirds spend no more than one hour in such preparation. Of the total number of teachers, 8.4 per cent have published books; 23.7 per cent are the authors of articles for professional journals; and 41.5 per cent have made, with some regularity, addresses before professional bodies. Thirty-two per cent of the number have recently completed, or are engaged in, professional research study, a considerable portion of which appears to be connected with advanced study toward graduate degrees. Slightly more than one-half, 55.6 per cent, of these teachers report membership in two or more recognized professional organizations, and 77 per cent are regular readers of three or more professional periodicals.

Keen professional interest and enthusiasm will lead teachers to desire to improve existing conditions, to associate on a professional plane with others, to share their discoveries, and to keep abreast of the progress that is being made in the field of their interest. The attitude back of such desires might properly be termed a research attitude—dynamic instead of static. Some educators do not consider research work a proper function for the staff of an undergraduate teacher-training institution. This position is taken apparently by most of the 178 members of the American Association of Teachers Colleges. In 1930 only thirteen members were reported to have established organized bureaus or departments of research,[24] and some of the institutions offer graduate work. Efficient teaching on a full schedule requires most of the time and the full abilities of a teacher,

[24] Whitney, F. L. "Organization, Scope, and Cost of a Department of Research," *Ninth Yearbook of the American Association of Teachers Colleges*, pp. 114-30, 1930.

and is not strictly compatible with formal research.[25] That there is a very general interest in the improvement of college teaching is evidenced by the material presented in the 1928 *Yearbook of the National Society of College Teachers of Education*, and by supplementary summaries published in the *Bulletin of the Bureau of School Service of the University of Kentucky*, Vol. 1, No. 2, December, 1928. The literature dealing with teacher training seems to present very generally unanimous opinions that the efforts of teachers colleges should primarily be centered in skillful teaching and the improvement of teaching, and that research work should come as an auxiliary to that fundamental function.[26]

An effort was made to ascertain the opinions of members of the faculties regarding the conditions surrounding their teaching, and their ideas as to what means the institutions might employ to promote the professional growth of teachers. Incomplete replies were made to questions bearing on these points, but it is considered that those received were indicative of the trend of faculty sentiment. Sixty-eight per cent reported a satisfactory degree of academic freedom in their teaching; others neglected to answer the question, and two individuals confessed to being hampered. Eighty-four per cent answered the question regarding the presence of supervision, and half of this percentage reported that they had some supervision and the other half that they had none. An examination of the replies shows that most of the training-school teachers have regularly appointed supervisors, but the only supervision apparent in the college departments is the general oversight and advice of the heads of the several departments. Most of the college teachers expressed themselves as opposed to formal supervision, but a few admitted that they would welcome supervisory assistance by a dean of instruction. To the question: "Do you and your colleagues participate to a desirable extent in determining the educational policies of your school?" 61 per cent replied that they did, while 14 per cent felt that these policies were largely determined for them. The proportion of negative replies ranged from one-seventh to one-third of the number re-

[25] Carnegie Foundation for the Advancement of Teaching. *Bulletin, No. 14*, pp. 110-12.

[26] *Ninth Yearbook of the American Association of Teachers Colleges* presents five papers on this topic: Chandler, Paul G. "The Quality of Instruction in Teachers Colleges," pp. 136-41; Moehlman, Arthur B. "Appraisal of Teaching," pp. 141-48; Alger, John L. "Forces Producing the Greatest Improvement in Instruction at Rhode Island College of Education," pp. 144-50; Cooper, H. E. "What I Am Doing to Improve Instruction at My Institution," pp. 150-52; Thomas, Frank W. "What I Am Doing to Improve Instruction at My Institution," pp. 152-55.

porting, and was especially noticeable from three institutions. Estimates of the teachers indicate that general faculty meetings are irregularly held, with approximately 38 per cent of the time of such meetings devoted to details of administration, 32 per cent to the discussion of educational policies, 22 per cent to a consideration of professional improvements, and 8 per cent to miscellaneous topics. Reports of teachers give the impression that departmental meetings are not held according to a set schedule. It appears that the departments of education, science, industrial education, physical education, and training teachers, devote an average of an hour or more per month to such meetings. Meetings of teachers in the departments of English, history, social studies, fine arts, and languages average less. The expressions of teachers indicate that professional growth on their part is expected and encouraged by each of the colleges, but that no definite plans have been put into effect to lessen the financial burden incurred by them for study, travel, research or participation in professional organizations.

Some typical suggestions from the original replies to the question as to what the institutions might do to stimulate growth are quoted here: "Better salaries"; "Part pay during leaves of absence for study"; "Professional growth is a personal matter, and an ambitious teacher grows according to his own ideals"; "Provide means for the faculty to become conversant with the work and status of the public schools"; "Provide recognition and salary advance according to scholarship and successful teaching"; "Set up a definitely graduated salary schedule including provision for sabbatical leave"; "Exchange teachers among the colleges"; "Make an adjustment of the service load among the teachers"; "Provide pecuniary assistance in conducting research work."

Data on the teaching loads of the faculties were obtained from reports made by the heads of the departments in each of the colleges. Five of these reports were received too late to be included in the tabulations and some of the department heads did not report the number of hours and number of students for each teacher in the department. In each of the institutions certain individuals teach classes in more than one department and others teach a few hours per week, devoting most of their time to other duties such as those of placement service, registrar, business manager, and others. The reports received gave the number of recitation periods per week for teachers, and these periods are 50 and 55 minutes in the Texas teachers colleges. Section

VI of the standards for accrediting teachers colleges[27] sets the following as the standard regarding the teaching load of the faculty:

> The following teaching loads shall be the maximum for a teachers college or normal school faculty: 16 recitation periods of at least 50 minutes each per week or its equivalent. Equivalence shall be based upon the ratio of one class period to one and one-half class periods in shop, laboratory work, and physical education.

The median class-period load for each of the colleges is seen from Table 54 to fall within the maximum set by the standard of the

TABLE 54

DISTRIBUTION OF TEACHERS SHOWING NUMBER OF CLASS PERIODS PER WEEK IN EACH COLLEGE*

No. of Periods	Alpine	Canyon	Commerce	Denton	Huntsville	Nacogdoches	San Marcos	Total
3	0	0	4	2	1	3	2	12
4	0	0	1	0	1	2	2	10
5	0	1	0	1	2	0	1	5
6	1	0	1	3	4	3	3	15
7	0	0	0	1	1	1	1	4
8	0	0	0	3	0	1	1	5
9	1	5	1	1	2	3	2	15
10	1	1	1	5	2	2	0	12
11	1	1	0	4	0	0	1	7
12	3	1	0	5	1	4	2	16
13	3	2	0	14	1	3	1	24
14	0	0	1	3	11	1	2	18
15	1	9	27	15	13	15	18	98
16	1	0	4	5	0	2	4	16
17	3	3	1	7	1	4	6	25
18	0	1	4	7	4	2	6	24
19	0	5	3	6	4	2	1	21
20	0	2	3	0	0	4	2	11
More than 20	4	8	4	5	8	1	1	31
Median ...	13.8	15.9	15.7	15.1	15.2	15.2	15.5	15.47
Q_1	12.25	13.75	15.17	12.35	12.0	10.2	12.5	12.45
Q_3	17.75	19.85	18.25	17.46	18.5	16.87	17.33	17.79

* College Teachers; Association ratios used.

American Association of Teachers Colleges. From the quartile figures shown for all, it appears that of the total number of teachers reporting, 369, one-fourth have a class-period load of less than 13

[27] *Ninth Yearbook of The American Association of Teachers Colleges,* p. 13, 1930.

periods per week, while one-fourth have a load in excess of 17 periods per week. In general a similar situation obtains at each of the colleges, as is seen from the several quartile points. So far as the reports received are representative, these figures mean that the class-period load is not evenly distributed among the members of the teaching staffs at these institutions. Those having a light teaching load are probably carrying additional duties, but no explanation can be offered for the fact that one-fourth of the teachers are carrying more than 17 periods per week. There have been some noticeable changes in the median number of class periods per teacher at the Texas teachers colleges since 1924. The medians for that year were found to be as follows:[28] at Alpine, 16.0; at Canyon, 16.10; at Commerce, 15.05; at Denton, 17.48; at Huntsville, 14.81; at Nacogdoches, 18.2; and at San Marcos, 15.68. The same report shows the medians at the State University to range from 11.48 to 12.21; at A & M College from 13.59 to 14.81; and at the College

TABLE 55

AVERAGE CLASS HOURS PER WEEK PER TEACHER BY DEPARTMENTS*

Department	Total No. Periods	No. Teachers Reported	Average Periods per Teacher
Art	211.9	14	15.13
Agriculture	191.7	13	14.74
Biology	253.1	17	14.9
Business Administration	216.8	15	14.45
Chemistry	199.5	13	15.34
Education	533.1	44	12.11
English	730.3	53	13.8
Languages	243.0	17	14.3
Economics and Sociology	88.0	8	11.0
Geography	175.8	12	14.65
Government	87.0	6	14.5
History	320.0	24	13.33
Home Economics	388.4	25	15.53
Industrial Education	220.1	12	18.34
Latin	87.0	7	12.42
Mathematics	277.3	20	13.86
Music	284.5	18	15.8
Physical Education	447.2	26	17.2
Physics	93.8	6	15.63
Speech Arts	148.6	8	18.57
Library Science	26.5	5	5.3

* Association ratios used.

[28] Educational Survey Commission. *Texas Educational Survey Report,* Vol. VI, pp. 206-7. Austin, Tex.

of Industrial Arts from 13.99 to 15.99, according to the academic rank of the teachers. The median number of teaching hours per week in Missouri teachers colleges was found in 1929 to be 13, 14, 15, and 16; slightly more than one-fourth the teachers were carrying more than 17 hours per week.[29] It is recommended in the Missouri report that each institution carefully scrutinize its records regarding teaching loads and adjust them to the commonly accepted standard of 16 hours per week.

To determine differences in the class-period loads among the different departments of the colleges, Table 55 was constructed. The total number of class periods of the teachers in each department in all the colleges was found, and the average number per teacher calculated as shown in the table.

No very significant differences among departments are to be noted from this table except that the departments of speech arts, industrial

TABLE 56

AVERAGE NUMBER OF STUDENTS PER TEACHER IN EACH COLLEGE BY DEPARTMENTS

DEPARTMENT	ALPINE	CANYON	COMMERCE	DENTON	HUNTSVILLE	NACOGDOCHES	SAN MARCOS	AVERAGE ALL COLLEGES
Art	19	72	28	50	81	56	70	50
Agriculture	*	48	84	*	36	41	62	54
Biology	65	60	80	67	64	80	35	64
Business Adm.	51	112	145	92	32	36	64	76
Chemistry	31	72	56	73	65	46	72	59
Education	100	99	120	94	91	76	104	97
English	54	108	84	92	94	81	75	84
Languages	33	81	108	57	48	118	44	70
Econ. & Sociol.	*	107	117	50	31	41	80	71
Geography	12	82	132	88	67	118	108	87
Government	30	128	90	152	*	†	107	101
History	62	118	107	89	61	65	124	89
Home Econ.	37	34	59	64	51	48	27	46
Indus. Educ.	34	45	50	80	30	*	46	48
Latin	6	18	35	37	29	24	6	22
Mathematics	31	67	79	73	75	43	38	58
Music	17	41	123	87	48	76	123	74
Physical Ed.	47	*	198	116	54	94	158	111
Physics	5	75	30	100	33	18	90	50
Speech Arts	60	122	69	73	106	*	‡	84
Library Sci.	5	15	*	14	*	11	10	11

* None reported.
† With History Department.
‡ With English Department.

[29] *Report on Publicly Supported Higher Education*, p. 362.

education, and physical education show more than 16 hours. The light load in library science is probably attributable to the fact that teachers in that department devote most of their time to work in the libraries. McMullen shows in his study the departments, out of 13 listed, which report more than 16 hours per week: manual arts, music, commerce, and science.[30]

The reports of department heads indicate the number of students in all the classes of each instructor. A wide range in the number of students per teacher is noticed, in the original reports, among the various departments of each college. The average number per teacher in each department of each institution, and for all, is shown in Table 56.

It was found that, in departments where very few students per teacher are shown, teachers have charge of classes in other departments or have administrative duties, and an examination of catalogues and class-hour schedules indicates that courses are given in the subjects for which no separate departments are reported. This is true in all cases where no data are shown in Table 56 except agriculture at Denton, industrial education at Nacogdoches, and library science at Commerce. Such situations suggest the possibility that some teachers are working in subject matter fields with insufficient preparation to meet collegiate standards. A report of a recent study of the training of faculty members in teachers colleges shows that slightly more than one-half the teachers in college departments lack preparation to meet such standards.[31]

Professor Harris Cook of the Teachers College at Canyon, Texas, in his study of this problem set up the following amounts of training in each subject taught as standard: 24 semester hours of undergraduate work and 15 hours of graduate work, or a total of 39 hours.[32]

McMullen divides activities of teachers college teachers as follows:

> (1) Direct school work for which remuneration is received from the employing institution (referred to hereafter as "service load"), and (2) incidental activities for which remuneration is not received from the institution but which grow out of the work of teaching and contribute indirectly to its efficiency through the growth of the teacher or through the advance of education in general.

[30] McMullen, L. B. *Service Load in Teacher Training Institutions,* p. 26. Contributions to Education, No. 244. Bureau of Publications, Teachers College, Columbia University, 1927.

[31] Phelps, Shelton. "Some Phases of the Training of Faculty Members of Teachers Colleges," *Ninth Yearbook of the American Association of Teachers Colleges,* pp. 91-99. (Based on data collected by Harris Cook.)

[32] Cook, Harris. *The Training of Teachers College Faculties.* George Peabody College for Teachers, Contributions to Education, No. 86, 1930.

In the first group are (1) class work, (2) daily preparation for class work, (3) routine work incident to class work or to faculty organization, and (4) work with students in conferences or otherwise, outside of class. The second group includes (1) exercise or recreation needed for physical or mental efficiency, (2) work outside of class hours including work for pay which in some cases bears a return to the school in increased efficiency or in advertising, and (3) work of a miscellaneous nature for the betterment of the individual teacher, of the social community, and of the professional group to which the teacher belongs.[33]

An effort was made to determine the total service load in Texas teachers colleges in hours per week. The replies on which estimates of the time devoted to elements in service load, other than class periods, are based, were incomplete and in some cases seemingly improbable. Reports from college teachers were received as follows: from 82 per cent on time spent in work connected with teaching outside of class periods and preparation; from 44 per cent on time spent with students; and from 35 per cent on time devoted to committee work. An average of 16 hours per week was reported for work connected with teaching, exclusive of time spent in class and direct preparation; 1 hour for working with students, and 2.5 hours for committee work and administrative routine. These, added to the median of 15 periods class work and 15 hours direct preparation, (one hour for each period) give a total average service load of 49.5 hours per week. This is noticeably greater than the standard service load of 42 hours set up by McMullen;[34] and higher than the medians found in the Missouri state teachers colleges, which ranged from 36 to 40 hours. However, the ranges of the middle 50 per cent at those colleges varied from 29 to 51 hours.[35]

The replies of training school teachers as to hours spent in the various elements of service loads were also incomplete. The impression gained from a study of these replies is that there is an unequal division of work among individuals in several of the institutions. The one at Alpine is the only teachers college that does not maintain a training school as a part of the college plant, but uses the public schools of the town for training purposes. Seventy-four per cent of all training teachers submitted usable reports concerning the service load. The average number of hours devoted to class teaching is 16; to other duties, 17, making a total service load of 33 clock-hours per week. Twelve teachers reported a total load of more

[33] McMullen, L. B. *Op. cit.*, p. 14.

[34] *Ibid.*, p. 71.

[35] *Report on Publicly Supported Higher Education*, p. 368.

than 40 hours, the average being reduced apparently by incomplete reports on some items. The average number of pupils per teacher is 55, and the average number of student teachers under the direct supervision of each training teacher is 7. The modal number of pupils per teacher in the elementary grades in training schools which belong to the colleges is approximately 25, but the number in high school classes where departmental work is done runs considerably higher, bringing the average up to 55.

Summary

The 460 teachers in the Texas teachers colleges are largely native Texans, and most of them come from families belonging to the agricultural and small-business groups, the professions producing from ten to eighteen per cent. The median ages at the several colleges, 35 to 44 years, are about the same as have been found in similar groups elsewhere, and the proportion of those 25 years of age or younger is higher than that found in some other places. A decided majority come from families in which other members have been teachers; also the greater proportion say they would choose teaching if they had an opportunity to select an occupation now. Nearly half the total number are men, 79 per cent of whom have from one to four persons entirely dependent upon them for support. A smaller per cent of the women report dependents. Neither men nor women, with very few exceptions, have an appreciable income apart from their salaries, of $2343.50 and $1896.65, medians of college and critic teachers, respectively. The training of these staffs has followed largely the traditional academic sequence, and, as represented by academic degrees, has greatly improved during the past eleven years in both the college departments and the training schools. Approximately three-fourths of the former and 39 per cent of the latter hold graduate degrees, and the training of all is being continued, as is evidenced by the fact that 8.5 per cent were on leave of absence for study, and 15.8 per cent were taking extension courses during 1930. A decided majority had teaching experience in public schools before entering teacher-training institutions, the median number of years of such experience for college teachers being 6.15, and for training teachers 4.77. The median teaching load is approximately 16 hours per week, with the third quartile point falling at 17.79 hours. The total service load appears to vary widely among the individuals of the several staffs.

A peculiarity of the profession of college teaching is pointed out by Chandler in the following paragraph:

> There is no profession where the opportunities for slighting one's work are as great as in college teaching. On the other hand there is no profession where excellent work comes so little to the attention of the public, even of the educational public. This is because there are no immediate or objective checks on the college professor's work. There are neither checks within the profession nor without, as in other occupations. College students are at an age when they are supposed to be very discerning of shams and no doubt do recognize incompetence in professors. But their opinions do not influence the teaching. Students desire above all else to get credit in a course and criticism of one's teachers is not conducive to getting credit. For more or less obvious reasons their opinions, when expressed, do not carry weight with the teacher or with the administration.[36]

Proposals

1. That an established policy be set up of selecting ambitious teachers from the lower academic ranks and encouraging them to proceed with advanced training with the assurance of promotion.
2. That an adequate system of retirement, which has been discussed by the Board of Regents on several occasions, be established to provide for the economic security of teachers who have served long and faithfully, and who, because of advanced age or physical disability, are unable to carry the regular load to their own satisfaction or as the best interest of the institution demands.
3. That provision be made for leave of absence with part salary for members of the teaching staffs who are deemed able to profit by advanced study and who will be able to increase the efficiency of the institutions because of such study. This provision should be extended to members of the administrative staffs.
4. The provisions for retirement and pay for leave of absence should be incorporated in a permanent graduated salary schedule which would be free from the uncertainties of biennial appropriations, and which would make certain pecuniary reward for efficient service and increased scholarship.
5. Such a salary schedule should place training teachers on the same basis of salary and qualifications as teachers in the college departments.
6. A year of graduate study, presumably represented by the master's degree, should be the minimum requirement in training for both college and training teachers.

[36] Chandler, Paul G. "The Quality of Instruction in Teachers Colleges," *Ninth Yearbook of the American Association of Teachers Colleges*, p. 136, 1930.

7. That clerical assistance be furnished to all members of teaching staff who show that they are able to make profitable use of it.

8. That a continuous study of the service load of teachers be made by administrative officers to the end that such load be equitably distributed and that it fall within limits set by recognized standards.

9. That skillful supervision of instruction could profitably be set up in order to integrate the work being done by each institution toward professional objectives, and to prevent the working at cross purposes that is likely to result when direction and oversight are left entirely in the hands of department heads and their assistants.

10. That faculty members continue to be relieved of as much administrative routine as possible, but that they be expected to make contributions to the educational and professional policies of the several institutions.

11. That the budget of each institution make provision for subsidizing research work on the part of faculty members when such research is considered to be of potential value to education within the state.

12. That plans be developed to insure that teachers in the teachers colleges keep in continuous contact with the work being done in the public schools of the state.

13. That close attention be given to the kind as well as the amount of training possessed by teachers. A part of the graduate work should deal with the professional preparation of teachers for the public schools, and should be done in institutions which are in sympathy with the work and with the scientific study of education.

14. A permanent salary schedule for the teachers colleges, with provisions for retirement and leave of absence can hardly be expected under the present method of support for the state colleges. Institutional autonomy, with the resulting rivalry in bidding for students and in asking for appropriations, will continue to operate against such a schedule. Some stable arrangement such as that proposed in a later chapter should be set up by the state in the near future.

CHAPTER IV

CURRICULA AND THE PLACEMENT OF GRADUATES AND EX-STUDENTS

Portrayal of complete and detailed curricular practices is always beset with difficulties, especially when it is attempted within limited space. There are several reasons for such difficulties, all of which affect the present study: (1) the absence of a coördinating agency on curriculum among the seven colleges; (2) the resulting diversity of detailed practice; (3) the lack of centralized supervisory authority within the several institutions, which leaves the actual construction and handling of courses to the department heads and teachers; (4) the frequent changes that have occurred during recent years; (5) the generally recognized brevity and ambiguity of catalogue statements; and (6) the exceptions to general curricular requirements that each institution considers it proper to make, for curriculum procedures are necessarily identified with the handling of individual students. The following sources of information have been used in this section of the study: the minutes of the Board of Regents from 1921 to 1929; the minutes of the Council of Teachers College Presidents; the minutes of the organization of presidents of all state colleges; personal visit to each of the colleges and conferences with teachers and administrators; 1929-30 editions of the catalogues; data sheets prepared and submitted by each of the deans and directors of the training schools. The purpose is to show a general picture of the present curricula, to compare them with standards set up in the literature on teacher training, and to point out those aspects which are capable of improvement in the light of these standards. It is evident that definite curricula that are comparable to those for other professions, and different from the traditional academic curricula out of which they grew, are being developed for the professional training of teachers.[1]

An examination of the minutes of the Board of Regents covering

[1] In the following pages specific references are made to outstanding contributions dealing with the curricula for professional training of teachers.

approximately the period during which the colleges have operated as four-year institutions shows that this board has given little official attention to their curricula. The following represent the types of action taken on that phase of administration: ordering the discontinuance of sub-college work; authorization of vocational training leading to certificates at certain of the colleges; giving some of them authority to affiliate with the public schools of the town where they are located to provide facilities for observation and practice teaching; requesting the presidents to prepare information relative to the offering of a year of graduate work at some of the institutions. Neither the organization of Presidents of the State-Supported Colleges nor the Council of Presidents of Teachers Colleges has recorded in its minutes evidences of a concerted attack upon the problems of curriculum building,[2] yet, with the exception of vocational agriculture and vocational home economics, all the teachers colleges offer in general very similar programs. Each is training teachers for all branches and grades of the public school service, and also offering academic work which can be used to satisfy the pre-professional requirements of institutions which train for other professions. Each of the other state colleges also is training teachers for the public schools.[3] The curricula of each college seem to have been constructed by the staff of that college, without coöperation with the staffs of the others, and with no study of requirements of the state as a whole.

The American Association of Teachers Colleges, in its standards for accrediting teacher-training institutions, sets up certain requirements regarding the curriculum which will be used as part of the criteria for evaluating the curricular practices in the Texas colleges. These requirements are published by the Association under the following sections: II. Requirements for Admission; III. Standards for Graduation; VII. Training School and Student Teaching; VIII. Organization of the Curriculum.[4] Standard VIII reads as follows:

> A. The curriculum of the teachers colleges must recognize definite requirements as regards sequences of courses. Senior college courses must not

[2] A Council of Deans of Teachers Colleges began holding meetings at irregular intervals about 1922. Minutes of all these were not available. The latest meeting was held in April, 1930—the first in two years. This organization has made certain recommendations to the presidents regarding requirements for degrees, extension courses, and on similar subjects. It appears that these recommendations are put into effect by each college at its option.

[3] A study of the scope of work and internal organization of the state-supported colleges in Texas is found in *Texas Educational Survey Report,* Vol. VI, Chap. 2.

[4] "Standards for Accrediting Teachers Colleges," *Ninth Yearbook of the American Association of Teachers Colleges,* pp. 9-19, 1930.

be open to freshmen who have not taken the prerequisites for these courses. Programs consisting mainly of freshman and sophomore courses carrying full credit shall not be available for students in the junior and senior years. Coherent and progressive lines of study, leading to specific achievement within definite fields, must be characteristic of the college curriculum. Every teachers college must, therefore, adopt an organization of its curricula which will provide in its junior and senior years courses which require prerequisite courses in the freshman and sophomore years or courses which are open only to juniors and seniors. The number of such courses taken by a student in the junior and senior years must total at least one-third of the requirements for the completion of the four-year college curriculum. It is recommended that teachers colleges adopt a system of numbering courses or of catalogue description which will indicate the year in which the course should be taken.

B. In a normal school with a three-year curriculum, two-thirds of the work of students in the last year shall consist of advanced courses to which freshmen are not admitted.[5]

The literature on teacher training seems to agree on certain underlying principles of curriculum construction which are more rigidly professional than any that the standards of the American Association of Teachers Colleges have yet embodied.[6] A summary of these, as they apply to four-year institutions, is used to supplement the Association standards as criteria for evaluating the curricula of the Texas colleges.

1. Curricula should be differentiated to give specific preparation to primary teachers, intermediate teachers, rural teachers, junior- and senior-high-school teachers, and administrators.

2. Within each curriculum relatively little free election should be allowed. The student selects his curriculum rather than courses or subjects.

3. The four years of training should provide adequate background in the major fields of human knowledge—language, mathematics, social sciences, literature, natural and physical sciences, the arts, and health—with intensive preparation in the specific fields in which the student is preparing to teach.

[5] *Op. cit.*, p. 14.

[6] Helpful contributions in this field are: Carnegie Foundation for the Advancement of Teaching, *Curricula Designed for the Preparation of Teachers of American Public Schools,* 1917; Carnegie Foundation for the Advancement of Teaching, *Bulletin, No. 14,* Chap. VII; *Report on Publicly Supported Higher Education,* Part II, Chap. 2; Louisiana Survey, *Report of the Survey Commission,* pp. 120-22; Hill, C. M. *A Decade of Progress in Teacher Training,* Chap. IV; Pryor, H. C. *Graded Units in Student Teaching,* Contributions to Education, No. 202, Teachers College, Columbia University, 1926; Evenden, E. S. "The Critic Teacher and the Professional Treatment of Subject-Matter," *Report of the Ninth Annual Session of Supervisors of Student Teaching,* pp. 39-48, 1929.

4. Subject-matter courses in any curriculum, in addition to providing academic scholarship, should be treated in a professional manner to meet the future needs of active teachers of children.

5. Each curriculum should provide training in educational theory, science, and practice extensive enough to equip the future teacher with controls and skills beyond the limits of the minimum requirements of the work he expects to do.

6. All courses in each curriculum should be directly contributory to the academic, cultural, or professional requirements of the branch of the teaching service for which the curriculum prepares the student. The requirements should be considered as including generous margins beyond the minima set by current practice.

7. It is generally regarded as important that all curricula provide facilities for developing the social and personal abilities of prospective teachers. This provision should include training for the planning and conduct of some forms of the so-called extracurricular activities which have value in the public schools.

8. The curricula of a college which prepares for the active practice of the teaching profession should establish ideals and develop abilities beyond the present general usage and requirements of the public schools.

In order to achieve the values suggested by the foregoing principles, each curriculum should be set up and arranged in psychological order to present a systematic pattern which would include the following:

1. Introductory and orientation courses for the purpose of providing outlooks and over-views in the field of education and practical school service, and to some extent in the academic fields. Such courses might be expected to furnish help to students in the choice of a curriculum.

2. Definite professional courses which are technical in character and which properly integrate educational theory and practice.

3. Professionally treated courses in subject matter which accompany the technical courses and contribute the materials and agencies of education to the prospective practitioner. Such courses are in no sense merely reviews of elementary and secondary subjects, but are entirely on the collegiate level.[7]

4. Properly graded observation, participation, and practice teaching which parallel most of the courses in each curriculum. Guidance

[7] Randolph, E. D. *The Professional Treatment of Subject-Matter,* especially Chap I. Warwick & York, Inc., Baltimore, 1924.

and direction of such activities should be shared by teachers in the field of education and in the subject-matter departments.

5. The arrangement and conduct of courses given by all departments so that all contribute as integrated units toward the objective of preparing efficient teachers for the public schools.

6. Final courses in each curriculum which are generalizing and synthesizing and which lead students toward an open-minded and progressive philosophy of education.

The first principle in regard to differentiation of curricula according to the type of work the student expects to do, together with the collegiate character of the courses offered, suggests the necessity of definite standards of admission to the teachers colleges and possibly some methods of selection of prospective teachers in addition to the standards set up by accrediting agencies. The Texas teachers colleges have not set up the additional selective means for the apparent reason that all the other state institutions of college rank, and all private, denominational, and public junior colleges are training teachers, and no selective measures, other than the common requirement of high school graduation, have been adopted by any of them. Such a situation forces the teachers colleges into competition with every other college in the state regardless of their desires in the matter. The state medical college is in a different position. Admission requirements of the teachers colleges are uniform, as stated in their catalogues, and comply with Standard II of the American Association of Teachers Colleges. Fifteen units of accredited secondary work, or the equivalent by examination, are required, eight of which are prescribed as follows: three in English, two in social science, two in algebra, and one in plane geometry. A first-grade certificate or high-school certificate of the second class may be used to absolve 8½ units, and a permanent certificate, 12½ units. Persons over twenty-one years of age who show ability to do college work are admitted to the freshman class on approval, as permitted by the Association standard.[8]

The study of the Missouri teachers colleges made in 1929 reports that at least three of them made definite bids, in their catalogues, for students preparing for professions other than teaching.[9] The Texas colleges, through their catalogues, have given no general evidence of efforts to meet the needs of pre-professional students except that the bachelor's degree may be obtained without taking the

[8] *Ninth Yearbook of the American Association of Teachers Colleges,* Chap. II, p. 2.

[9] *Report on Publicly Supported Higher Education,* pp. 258-59.

courses in education required for the permanent certificate.[10] The attitude of these institutions is expressed by the following statement taken from the catalogue of the college at Huntsville:

> The Texas State Teachers Colleges were established and are maintained for the definite purpose of preparing competent teachers for the public schools of the state. The field of service of the Sam Houston State Teachers College, therefore, includes the education of teachers for all departments of the public schools from the kindergarten to the high school, including the preparation of teachers of the special subjects taught in the public schools of Texas. It is not the function of the Teachers College to educate engineers, lawyers, physicians, milliners, dietitians, artists, nor to give general university education. Other agencies are maintained by the state for these purposes, and the Teachers College does not attempt to invade their fields of service.[11]

The degrees and certificates offered by each of the colleges in 1929-30 are shown in the following list:

B. A. Degree with permanent certificate
B. S. Degree with permanent certificate
B. A. Degree without permanent certificate
B. S. Degree without permanent certificate.
Upon completion of the freshman year, a four-year elementary or a two-year high-school certificate.
Upon completion of the sophomore year, a permanent elementary or a four-year high-school certificate.
Upon completion of the junior year, a six-year high-school certificate.
Upon completion of the eleventh grade of the demonstration high school, a first class elementary certificate valid for three years, provided one unit of credit in education has been earned.

All certificates are issued by the State Department of Education upon proof submitted by the college that requirements have been met.

The differentiated curricula leading to certificates and degrees offered at each institution are shown in Table 57. The similarity of the curricula in the several colleges is noticeable and indicates that all are undertaking to prepare teachers for practically the same types of public-school positions. The prominent exceptions are: the vocational curricula under the Smith-Hughes Act at four of the

[10] That they seem however, to be meeting such demands is indicated by the data in Table 27, Chap. II.

[11] *Fiftieth Annual Catalogue of the Sam Houston State Teachers College,* 1928-1929, pp. 11-12.

TABLE 57

DIFFERENTIATED CURRICULA OFFERED BY THE TEXAS TEACHERS COLLEGES, 1929–30

CURRICULA	2-YEAR CURRICULA LEADING TO PERMANENT ELEMENTARY CERTIFICATE OR TEMPORARY HIGH SCHOOL CERTIFICATE*							4-YEAR CURRICULA LEADING TO DEGREE AND PERMANENT HIGH SCHOOL CERTIFICATE						
	A	C	Cm	D	H	N	S	A	C	Cm	D	H	N	S
Kindergarten-Primary	x	x	x	x	x		x	x	x	x	x	x		x
Primary	x	x	x	x	x	x	x	x	x	x	x	x	x	x
Intermediate	x	x	x	x	x	x	x	x	x	x	x	x	x	x
Junior High School														
Rural School		x	x	x	x	x	x		x	x		x	x	x
General								x	x	x	x	x	x	x
Supervision														
Administration		x							x					
Vocational or General Agric.†		x	x		x	x	x		x			x	x	x
Vocational or General H. Ec.‡	x	x	x	x	x	x	x	x	x	x	x	x	x	x
High School	x	x	x	x	x	x	x	x	x	x	x	x	x	x
Industrial Education	x	x	x	x	x		x	x	x	x	x	x		
Art	x	x	x	x		x	x	x	x	x	x			
Public School Music	x	x	x	x	x	x	x	x	x		x			
Reading (Speech)	x	x	x	x			x		x	x	x			
Commerce (Bus. Ad.)	x	x	x	x	x	x	x	x			x	x	x	
Physical Education	x	x	x	x	x	x	x		x		x		x	

A —College at Alpine
C —College at Canyon
Cm—College at Commerce
D —College at Denton
H —College at Huntsville
N —College at Nacogdoches
S —College at San Marcos

Note: x indicates that the curriculum is offered.

* Vocational training under the Smith-Hughes Act is offered at Huntsville.

† Vocational training under the Smith-Hughes Act is offered at San Marcos and at Denton. However, the latter does not receive financial aid under the terms of the Act.

‡ Temporary certificates are authorized by law in the special subjects of agriculture, domestic art, domestic science, commercial subjects, public school drawing, expression, manual training, public school music, vocal music, instrumental music, industrial training, and foreign languages.

colleges; the absence of four-year rural school curricula at two; and emphasis on certain of the special subjects at each. No distinct curricula are offered for the preparation of teachers in junior high schools, or for supervisors; and only the college at Canyon shows a curriculum for the training of administrators. The absence of a central coördinating agency, which was noted above, would lead one to regard the similarity in curricula as the result of emulation rather than of a well-planned effort at uniformity. The catalogues do not specify completely even a majority of the courses which make up the four-year curricula, with the exception of curricula in vocational agriculture and vocational home economics. The differentiation, therefore, is principally based on differences in major and minor subjects. The requirements for degrees, with a few exceptions, are uniform in all the colleges. They are stated in the catalogues[12] as follows:

Education, a minimum of 36 term-hours if the permanent certificate is applied for; 27 if no certificate is desired.

A major subject, a minimum of 36 term-hours, 18 of which must be in advanced courses.

A first minor subject, 27 term-hours, 9 of which must be in advanced courses.

A second minor subject, 18 term-hours. A foreign language, for the B. A. Degree, a minimum of 18 term-hours; 27 if none is offered for admission.

English, 18 term-hours.

Social science, 9 term-hours.

Laboratory science, 9 term-hours.

Total advanced courses, a minimum of 45 term-hours.[13]

Advanced courses taken in residence, a minimum of 36 term-hours.

Physical training, 18 term-hours. Electives, to make up a total of 180 term-hours.

The exceptions to the above requirements are: the college at Denton requires only 18 term-hours in education of students who do not apply for the permanent certificate; and the college at Denton and that at Nacogdoches require 18 term-hours of laboratory science. Variations in major and minor requirements in different departments are found in each of the colleges which specify credits in the major and minor subjects in excess of the minima stated above.

The importance of a skillful selection of those who are admitted to training for the teaching profession, of a functional differentiation of the training curricula, and of the attack on these problems by the entire training institution rather than by departments is rendered more significant by the results of *The Commonwealth Teacher-*

[12] Sul Ross State Teachers College at Alpine, *Bulletin 31,* p. 51, 1929-1930; West Texas State Teachers College at Canyon, *Bulletin No. 53,* p. 72, 1929-1930; East Texas State Teachers College at Commerce, *Catalogue,* p. 30, 1928-1929; North Texas State Teachers College at Denton, *Catalogue,* p. 65, June, 1929; Sam Houston State Teachers College at Huntsville, *Fiftieth Annual Catalogue,* p. 51, 1928-1929; Stephen F. Austin State Teachers College at Nacogdoches, *Bulletin No. 25,* p. 32, 1929-1930. Southwest Texas State Teachers College at San Marcos, *Catalogue,* p. 53, 1929-1930.

[13] The catalogues prepared in the spring of 1930 have changed this minimum to 60 term-hours to conform to Standard VIII of the American Association of Teachers Colleges.

TABLE 58

MAJORS OFFERED IN TEXAS TEACHERS COLLEGES BY DEPARTMENTS, AND NUMBER OF TERM COURSES BY YEARS

DEPARTMENT	ALPINE						CANYON						COMMERCE					
	No.* Yrs. Work (3 Terms Each) Offered	No. Terms Advanced Work Above 4 Yrs.	No. Term Courses Offered in Each Year				No.* Yrs. Work (3 Terms Each) Offered	No. Terms Advanced Work Above 4 Yrs.	No. Term Courses Offered in Each Year				No.* Yrs. Work (3 Terms Each) Offered	No. Terms Advanced Work Above 4 Yrs.	No. Term Courses Offered in Each Year			
			Fr.	Soph.	Jr.	Sr.			Fr.	Soph.	Jr.	Sr.			Fr.	Soph.	Jr.	Sr.
Agriculture	1	—	3	0	0	0	4	3	8	4	4	5	3	0	7	6	3	—
Art	4	0	3	5	3	0	4	3	3	10	6	3	4	3	3	5	3	6
Biology	4	1	3	3	3	4	4	—	3	3	3	3	2	0	6	7	—	—
Business Administration	4	0	6	7	3	3	2	0	12	4	0	0	2	0	6	10	—	—
Chemistry	4	0	3	4	3	3	4	1	3	3	3	4	3	0	3	6	3	—
Education	4	6	4	10	9	3	4	8	6	13	6	8	4	25	9	17	17	14
Economics and Sociology	2	0	0	6	6	0	3	0	0	3	3	3	4	1	3	3	4	3
English	4	10	4	8	9	7	4	17	3	14	13	10	4	18	4	4	12	12
French	2	0	6	3	3	0	3	0	3	3	3	0	4	1	6	3	4	3
Geography	1	0	3	0	0	0	4	1	3	4	3	4	4	0	4	6	3	3
Government	1	0	3	0	0	0	4	0	0	7	3	3	1	0	0	3	—	—
History	4	2	6	4	6	4	4	3	3	4	3	6	4	2	8	11	4	4
Home Economics	4	7	7	6	7	6	4	7	9	8	5	8	4	8	8	9	9	5
Latin	1/3	0	6	7	—	—	4	2	4	3	4	4	4	4	11	4	6	4
Industrial Education	4	3	7	5	5	4	4	3	3	6	3	6	4	5	7	9	8	3
Mathematics	4	0	4	4	3	4	4	2	7	9	5	3	4	7	6	5	6	7
Music	4	0	6	6	3	3	4	0	3	3	3	3	3	0	6	8	3	—
Physical Education—Men	2	0	3	3	0	0	4	1	7	9	3	4	2	0	2	5	1	—
Physical Education—Women	2	0	3	3	0	0	2	0	12	9	—	—	2	0	6	15	2	—
Spanish	4	7	6	3	6	7	4	6	3	3	4	8	4	5	6	3	4	7
Speech Arts	3	0	6	6	3	0	4	1	7	3	4	3	4	1	3	4	4	3
Library Science	3	0	3	3	3	0	3	3	0	3	6	3	—	0	—	—	—	—
Physics	2	0	3	3	0	0	4	5	3	3	7	4	4	0	3	6	3	3
German													2	0	3	3	—	—
Bible																		

* Four years' work equals a major.

TABLE 58 (*Continued*)

MAJORS OFFERED IN TEXAS TEACHERS COLLEGES BY DEPARTMENTS, AND NUMBER OF TERM COURSES BY YEARS

DEPARTMENT	DENTON						HUNTSVILLE						NACOGDOCHES						SAN MARCOS					
	No.* Yrs. Work (3 Terms Each) Offered	No. Terms Advanced Work Above 4 Yrs.	No. Term Courses Offered in Each Year				No.* Yrs. Work (3 Terms Each) Offered	No. Terms Advanced Work Above 4 Yrs.	No. Term Courses Offered in Each Year				No.* Yrs. Work (3 Terms Each) Offered	No. Terms Advanced Work Above 4 Yrs.	No. Term Courses Offered in Each Year				No.* Yrs. Work (3 Terms Each) Offered	No. Terms Advanced Work Above 4 Yrs.	No. Term Courses Offered in Each Year			
			Fr.	Soph.	Jr.	Sr.			Fr.	Soph.	Jr.	Sr.			Fr.	Soph.	Jr.	Sr.			Fr.	Soph.	Jr.	Sr.
Agriculture	—	—	—	—	—	—	4	12	9	10	9	9	4	4	15	3		10	3	0	5	1	3	
Art	4	3	4	3	3	6	3	0	4	4	5	0	3	0	7	2		3	3	0	7	0	3	
Biology	4	4	3	6	6	4	4	0	10	6	3	3	4	0	9	6		6	4	3	6	7	7	
Business Administration	4	3	6	11	5	4	4	3	3	9	5	4	4	2	6	6		8	3	0	3	8	7	
Chemistry	4	4	4	6	7	3	3	0	6	3	3	0	4	0	3	6		6	4	1	3	6	7	
Education	4	18	7	12	19	5	4	15	7	18	10	11	4	17	3	11		23	4	13	7	10	14	
Economics and Sociology	4	3	0	6	6	3	2	0	—	12	0	0	4	3	0	6		9	4	0		7	6	
English	4	12	3	9	10	3	4	7	12	9	6	7	4	13	6	5		19	4	13	3	6	6	13
French	2	0	6	3	0	0	3	0	3	6	3	0	2	0	3	3		0	1	0	6	3	00	0
Geography	4	2	3	7	5	3	4	0	3	4	3	3	4	0	3	5		6	3	0	5	1	3	
Government	4	0	3	3	3	3	2	0	3	4	0	0	2	0	1	3		3	4	0	2	3	6	
History	4	6	6	7	7	5	4	6	3	19	6	6	4	0	12	7		6	4	6	6	7	12	
Home Economics	4	3	9	4	5	8	4	3	4	6	4	5	4	4	11	1		10	4	10	6	3	12	4
Latin	4	3	13	8	3	6	3	0	6	6	3	—	4	0	6	4		6	3	0	12		3	
Industrial Education	4	3	9	18	6	3	4	2	5	9	5	3	—	—	—	—		—	3	0	6	2	3	
Mathematics	4	3	3	4	4	5	4	0	3	3	3	3	4	3	4	8		9	4	3	8	3	6	3
Music	4	0	4	11	3	3	2	0	10	8	0	0	3	0	4	5		3	2	0	7	2	0	0
Physical Education—Men	4	4	5	9	6	4	3	0	3	4	3	3	3	0	6	0		3	2	0	5			
Physical Education—Women	4	4	5	9	6	4	3	3	3	4	4	5	4	0	9	0		6	2	0	4			
Spanish	4	6	6	3	9	3	3	0	4	5	3	0	4	5	7	4		11	4	6	9		12	
Speech Arts	3	0	3	6	3	0	1	0	3	0	0	0	1	0	3	0		—	2	0	1	4	2	
Library Science	1	0	1	0	0	0	1	0	3	0	0	0	1	0	3	—		—	1	0	0	3		
Physics	4	0	4	3	3	3	3	0	3	5	5	0	2	0	3	3		—	4		3	4	6	
German																			4	0	9		6	
Bible													2	0	4	3		—	2					

* Four years' work equals a major.

Training Study.[14] These, based on elaborate job and trait analyses, show that the personal characteristics and traits, together with the duties, activities, and responsibilities of successful teachers in various kinds of teaching positions differ markedly. The conclusion is that training institutions have the obligation of supplying teachers who possess the particular personal and professional characteristics to fill specific positions successfully. A study of the curricular practices of many teacher-training institutions would lend confirmation to the following indictment of the usual methods of organizing curricula which is made in *The Commonwealth Teacher-Training Study.*

> A radical reorganization of the curricula of teacher-training institutions is demanded by a variety of conditions. Teacher-training curricula, like others, have been developed without clear definition of objectives and with no logical plan of procedure. The custom of writing to discover what other schools are doing, when the revamping of old courses or the installation of new ones is under consideration, bespeaks the powerful influence of common practice and tradition. The preferences and special abilities of faculty members likewise exert stubborn and resourceful pressure. An instructor may request or demand the inclusion of a certain course because he has recently mastered the material in the graduate school or because he wishes to study the subject more elaborately, or because he has found an interesting text that he wishes to evaluate. Likewise, the preferences common to several individual instructors lead to wide overlapping and duplication among the various departments and courses. Evidence of this tendency has been found by recent studies showing that the same specific topics are given major treatment in several different courses enrolling the same students, and—curious proof of overlapping—that a large percentage of the students passed the final examination of one university course in education on the day they entered it.[15]

Table 58 was constructed to show further facts in regard to the various offerings as the departments seem to influence them. The facts were obtained from data sheets submitted by each college, supplemented by reference to catalogues. The table gives the number of years of work offered by each department; the number of advanced courses, or thirds, above the number required for a major of four years; and the number of courses, or thirds, that belong in each of the four collegiate years. It will be seen that several of the institutions have not definitely placed all the courses as to the year in which they belong. This is especially true of junior and senior courses, and, in some instances, of freshman and sophomore courses.

[14] Charters, W. W. and Waples, D. *The Commonwealth Teacher-Training Study,* University of Chicago Press, Chicago, 1929. (See Chap. I for a summary of the study.)

[15] *Ibid.,* Preface p. v.

The system of numbering courses is not uniform. Five departments of the twenty-five listed in the table—education, English, history, home economics, and mathematics—offer four years of work (or a major) at each institution. Three other departments—art, chemistry, and Spanish—offer three or four years at each. No evidence is at hand to indicate what influences have determined the amount of work offered by the several departments. The demands of the public schools, qualifications of faculty members, or the zeal of department heads in pressing the claims of their departments before the curriculum committees may have been factors in this determination. It is doubtful whether the number of advanced courses offered in the departments of English, history, home economics, mathematics, Spanish, and possibly others are in response to the direct needs of the teaching service. Such would, however, prepare students for graduate work at the universities.

Differentiation of training curricula is not especially encouraged by the certification laws of the state.[16] The principal differentiation in certificates is between those valid in elementary schools and those valid in high schools. However, the holder of a high school certificate of any grade may contract to teach in an elementary school, or to teach any subject in a high school whether he has had adequate preparation in that subject or not. An exception to the principal difference is made by provisions for special certificates in the following subjects: agriculture, domestic art, domestic science, commercial subjects, public school music, public school drawing, expression, manual training, vocal music, instrumental music, industrial training, foreign languages, kindergarten.[17] The minimum requirement for such certificates is two years of college work, with the exception of a two-year kindergarten certificate which is awarded upon completion of one year of work.

A more accurate picture of the actual differentiation among curricula that obtains in these institutions is presented in Table 59, which shows the specific courses required for the various degrees and certificates. Table 57 appears to represent the aims of the several colleges, and possibly their actual attainments, toward the preparation of teachers for specific positions, but the data presented in Table 59 indicate that these objectives are accomplished by the elective system rather than by definitely required curricula. Direct reports

[16] *Laws, Rules, and Regulations Governing State Teachers' Certificates.* Bulletin of State Department of Education, No. 252, Feb., 1929, Austin, Tex.

[17] *Ibid.*, pp. 9, 25-28.

from administrative officers, and the catalogue announcements for 1929-30, were used as sources of information. No courses are shown as required if they belong to a group from which one or more must be chosen. Some difficulty was experienced in checking the direct reports with catalogue statements. This was likely due to the general character of the latter. As can be seen from Table 59, the courses actually required for degrees and certificates at all institutions are: educational psychology, English composition, and a course in government which is a study of Federal and Texas constitutions required by statute. Courses in general method with observation are uniformly required, but are differentiated for the training of elementary and high school teachers. Six institutions include literature among the requirements. Practice teaching is everywhere required for all degrees which carry a permanent certificate. For degrees in elementary education at each institution courses are required in all or some of the following subjects: biology, public school music, art, speech arts, penmanship, and geography. The requirement in social science permits election of history, economics, or sociology. Election is also provided among the subjects named above to meet requirements for the 90-hour certificate. A careful examination of Table 59 indicates that the setting up of definite curricula has been begun by certain colleges and carried farther than the general certificate laws of the state demand. The writer's knowledge of conditions leads to the conclusion that the absence of specific requirements for practice teaching in all the 90-hour curricula is due to the lack of adequate laboratory school facilities to accommodate the large enrollments.

The following extracts from letters received from deans throw additional light on the differentiation of curricula obtaining in present practice.[18] One letter, in discussing the requirements for the 90-hour permanent certificate issued to kindergarten-primary, intermediate, and rural teachers, and temporary certificates to teachers of special subjects, reads:

> Permit me to point out that since the two-year curricula mentioned above all lead to a permanent certificate upon completion thereof it is misleading to speak of four-year curricula in the aforementioned fields leading to a degree and permanent certificate. What happens is that the student who has received a permanent certificate under one of the aforementioned two-year curricula pursues two years' work additional entitling him to a degree, in which work he satisfies all academic requirements for such a degree with

[18] Letters are on file with original data.

TABLE 59

DIFFERENTIATION ACCORDING TO SUBJECTS REQUIRED FOR DEGREES AND 90-HOUR CERTIFICATES, 1929–30

SUBJECT	ALPINE							CANYON							COMMERCE							DENTON							HUNTSVILLE							NACOGDOCHES							SAN MARCOS						
	1	2	3	4	5	6	7	1	2	3	4	5	6	7	1	2	3	4	5	6	7	1	2	3	4	5	6	7	1	2	3	4	5	6	7	1	2	3	4	5	6	7	1	2	3	4	5	6	7
Introduction to Education	x	x	x	x	x	x	100															x	x	x	x	x	x	100								x	x	x	x	x	x	100							
Educational Psychology	x	x	x	x	x	x	100	x	x	x	x	x	x	100	x	x	x	x	x	x	100	x	x	x	x	x	x	100	x	x	x	x	x	x	100	x	x	x	x	x	x	100	x	x	x	x	x	x	100
History of Education																																																	
Elementary Meth'ds with Observat'n	x		x		x		50	x		x		x		50	x	x	x	x	x	x	100	x		x		x		50	x		x		x		50	x		x		x		50	x		x		x		50
Practice Teaching	x	x	x	x	x	x	100	x	x	x	x	x		83	x	x	x	x			66	x	x	x	x	x		83	x	x	x	x	x	x	100	x		x		x		50	x	x	x	x	x		83
Educational Statistics																																																	
Tests and Measurements								x		x				33															x	x	x	x			66														
Curriculum Construction									x		x			33									x		x			33																					
Junior High School																														x		x			33		x		x		x	50							
Child Psychology								x		x		x		50									x		x			33	x		x		x		50														
Extracurricular Activities																																																	
School Administration																														x		x			33														
Supervision																													x						16														
Philosophy of Education																																																	
English Composition	x	x	x	x	x	x	100	x	x	x	x	x	x	100	x	x	x	x	x	x	100	x	x	x	x	x	x	100	x	x	x	x	x	x	100	x	x	x	x	x	x	100	x	x	x	x	x	x	100
Literature	x	x	x	x			33	x	x	x	x	x	x	100	x	x	x	x	x	x	100	x	x	x	x	x	x	100	x	x	x	x	x	x	100	x	x	x	x	x	x	100	x	x	x	x	x	x	100
Mathematics																																																	
American History																																																	
English History																																																	
Foreign Language			x	x			33			x	x			33			x	x			33			x	x			33																	x	x			33
Biology																						x	x	x	x			66	x	x	x	x	x	x	100	x		x		x		50			x				16
Chemistry																																																	
Physics																																																	
Music								x		x				33								x		x				33								x		x		x		50			x		x		33
Art								x		x				33								x		x				33	x		x				33	x		x		x		50			x		x		33
Speech																						x		x				33																					
Penmanship																						x		x				33																					
Geography																						x		x				33																	x		x		33
Social Science															x	x	x	x			66	x	x	x	x	x	x	100	x	x	x	x			66	x	x	x	x	x	x	100	x	x	x	x	x	x	100
Government	x	x	x	x	x	x	100	x	x	x	x	x	x	100	x	x	x	x	x	x	100	x	x	x	x	x	x	100	x	x	x	x	x	x	100	x	x	x	x	x	x	100	x	x	x	x	x	x	100
High School Methods with Observation		x		x		x	50		x		x			33									x		x		x	50		x		x		x	50		x		x		x	50		x		x			33

1—B. S. for elementary teachers.
2—B. S. for high-school teachers.
3—B. A. for elementary teachers.
4—B. A. for high-school teachers.
5—Sophomore certificate for elementary teachers.
6—Sophomore certificate for high-school teachers.
7—Per cent of curricula in which each subject appears.

reference to academic major and first and second minors without necessarily pursuing additional courses in education. If he does, they may be additional courses in education dealing with the kindergarten-primary or intermediate fields leading to further specialization in such fields without leading to additional certification; or they may be courses in education dealing with the secondary field that enable the student to satisfy all requirements for the permanent high-school certificate at the time of graduation. In fact, it is common practice for a student, after having finished a two-year curriculum and having a permanent elementary certificate, to transfer to the curriculum for high-school teachers at the beginning of the junior year.

This letter expresses the opinion that these facts obtain in all teachers colleges of Texas. A letter from another institution has the following to say in regard to differentiation of curricula:

We do not line up many curricula in our catalogue. Our policy is to start with the minimum requirements for certificates and degrees and from this as a nucleus, the student himself under guidance selects his own curriculum. In this way the student may build almost any kind of curriculum so far as our offerings will permit.

Requirements looking to coherent and progressive lines of work are stated by the catalogues in regulations governing majors, minors, and advanced courses. Freshman courses must be completed before junior or senior work is undertaken.[19] Advanced courses are credited as such only after the prerequisites have been met. A major requires not less than eighteen term-hours of advanced work, and a first minor not less than nine; while a total of sixty term-hours of the one hundred and eighty required for a degree must be done in advanced courses. In order to determine more accurately the actual continuity and sequence of the work in these colleges Table 60 was constructed. The number and per cent of advanced courses in the principal fields which are counted as independent thirds are shown. There is nothing in the catalogue announcements to indicate that these courses must be taken in sequence with other advanced courses. The totals show a wide variance in the per cent of these independent thirds among the several colleges—ranging from thirty-five per cent to seventy-seven per cent. The reason for such a situation is not apparent from data available, but the general conclusion seems warranted that the required coherence and continuity in advanced work are in inverse proportion to the number of independent courses. Whatever coherence and continuity are attained are likely the result of the individual student's election under such guidance as is provided. A

[19] Catalogues referred to: Alpine, p. 46; Canyon, p. 66; Commerce, p. 27; Denton, p. 66; Huntsville, p. 47; Nacogdoches, p. 28; San Marcos, p. 43.

TABLE 60

NUMBER AND PER CENT OF ADVANCED COURSES (3 TERM-HOURS) THAT ARE COUNTED AS SEPARATE THIRDS—NOT REQUIRED IN SEQUENCE WITH OTHERS

Department	Alpine		Canyon		Commerce		Denton		Huntsville		Nacogdoches		San Marcos	
	No.	%	No.	%	No.	%	No.	%	No.	%	No.	%	No.	%
Agriculture	—	—	7	77.7	3	100	—	—	13	72.2	1	10.0	3	100
Art	3	100	1	11.1	2	22.2	0	0	—	—	0	0	0	0
Business Administration	1	16.6	—	—	—	—	9	100	5	62.5	2	25.0	2	40.0
Education	6	50.0	11	78.5	32	78.0	18	75.0	19	94.2	22	95.6	4	28.5
English	4	25.0	14	60.8	5	20.8	16	88.8	13	100	11	57.9	19	100
Biology	1	14.2	2	33.3	—	—	1	10.0	6	100	0	0	1	14.2
Chemistry	1	16.6	4	57.1	0	0	4	40.0	0	0	7	100	2	25.0
Physics	—	—	3	42.8	0	0	1	16.6	5	100	—	—	5	100
History	1	10.0	9	100	5	62.5	7	58.6	0	0	1	12.5	10	66.6
Geography	—	—	7	100	4	66.6	3	37.5	6	100	6	100	3	100
Sociology	—	—	6	100	4	57.1	6	100	—	—	1	33.3	1	33.3
Economics	0	0	—	—	—	—	3	100	—	—	4	66.6	0	0
Government	—	—	—	—	—	—	0	0	1	33.3	3	100	0	0
Languages	1	6.2	20	86.5	15	62.5	0	0	9	100	5	29.4	7	33.3
Mathematics	1	14.2	5	62.5	4	30.7	3	33.3	4	66.6	5	55.5	3	33.3
Home Economics	9	75.0	4	30.7	12	85.7	4	30.7	8	88.8	10	100	8	50.0
Industrial Arts	9	100	2	22.2	3	27.2	0	0	6	75.0	—	—	3	100
Music	4	57.1	0	0	—	—	0	0	—	—	1	33.3	—	—
Physical Education	—	—	7	100	3	100	10	100	7	100	6	85.7	—	—
Total	41	35.0	102	62.6	92	77.3	85	47	102	70.0	84	64.1	71	58.2

A dash in the No. and % columns means that no advanced courses are offered, while 0 means that none are counted as separate thirds.

similar variation in percentages of independent courses is seen in each subject in the several institutions, with the exception of physical education in which separate thirds are the rule. Differences just as noticeable are shown among the various subjects in each college. With the exception of one institution, half or more of the advanced courses in education are not required in sequence with others. It is at least doubtful whether such an arrangement can be relied on to give the thorough training in educational theory, science, and practice demanded by the fifth principle stated above. Neither is it certain that specific achievement within the subject-matter fields would result if students were left to choose at random among a large number of independent three-term-hour courses. A predominance of such courses seems to indicate that the program of the department offering them has grown by accretions instead of developing systematically to meet definite professional objectives. There seems to be nothing inherent in or peculiar to any subject that makes a large number of independent thirds necessary among advanced courses, with the possible exception of physical education. Practically all subjects show a high percentage of such courses in certain colleges and a comparatively low percentage in others. The offering of independent thirds, whether comparatively few or many, appears from the facts presented in Table 60 to be due to the ideas of teachers in the various departments who participate in the preparation of the catalogues.

The fourth principle or criterion of teacher-training curricula, which demands that subject matter be organized and presented in a professional manner, presents a difficult problem in attainment, and in evaluating the work of any institution. Hill[20] claims that teachers colleges throughout the country show their greatest weakness in failing to give professional treatment in actual class instruction. He says:

> The situation is largely due to the fact that any excellent teachers in teachers colleges are still of the opinion that no special treatment of subject matter for teachers is necessary. They expect young teachers to be able to apply the principles they learn in the education courses in the selection of subject matter for their students, and therefore leave the most difficult of all the teacher's problems for her to work out unaided. The almost total lack of textbooks written to exemplify this point of view has made it difficult for teachers who have had little or no training in the professionalization of courses to make modifications in their syllabi which result in a professional treatment of the subject.[21]

[20] Hill, C. M. *A Decade of Progress in Teacher Training.* Contributions to Education, No. 233. Bureau of Publications, Teachers College, Columbia University, 1927.

[21] *Ibid.,* pp. 123-24.

The evaluation of the work of institutions on this point will likely be inadequate because of the practical impossibility of securing concrete data, for actual classroom work may be different from anything printed in syllabi and catalogues.

As a brief definition of such handling of subject matter in the teacher-training institution, Randolph offers the following:

> Reduced to its lowest terms the idea of the professional treatment of subject matter implies: (1) on the side of scholarship such "new views" of generally familiar material as will reveal its racial significance and its potentialities for public education, and such extensions of scholarship as will be most likely to insure flexible control of the problems of utilizing the study for social purposes in a particular teaching position; and (2) on the side of method it implies a conscious organization of instruction in subject-matter with reference to the professional responsibilities of the future teacher—which among other things involves the transmitting of a fruitful method of study and the purposeful affecting of attitudes and technique.[22]

Table 61 shows the extent to which professional treatment is being given in the various fields by each of the Texas teachers colleges, as accurately as this can be ascertained from course descriptions in their catalogues. In preparing this table a course was considered to have some professional treatment if the description made any mention of its being designed or used to train teachers. Several of the courses so counted were methods courses in different subjects. In some departments, indicated by an asterisk in Table 61, the statements introducing course descriptions point out that all courses are designed to prepare teachers, and in such departments all courses were counted as having professional treatment. The totals show that not more than 28 per cent of all courses in any institution differ, as judged by their descriptions, from similar courses in a liberal arts college. That percentage ranges downward among the other institutions to 11 per cent. Only slightly higher percentages were found in the five state teachers colleges in Missouri by a study made in 1929,[23] the range there being from 30.1 per cent to 15.1 per cent. Armentrout found that two-thirds of the courses in state teachers colleges are mainly academic with no apparent difference in the work done in a liberal arts college.[24] The

[22] Randolph, E. D. *Op. cit.*, p. 133.

[23] *Report on Publicly Supported Higher Education*, p. 279, 1929.

[24] Armentrout, W. D. *Student Teaching in State Teachers Colleges*, p. 37. Colorado State Teachers College, Greeley, Colo., 1927.

TABLE 61

PER CENT OF TERM COURSES OFFERED IN VARIOUS FIELDS, THE CATALOGUE DESCRIPTION OF WHICH GIVES EVIDENCE OF PROFESSIONAL TREATMENT

SUBJECTS	ALPINE		CANYON		COMMERCE		DENTON		HUNTS-VILLE	
	No. Profs.	% Profs.	No. Profs.	% Profs.	No. Profs.	% Profs.	No. Profs.	% Profs.	No. Profs.	% Profs.
Agriculture	0	0	5	23.8	1	16.2	not offered		5	12.1
Art	5	45.4	1	4.5	4	23.5	7	43.7	3	37.4
Business Administration or Comm.	19	100 *	16	100 *	1	15.2	4	16.0	7	35.0
English	3	10.7	6	16.6	4	12.5	3	10.0		19.3
Social Studies, including History and Geography	2	5.4	4	8.1	4	6.9	2	2.8	7	11.6
Sciences	2	6.3	3	7.7	2	4.6	2	4.1	2	4.2
Languages	1	2.0	2	4.0	3	4.9	3	4.9	0	0
Mathematics	1	6.6	5	20.8	2	8.3	1	6.2	2	15.3
Music	8	40.0		100 *	4	21.0	7	31.8	11	61.1
Industrial Arts	21	100 *	3	16.6	2	7.4	2	8.7	5	22.7
Reading or Speech	15	62.5	2	11.7	2	14.2	5	38.4	1	33.3
Home Economics	2	8.0	2	6.6	4	12.9	5	20.8	0	0
Physical Education or Health	3	50.0	8	18.1	11	37.9	16	45.7	12	66.6
Total	82	28.1	57	15.6	44	11.0	57	12.2	61	17.9

* Introduction to course descriptions states that all courses in the department are designed for the training of teachers. Generally the descriptions of separate courses make no mention of professional function or treatment.

wide differences in the proportion of professionally treated courses among the departments in the same institution are noticeable, but not definitely explainable by means of concrete information at hand. A similar variance was found among departments in the Missouri schools. In general it appears that higher percentages of courses are professionalized in the subjects usually referred to as special subjects. The inference from data presented in this table, so far as they represent the actual situation, is that those responsible for the offerings in most subject-matter departments have been guided by academic traditions, and that there has been little integration, from the standpoint of professional requirements, in organizing courses throughout the institutions. The experience and observations of the writer, and the syllabi of courses examined, indicate that the proportions of professionally treated courses have not been underestimated.

A condensed summary of reports from administrative officers on certain practices relative to administration of curricula is shown in Table 62. A committee on course of study is common to all colleges.

TABLE 62

GENERAL INFORMATION CONCERNING THE ADMINISTRATION OF CURRICULA*

ITEM OF INFORMATION	ALPINE	CANYON	COMMERCE	DENTON	HUNTSVILLE	NACOGDOCHES	SAN MARCOS
By whom the course of study was made	Committee on Course of Study	Heads of Departments, Committee, and Dean	Heads of Departments and Committee	Dean and Committee	Dean, Associate Dean Head of Education Department	Dean and Heads of Departments	Committee, Dean, and Department Heads
Changes are made	Semiannually	Annually	Annually	Annually	Annually	Biennially	Annually
Concerted effort for harmony and curricula among colleges	No report	Presidents work on this each year	Course of study committee	Council of presidents and council of deans	Deans' meetings. None for 2 years	None	Council of presidents. Deans' recommendations.
Number of students admitted without 15 units from high school, '29–'30	No report	56	None	54	13	22†	19 by examination, 36 on approval
Length of time after opening of term students may enter with full program	10 days	1 week	1 week	10 days	3 weeks	1 week	1 week
Length of time with reduced program	midterm	1 month	2 weeks	20 days — very rare	6 weeks	20 days	2 weeks
Reduction required in number of courses because of late entrance	10 days late, 1 course; 20 days late, 2 courses	2 courses	1 course	1 and 2 courses, respectively	2/5 of load	1/5 to 2/5 of load	After first week, 1 course; after second week, on individual merit
Per cent of students permitted to deviate from sequence of courses in requirements for degree, '29–'30	5 per cent	Probably 1 per cent	None	Probably 3 per cent	.5 per cent	No report	No considerable number
Is there correlation and harmony between work of training school and college teachers of academic subjects?	Yes	Yes	Yes	Yes	Yes	Fairly satisfactory	Yes

* Data obtained from deans and other administrative officers.

† Individual approval, with one exception.

The dean is a member of this committee in all the colleges except one which does not list a dean among its administrative officers. Provisions for annual changes in courses and curricula are reported by five institutions. Noticeable variety of practice is apparent in the matter of admission of students after the opening of a term, and in the reduction in number of courses required because of late entrance. Deviation from stipulated sequence of courses seems to be generally allowed. However, evidence secured in conferences suggests that most of the cases in which deviation is permitted are occasioned by students who began work for degrees in former years when requirements and sequences were different. Conversations with members of the training school staffs give the impression that they do not perceive a high degree of correlation between the work of the teachers of academic subjects and that of the training schools. According to that source of information the subject-matter teachers in the colleges generally know little concerning the work of the training schools in relation to the integrated task of preparing teachers for the public schools. Reports summarized in this table give support to statements made early in this chapter to the effect that although the seven colleges are governed by a single board, the internal administration is very nearly autonomous.

For several years the Texas teachers colleges have been enlarging the work offered by extension and correspondence. The objectives of such work, as stated in some of the catalogues, are the improvement of teachers in service, and the provision of opportunity for the earning of certificates and degrees without loss of time from teaching positions, and with a minimum of expense. The Council of Presidents at the summer meeting in 1930 limited the extension teaching of individual teachers to one term of a collegiate year. All colleges accept such courses for credit. Standard III of the American Association of Teachers Colleges sets a definite limit to the amount of extension and correspondence work that can be accepted for degrees, certificates, or diplomas as follows:

> Not more than one-fourth (¼) of any curriculum leading to a degree or certificate or diploma in a teachers college or normal school shall be taken in extension classes or by correspondence.[25]

The amount of work offered by correspondence and extension during 1929-30 is shown in Tables 63 A and 63 B. The number of term courses in each department given by each institution is tabulated and

[25] *Tenth Yearbook of the American Association of Teachers Colleges,* p. 13, 1931.

TABLE 63 A

Number of Extension and Correspondence Courses by Departments

Departments	Alpine*				Canyon				Commerce‡				Denton‡				Huntsville				Nacogdoches‡				San Marcos‡			
	Extension		Correspondence		Extension		Correspondence		Extension		Correspondence		Extension		Correspondence		Extension		Correspondence		Extension		Correspondence		Extension		Correspondence	
	T†	A†	T	A	T	A	T	A	T	A	T	A	T	A	T	A	T	A	T	A	T	A	T	A	T	A	T	A
Art							3																					
Agriculture							3	1	1										10	5								
Biology							8	4					3				2	1	2									
Business Administration			6				3						1						5	2								
Chemistry							3																					
Education			6		5	4	8	2	12	12			8	8			12	6	5		7	6			1			
Social Science									3				1				3											
English			6		4	4	8	2	3	3			10	6			12	8	13	6	2	2			3			
French													1						9	3								
Geography			3				3						2						2									
Government			1		4	3	7		1				3				2		1		5				1			
History			3		1	1	6		3	1			3	2			9	6	12		3							
Home Economics							3																					
Latin							12												6									
Manual Training			3																									
Mathematics			3				13	3	1										3									
Music							3																					
Physical Ed. (w)																												
Physical Ed. (m)																												
Spanish			3	3			7	3					1						12	3								
Speech																												
Lab. Science																												
Physics							3																					
Other													2															
German							3																					
Total			34	3	14	12	96	15	24	16			35	16			40	21	80	19	17	8			5			

* No courses by extension; † T—Total, A—Advanced; ‡ No courses by correspondence.

TABLE 63 B

MISCELLANEOUS FACTS REGARDING EXTENSION AND CORRESPONDENCE COURSES

	ALPINE	CANYON	COMMERCE	DENTON	HUNTSVILLE	NACOGDOCHES	SAN MARCOS
Is college credit given for extension and correspondence courses?	Yes	Yes	Yes	Yes	Yes	Yes	Yes
Number of term-hours of extension and correspondence toward a degree	21	¼	No report	60 term-hours	60	45	45
How many term-hours in advanced courses?	9	9	No report	*	0–100%	15	*
Fees for each extension course (per term)	No courses	$10–$12	No report	$12 (min.)	$8	$10	$10
Fees for each correspondence course (per term)	$8 per 3 terms work	$10	No report	No courses	$8	No courses	No courses
Per cent paid to instructor ..	75%	0	No report	†	62½%	‡	75%
Per cent paid to college funds	12½%	100%	No report	100%	37½%	No report	25%

* No limit other than that 36 term-hours of advanced work must be done in residence.
† Teacher paid flat sum of $100 a course.
‡ Depends on size of class—$60 term+expenses for all work.

the number of advanced courses is shown in separate columns. It appears from the totals that correspondence courses are more popular than those given by extension, and that a greater number of departments offer such courses. Very few extension courses are offered on the campus of any institution, and it can be seen that half or more of such courses are of advanced character. The departments of education, English, and history are most consistently represented by extension courses. Reports not included in the tabulation show that term fees for extension and correspondence courses vary from eight to twelve dollars per student, and that instructors in charge of such courses receive additional compensation.

The fourth step in the curriculum pattern outlined,[26] which would establish provision for properly graded observation, participation, and student teaching, and the demand for sufficiently extensive practice in the fifth principle of curriculum construction,[27] suggests the desirability of studying the training school facilities of the Texas teachers colleges.

The training school was established to aid in the training of teachers, and has always found its justification in the principle that "we learn to do

[26] *Tenth Yearbook of the American Association of Teachers Colleges*, p. 5.
[27] *Ibid.*, p. 4.

by doing." In all fields of endeavor, it has been found by practical experience that a knowledge of right practices does not give skill in the performance of such practices.[28]

The importance of the function of the training school is generally recognized by the literature on the preparation of teachers and is nowhere more directly presented than in the following principles:

1. Directed observation of skilled teaching in any subject or field is essential to thorough training in that subject or field.
2. Practice or participation in teaching is essential for the development of skill and insight.
3. Every course in a teachers college that touches either the subject-matter or the theory of teaching should be actively related to the practice or demonstration school. . . .
4. Every teacher in the college should contribute to the training of the young teacher, and to this end he should observe that teacher in practice.
5. The director of training should be a coördinating agent focusing the work of the college upon the development of efficient teachers.
6. There should be no more gap between college classes and this laboratory than between the chemistry lecture room and the chemistry laboratory.
7. The teachers in the training school should be equally as well trained for their work as are any other members of the faculty.
8. The training school is the central department of the institution and the proving ground of every other department.[29]

Pryor has worked out a series of graded units, graduated as to difficulty, by which the teachers college student is introduced according to psychological principles to an actual teaching situation, and shows in his study that such a plan is being used in several teacher-training institutions.[30] One of the objectives sought by such procedure is the reduction in the proportion of strictly theoretical courses in the field of education which do not serve to satisfy felt professional needs. The first contact with the teaching situation is furnished by the observation of skilled teaching. This is followed by participation in which the student shares the work of the skilled teacher. As a climax to the series of units the student serves as teacher with full responsibility for directing the work of the classroom. The effective employment of such a plan obviously depends upon adequate and properly administered training school facilities.

[28] Garrison, N. L. *The Status and Work of the Training Supervisor,* p. 1. Contributions to Education, No. 280. Bureau of Publications, Teachers College, Columbia University, 1927.

[29] Selected from the *Report of the Louisiana Survey,* p. 191.

[30] Pryor, H. C. *Graded Units in Student-Teaching,* especially Chap. I. Contributions to Education, No. 202. Bureau of Publications, Teachers College, Columbia University, 1926.

By means of tabulated information, which was secured from catalogues, conferences, and reports, and which is presented in Tables 64, 65, 66 A, 66 B, and 67 it is shown that the Texas colleges are lacking in adequate training school facilities in proportion to their enrollments, although they comply with the standards of the American Association of Teachers Colleges[31] in maintaining training schools under their control. Six colleges have their own campus schools and one uses the public schools of the town in which it is located—except that it houses the high-school division in the college buildings. Judging from reports received, the public schools of other towns are not used for student teaching. Catalogue statements are indefinite as to the actual conduct of and time devoted to observation, partici-

TABLE 64

REQUIREMENTS IN PRACTICE TEACHING*

	In Elementary Curriculum	In High-School Curriculum
Alpine	1, 2, or 3 term-hours during the sophomore year. 1 hour per day.	Three periods per week for three terms during the senior year.
Canyon	90 to 180 clock hours during the sophomore year. 1 hour per day.	90 to 180 clock hours during the senior year. 1 hour per day.
Commerce	120 clock hours during the sophomore year, except 60 hours for students with experience. 1 hour per day.	120 clock hours during junior or senior year, except 60 hours for students with experience. 1 hour per day.
Denton	40 clock hours in sophomore year; and 60 hours in the senior year. 1 hour per day.	60 clock hours during the senior year. 1 hour per day.
Huntsville	60 clock hours during the sophomore year, and 60 during the senior year. 1 hour per day.	60 clock hours during the sophomore year, and 60 during the senior year. 1 hour per day.
Nacogdoches	48 clock hours during the sophomore year. 1 hour per day, except each student teaches one whole day.	48 clock hours in junior year for 6-year high-school certificate; 48 hours in senior year. 1 hour per day, except each student teaches one whole day.
San Marcos	Two terms during the sophomore year. 1 hour per day, 5 days a week.	One term in the junior year and one in the senior or two in the senior. 1 hour per day, 5 days a week.

*Based on Catalogue Statements.

31 *Ninth Yearbook of the American Association of Teachers Colleges,* pp. 13-14.

pation, and practice. The information summarized in Table 64 was secured from catalogues, reports of, and conferences with, administrative officers, and is shown in the terms in which it was obtained. Some practice teaching is done in college classes and not in the training school, usually in freshman courses in science, business administration, and other freshman subjects, but the exact amount cannot be determined, nor is it certain that requirements shown in the table are uniformly and exactly followed. Practice teaching seems to be "distributed" in that the student teaches one period each day. Judging from evidence presented in other tables, this is likely determined by administrative convenience and the lack of facilities for "concentrated" practice, in the sense that the student devotes at least most of his time to teaching under guidance for a stated period.[32] It appears that student teaching is almost uniformly confined to the sophomore and senior years, and that less of such practice is required of students taking the high-school curriculum.

A summary of information concerning the training schools and the student-teacher load, presented in Table 65, shows a general picture from which significant inferences can be drawn. A very obvious fact is that none of the colleges possess complete modern plants for the education of boys and girls in the elementary and high-school grades. Laboratories, shops, auditoriums, and gymnasiums, while shown at certain colleges, are not generally found belonging distinctly to the training schools. Where such facilities are lacking, the training schools use those primarily intended for college classes. Such a situation is not typical of conditions in the public schools; is not desirable from the standpoint of effective handling of pupils; and is rarely satisfactory to the college departments whose facilities are used. Teachers in these departments are inclined to look upon training school pupils as interlopers. In Chapter I, it was shown that the total enrollment at each college in the summer is practically double that of any term of the regular session. Approximately the same proportions of student teachers, in summer and winter terms, are shown in this table, yet only the college at Denton reports the use of additional facilities for practice teaching in the summer. At Denton slightly more than a fifth of the student teachers are cared for in public schools. By reference to data in Chapter I it is found that the following percentages of the entire enrollment at each

[32] For a discussion of "concentrated versus distributed practice teaching" see *Bulletin No. 14* of the Carnegie Foundation for the Advancement of Teaching, pp. 222-24.

TABLE 65

FACTS CONCERNING TRAINING SCHOOLS

		No. of Student Teachers					No. Laboratories and Shops Belonging to Training Schools				No. of Auditoriums	No. of Gymnasiums
		In Local Town Schools		In Campus Schools		Total						
		Elementary	High School	Elementary	High School		Science	Home Economics	Manual Training	Commercial		
Alpine	Summer 1929	79	0	0	10	89						
	Winter 1930	26	0	0	30	56	0	0	0	0	0	0
Canyon	Summer 1929	0	0	60	22	82						
	Winter 1930	0	0	7	22	29	2	0	0	0	1	1
Commerce	Summer 1929	0	0	82	62	144						
	Winter 1930	0	0	59	42	101	1	1	1	0	0	0
Denton	Summer 1929	27	37	141	71	276						
	Winter 1930	0	0	23	43	66	0	0	0	0	0	0
Huntsville	Summer 1929	0	0	97	72	169						
	Winter 1930	0	0	40	65	105	0	0	1	0	1	0
Nacogdoches	Summer 1929	0	0	54	34	88						
	Winter 1930	0	0	8	12	20	0	1	0	0	0	1
San Marcos	Summer 1929	0	0	157	63	220						
	Winter 1930	0	0	79	80	159	0	0	1	0	1	1

institution were engaged in practice teaching during the summer and winter terms, respectively:

Town	Per Cent in Summer	Per Cent in Winter
Alpine	14.0	19.9
Canyon	7.2	4.0
Commerce	6.0	8.7
Denton	8.3	4.1
Huntsville	11.0	14.5
Nacogdoches	8.2	3.7
San Marcos	10.6	15.0

The variation in these percentages among the colleges is noticeable, but may result from differences in scheduling practice work. However, the generally small proportions of students engaged in practice lead to the conclusion that student teaching is not given a prominent place in the programs of the Texas colleges.

Additional facts concerning enrollments and teachers in training schools, shown in Tables 66 A, 66 B, and 67, suggest that the primary factor in the lack of prominence given to practice is the comparatively small number of pupils available to the Texas colleges. If large numbers of pupils were at hand, the chances are that necessary physical equipment would be forthcoming. That these institutions have recognized the importance of training facilities is evident from the fact that each has made an effort to provide them, and in former years special pride was felt in this distinctive part of their teacher-training equipment. However, in the rapid development of these institutions, the student enrollment has outstripped the growth of the training schools. Such a situation is not confined to Texas, as is indicated by the following statement from a bulletin of the Carnegie Foundation for the Advancement of Teaching: "The training school constitutes the characteristic laboratory equipment of a normal school or teachers college, and the courses in observation, participation, and practice teaching should be looked upon as the central and critical elements in each of the curricula. An examination of these courses as they are actually administered in the Missouri normal schools leads one to the conviction that, fundamental as the work is asserted to be, its theoretical values are seldom realized in practice. It is not too much to say, indeed, that the training department is the weakest part of the structure, and the same thing is probably true in many, if not most, of the state normal schools in this country."[33] The Texas colleges are located in small communities, as has been shown in an earlier chapter. As suggested by the Carnegie Bulletin,[34] this is probably the primary cause of the difficulty they are having in securing enough pupils to build up training schools of sufficient size to give thorough professional training to the increased number of college students.

The first of the tables under discussion (Table 66 A) shows the number of critic teachers, the enrollment of pupils by grades and totals, for a summer term and a winter term, in the elementary division of the several training schools. The number of sections and students scheduled for practice in these grades, together with the number of hours expected in each activity, is included in the table. Similar facts for the high-school division at each college are given in the table that follows. It is seen from the totals for all colleges that the number of critic teachers and the enrollment in the elementary schools are smaller in the summer term, notwithstanding the fact that the student load is practically three times that of the winter term. The figures for the high-school division show nearly an equality in the size of training school personnel in the two terms, although the student load is noticeably increased in the summer, and would be further increased in each term if more nearly equal requirements as to participation and practice were included in the secondary curricula. It should be remembered in studying these tables that the same critic teachers and pupil groups who guide and furnish opportunity for practice teaching must also provide the demonstrations for observers. The lack of enrollment in certain grades and small enrollment (less than 15) in others at certain institutions, are additional indications of deviation from reasonable standards in training facilities.

By a study of the schedules it was found that the number of student teachers is generally much greater in the spring term than in other terms of the regular session. However, since facts for the winter term were the latest obtainable, they were used to represent the situation in the regular session, and are the basis for the data shown in Table 67. The purpose of that table is to show the number of classes in principal subjects in high schools, and the number of critic and student teachers of each subject. The proportion

[33] Carnegie Foundation for the Advancement of Teaching. *Bulletin No. 14*, 1920, p. 192.

[34] *Ibid.*, p. 193.

TABLE 66 A

NUMBER OF CRITIC TEACHERS AND PUPILS IN TRAINING SCHOOLS (ELEMENTARY GRADES) WITH NUMBER OF STUDENT TEACHERS AND OBSERVERS

		Total No. of Critic Teachers	Enrollment by Grades								College Students			Hours Per Week	
											To Observe		To Practice	Each Section Observes	Each Student Teaches
			K	1st	2nd	3rd	4th	5th	6th	Total	No. Secs.	Students	Students		
Alpine	Summer 1929	2		24	35		16	22		97	4	79	79	5	5
	Winter 1930	2		51	49	62	39	32	59	292	4	26	26	3	3
Canyon	Summer 1929	7	18	20	12	12	23	17	18	120	6	36	60	5	5
	Winter 1930	7	17	18	16	10	13	15	13	102	6	52	7	5	3
Commerce	Summer 1929	7	24	24	24	24	24	24	28	172	4	140	82	5	5
	Winter 1930	7	24	24	24	24	24	24	26	170	2	60	59	5	3
Denton	Summer 1929	8	34	41	37	28	36	23	23	222	9	348	141	3	5
	Winter 1930	7	21	24	24	24	22	17	24	156	4	109	23	3	3
Huntsville	Summer 1929	6		20	22	17	19	20	17	115	10	336	97	1	5
	Winter 1930	7	27	23	26	20	22	26	18	162	4	82	40	1	3
Nacogdoches	Summer 1929	2		8	7			10	7	32			54		No report
	Winter 1930	4		22	11	15	16	13	19	96			8		No report
San Marcos	Summer 1929	3	17	12	12	11	11	10	16	89	3	113	157	5	5
	Winter 1930	5	14	25	22	11	15	6	21	114	6	45	79	5	3
Total	Summer 1929	35	93	149	149	92	129	126	109	847	36	1,052	670		
	Winter 1930	39	103	187	172	166	151	133	130	1,092	26	374	242		

TABLE 66 B

Facts Similar to Those in Table 66A for the High-School Grades of the Training Schools

		Total No. of Critic Teachers	Enrollment by Grades						College Students: To Observe		To Practice	Hours Per Week	
			7	8	9	10	11	Total	No. Secs.	Students	Students	Each Section Observes	Each Student Teaches
Alpine	Summer 1929	5				44	20	64	1	10	10	5	5
	Winter 1930	3				10	26	36	1	30	30	3	3
Canyon	Summer 1929	13	5	16	18	27	37	103		12	22	5	5
	Winter 1930	13	15	36	30	35	41	157		18	22	5	3
Commerce	Summer 1929	29	28	28	28	111	190	385	2	80	62	5	5
	Winter 1930	29	28	32	30	98	150	338	1	55	42	5	3
Denton	Summer 1929	21	23	36	41	87	192	379	10	323	71	3	5
	Winter 1930	11	19	19	18	17	111	184	5	153	43	3	3
Huntsville	Summer 1929	18	16	14	16	11	65	122	4	186	72	1	5
	Winter 1930	16	19	16	18	17	58	128	2	30	56	1	3
Nacogdoches	Summer 1929	5	7					7		*	34	*	*
	Winter 1930	9	16	21	13	15		65		*	12	*	*
San Marcos	Summer 1929	6				66	66	132	1	66	63	2	5
	Winter 1930	9½	29	30	22	23	115	219	1	29	80	2	3
Total	Summer 1929	97	79	94	103	346	570	1,192	18	682	334		
	Winter 1930	90½	126	154	131	215	501	1,127	10	315	284		

* No Report.

TABLE 67

RELATION OF CLASSES AND CRITIC TEACHERS TO NUMBER OF PRACTICE TEACHERS BY DEPARTMENTS IN TRAINING SCHOOLS OF TEXAS TEACHERS COLLEGES

	SCIENCE			ENGLISH			MATHEMATICS			HISTORY			EDUCATION			LATIN			SPANISH		
	C*	Cr*	P*	C	Cr	P	C	Cr	P	C	Cr	P	C	Cr	P	C	Cr	P	C	Cr	P
Alpine	2	½½	33	2	½	3	2	½		2	½	10	1	½					2	½	2
Canyon	4	1	1	8	2	4	4	1	3	4	1	3	2	1		4	1	2	3	1	3
Commerce	12	3	2	20	5	7	20	5	5	12	3	5	8	2		2	1	2	3	1	3
Denton	4	1	5	4	3	9	4	2	1	4	3	7	5	1		3	1	2	x	x	3
Huntsville	§	2	1	§	2	10	§	1	3	§	2	7	§			§	1	1	§	1	2
Nacogdoches	1	1		4	3	4	4	1	2	2	1								4	1	2
San Marcos	3	1	7	7	2	27	5	2	5	2	1	12	2	½		1	½		2	½	2

* C—Classes; Cr—Critics; P—Practice Teachers. x Subjects in training school taught by college teachers. § No report.

TABLE 67 (*Continued*)

	PHYSICAL EDUCATION			SOCIAL SCIENCE			HOME ECONOMICS			MANUAL TRAINING			ART AND MUSIC			COMMERCE		
	C	Cr	P	C	Cr	P	C	Cr	P	C	Cr	P	C	Cr	P	C	Cr	P
Alpine																		
Canyon	2	1		1	1	[illegible]	2	1	3	1	1	2						
Commerce	8	2	5	4	1	1	6	2	3	6	2	4	8	2	4			
Denton	x	x	7	x	x	[illegible]	x	x		x	x	4	x	x	4	x	x	5
Huntsville	§	1	3	§	1	[illegible]	§	1	5	§	1	1	§	1	2			
Nacogdoches	6	3	1	1	1				1									
San Marcos			3	5	1	[illegible]	2	½	6	2	½	2						2

* C—Classes; Cr—Critics; P—Practice Teachers. x Subjects in training school taught by college teachers. § No report.

of student teachers to critic teachers is not noticeably high in most of the cases tabulated, but in some instances there are ten or more student-teachers under the direction of one critic teacher. Such excessive proportions are known to exist quite commonly in the elementary grades during the spring term, for, as has been pointed out, sophomores as well as seniors in elementary curricula are expected to teach. The welfare of the pupils, together with the confidence of their parents in the training schools, demands that careful administrative attention be given to the number of student teachers assigned to each class of pupils. The recommendation of the American Association of Teachers Colleges, that at least two fifths of the teaching be done by regular teachers, should be interpreted to mean that not less than that proportion is to be done during any one term in any class.

According to the seventh curriculum principle[35] the Texas teachers colleges are offering a wide variety of opportunities for the personal and social development of students, and for training for the direction of extracurricular activities in the public schools. These opportunities have been analyzed on the basis of information gained from catalogues and from personal visits, and seem to fall in the following categories:

I. Social organizations, not Greek letter fraternities
   1. County clubs
   2. Out-of-state clubs
   3. Organizations of students with similar tastes
   4. Young women's forums

II. Literary societies

III. Athletics
   1. Intra-mural
   2. Intercollegiate (for men)

IV. Musical organizations
   1. Choruses
   2. Glee clubs
   3. Orchestras
   4. Bands

V. Student publications
   1. Weekly or biweekly newspapers
   2. Monthly or quarterly literary magazines
   3. Annuals

[35] P. 132.

VI. Student council or faculty-student council in at least five institutions to provide for student participation in control

VII. Annual Interscholastic League contests held at certain colleges

VIII. Religious organizations
1. Y. M. C. A.
2. Y. W. C. A.
3. Student volunteers
4. Organizations sponsored by denominations

IX. Debating
1. Intra-mural
2. Intercollegiate

X. Arts courses and assembly programs

XI. Scholarship societies

XII. Departmental clubs

The number and variety of these organizations differ somewhat among the institutions—apparently depending upon the enrollment. College credit is usually given for work in choruses, orchestras, debating, and, in some instances, for work on publications. Devices are used for limiting the number of these activities which individual students may engage in during a single term. Information shown in the last column of Table 30 in Chapter II indicates that participation in student activities is left largely to the discretion of students since the percentage of those so participating ranges from 59 per cent to 33 per cent. Clubrooms and other facilities to stimulate participation are provided by the colleges, but if student activities have value in the training of teachers, requirements to insure their benefits to all students would be justifiable.

In institutions maintained by the state for the purpose of preparing teachers for the state's public schools there ought to be a high degree of coördination between the functioning of the curricula and the work of placing students who have been graduated and certificated. The significance of that statement is emphasized by the finding of Brogan to the effect that

> Training institutions are by far the most important source of supply for new teachers.[36]

[36] Brogan, Whit. *The Work of Placement Offices in Teaching Training Institutions.* p. 2. Contributions to Education, No. 434. Bureau of Publications, Teachers College, Columbia University, 1930.

The same writer says

> Teachers colleges must realize that it is as much a part of education to see to it that trained people are in positions as it is to train them for positions.[37]

and that

> The policies of the placement office should reflect, as far as possible, the general policies of the training institution and be based on the principle that the work of the placement office is to serve the state by placing qualified teachers in the schools. The service of the office is primarily to the children in the classroom.[38]

The catalogues of the Texas colleges announce that facilities are provided to assist students, as they become qualified, to obtain teaching positions. In order to secure more detailed information as to the conduct of this service, reports from each institution were obtained, and the findings are summarized in Tables 68, 69, and 70. The first of these tables indicates that there has been no concerted study, by all institutions, of this phase of their work, and that no uniform procedures have been adopted. A separate placement office with a director in charge is reported by two, while in the others the work of placement seems to be carried on as a side line by faculty members or administrative officers. The service is without cost to students or employers except at one institution where an enrollment fee of $1.00 is charged the student. The approximate total cost to the college varies from $100 to $1,350. Two institutions report a definite follow-up system for the purpose of ascertaining the success of students who have been recommended for positions. Others depend on occasional reports and conferences for such information as is obtained. If records of in-service success thus secured are kept and used, reports do not so indicate. A systematic effort to secure and keep a continuous record of the teaching positions of ex-students for the purpose of assisting them in securing promotions is reported by two colleges. Brogan in his study[39] shows that the work of teacher placement has developed gradually as a function of training institutions in this country, and that it began in them as the responsibility of individual faculty members or loosely organized committees chosen more or less according to their willingness to undertake the task. In many cases secretaries and office assistants

[37] *Op. cit.*, p. 73.
[38] *Ibid.*, p. 43.
[39] *Ibid.*, pp. 3-7.

TABLE 68

ADMINISTRATION OF THE PLACEMENT SERVICE

	ALPINE	CANYON	COMMERCE	DENTON	HUNTSVILLE	NACOGDOCHES	SAN MARCOS
Is there a separate office?	No	No report	No	Yes	No	No	Yes
How is placement handled?	Committee, Head Education Department	Bureau and Committee	Dean, Chairman of Bureau	Director	Teacher, Stenographer	In office of History Department	
Number employed including director	2 commerce student assistants	No report	2	1 or 2	No report	Teacher, stenographer	Teacher, student stenographer
Cost to student for enrollment	Nothing	$1.00	Nothing	Nothing	Nothing	Nothing	Nothing
Cost to student for placement	Nothing	Nothing	Nothing	Nothing	Nothing	Nothing	Nothing
Cost to employer	Nothing	Nothing	Nothing	Nothing	Nothing	Nothing	Nothing
Approx. cost to college per year	No report	No report	$1350	$800–1000	$300	$100	$1100
Is there follow-up system?	No	Very limited	Yes	Yes	No	Limited	No
Source of information as to success of ex-students in service	Occasional conferences with superintendents, boards	Inquiries, school visiting	No report	No report	No adequate sources	Conferences when convenient	Voluntary reports of superintendents
Continuous records of teaching positions of ex-students	No	No	Yes	Yes	No	No	No

were largely depended upon to do the actual work. His recommendation is that the responsibility for placement, professional guidance, and recommendations be lodged with a distinct administrative officer who is provided with adequate facilities.

Table 69, by showing the numbers of graduates and undergraduates placed in various types of positions during 1928-1929, brings out significant facts in regard to the output of the five colleges which reported, and suggests a profitable field of continuous study for training institutions. The course of the investigation revealed the absence of complete records of the service positions of alumni and ex-students covering a period of years. This same difficulty was encountered by Benson[40] in his general study of the output of schools for teachers and is, therefore, not peculiar to Texas institutions. The figures shown represent only the individuals placed who had enrolled with the placement offices, and do not include those who secured positions independently. A fourth of the total number placed were graduates and they went into all types of positions. One hundred sixty-two, or 29 per cent, of these graduates were employed in small town and village high schools—communities of less than 5,000. Cities of more than 10,000 took much smaller numbers into high-school and grade positions—24 and 23, respectively. Of the total graduates and undergraduates, more than half went to teaching positions in the open country and in villages and small towns. The relatively small numbers placed as superintendents and supervisors are noticeable in view of the fact that all institutions offer four-year curricula. Benson's findings, based on data for 1910, 1915, and 1920, show smaller proportions going into rural schools, but more nearly similar proportions placed in town and village schools, and as superintendents and supervisors.[41] Records kept continuously of teaching positions of alumni and ex-students should prove valuable in curriculum revision and in enlarging the usefulness of teacher-training institutions. They should also form a significant part of the accounting rendered by these institutions to the state they serve, for in no more valid way could such schools justify their existence or support their requests for appropriations. The measure of definite service rendered by an educational institution is a more sound basis upon which to rest claims for financial support than mere enrollment figures. Should adequate records of this nature show that large pro-

[40] Benson, C. E. *Output of Professional Schools of Teachers,* Chap. I. Warwick & York, Inc., Baltimore, 1922.

[41] *Ibid.,* Chap. III.

TABLE 69

NUMBER OF GRADUATES AND UNDERGRADUATES PLACED IN VARIOUS TYPES OF POSITIONS IN 1928–29*

TYPES OF POSITIONS	ALPINE		CANYON		COMMERCE		DENTON		HUNTSVILLE†		TOTAL		GRAND TOTAL
	GRADUATES	UNDERGRADUATES	GRADUATES	UNDERGRADUATES	GRADUATES	UNDERGRADUATES	GRADUATES	UNDERGRADUATES	GRADUATES	UNDERGRADUATES	GRADUATES	UNDERGRADUATES	
Rural Schools		13	3	42	2	36	5	251	22	125	32	467	499
Primary grades in towns less than 5000		12	5	12	5	31	35	141		30	45	226	271
Primary grades in towns 5000–10,000			1	1	2	6	31	83	5	21	39	111	150
Primary grades in cities over 10,000	2	3	3	1	3	1	8	46	3	18	19	69	88
Intermediate grades in towns less than 5000		17	10	21	6	22	23	82	4	67	43	209	252
Intermediate grades in towns 5000–10,000		1	2	3	1	3	8	118	2	42	13	167	180
Intermediate grades in cities over 10,000		10	5	1	1		14	36	3	16	23	63	86
High schools in consolidated districts			9	15	2		11	16	10	21	32	52	84
High schools in towns less than 5000	3	1	40	5	50	28	63	8	6	32	162	74	236
High schools in towns 5000–10,000			4		15	9	3		3	12	25	21	46
High schools in cities over 10,000	3	1	5		12	1	2		2	8	24	10	34
Superintendents	4	2	14	1	4	1	4	8	6	4	32	16	48
Principals	2		11	5			21	112	2		36	117	153
Supervisors					1	1	2	1	1		4	2	6
Teachers of special subjects: art, music, etc.		3	8	3	4	11	5	25	3	2	20	44	64
TOTAL	14	63	120	110	108	150	235	927	72	398	549	1,648	2,197

* No reports were made by the colleges at Nacogdoches and San Marcos.

† Figures reported are estimates.

portions of the output of any institution are going to certain types of positions, careful attention should be given to curricula and facilities used in preparing students for successful work in them. On the contrary, curricula from which few students are placed in teaching positions could hardly be justified in a teachers college. Also, careful investigation might discover that the reason for small numbers being placed in certain types of positions lies in the poor, inadequate preparation being given for such positions and in the lack of confidence among school boards and superintendents in the value of such preparation.

The calls for teachers received by a teacher-training institution also constitute a valuable source of information for those of its staff who are responsible for curriculum making and for the guidance of students. Table 70 shows a classified summary of reports of such calls as they came from six colleges. Records of this nature appear to be kept with varying degrees of completeness and accuracy by the several institutions, for certain reports definitely state that records are kept of only those calls that come by mail or telegraph, or that the numbers given are merely estimates. Also, the fact that the total number of calls reported is nearly twice as large as the number of students placed, as shown in Table 69, (although numbers from only five colleges are given in that table) suggests that duplicates are included in the record of calls. This may be unavoidable since many requests are for combination teachers, especially in high schools, and calls are reported under each subject or type of position. Under *general high-school* were listed calls for teachers of all subjects commonly taught, including home economics. The totals indicate a strong demand for teachers in rural, consolidated, and village schools; for grade teachers in towns, and for high-school teachers. The number of requests for teachers of special subjects is noticeable and if data for past years were available, would likely be shown to be increasing. Analysis of reports shows that the greatest number of calls for high school teachers is for those qualified in sciences, English, mathematics, history, Spanish, home economics, and Latin—in the order in which they are named. Calls for teachers of agriculture, economics and sociology, and French, and for supervisors are not generally reported in noticeably large numbers. Certain reports name the types of positions for which it is most difficult to find qualified persons, as follows: mathematics-science, science-mathematics-athletics, mathematics-coaching, science-coaching, Latin-English, superintendents and principals, industrial education, home economics. It may be supposed from this that students are inclined to avoid the mathematics and science courses, or that curricula are not so arranged as to include the subject-

TABLE 70

NUMBER OF CALLS RECEIVED FOR VARIOUS TYPES OF POSITIONS 1928–29*

TYPES OF POSITIONS	ALPINE	CANYON	COMMERCE	DENTON	HUNTSVILLE	SAN MARCOS	TOTAL
Rural Teachers	36	21	10	15	200	57	339
Village, Cons'd	4	39	17	481	40		581
Superintendent	8	15	1	18	30	5	77
Principal	6	20	9	128	2	48	213
County Supervisors				4	1		5
Grade Teachers, Towns	76	134	67	361	62	181	881
General High School	39	183	168	440	112	268	1,210
Commercial	4	16	5	68	4	25	122
Manual Training	4	10	21	32	20	12	99
Physical Education	3	34	11	16	25	40	129
Auditorium		1	4	6		3	14
Art, writing	2	21	19	110	4	13	169
Music	3	17	13	101	6	14	154
Reading (speech)	14	12	4	48	5	14	97
Total	199	523	349	1,828	511	680	4,090

* No report from the college at Nacogdoches.

matter combinations most frequently desired by high schools seeking teachers. The importance of information of this character is evident if the needs of the public schools are to be accurately known and if they are to serve as a definite guide to the kind of preparation given.

SUMMARY

1. The Texas teachers colleges have definitely placed their work on the collegiate level and are maintaining membership in the American Association of Teachers Colleges, in the Association of Colleges and Secondary Schools of the Southern States, and in the Association of Texas Colleges.

2. Recognition of the need of "all-round" development of students is evidenced by the broad offerings in subject matter and in the number of majors provided.

3. Facilities of a wide variety for the personal, social, and general extracurricular development of prospective teachers have been set up. Opportunities for practice in self-control and in the develop-

ment of their own interests and abilities are offered to students by each institution.

4. Each college is apparently accepting the responsibility of preparing teachers for all types and levels of the public school service with the exception of certain vocational types.

5. The curriculum standards of the American Association of Teachers Colleges are being adhered to. In fact, visits and conferences in connection with this study afford reason to believe that efforts are being made in Texas to exceed the minimum curriculum standards of the Association.

6. Curricula for the professional preparation of teachers have not been studied coöperatively by these institutions with a view to meeting the needs of the entire state. The Council of Presidents, which is the only regular organization representing the teachers colleges, has been concerned chiefly with administrative problems.

7. Present curricula, therefore, are the result of institutional effort, and evidence points to the conclusion that the curricula at each institution have been developed by departmental initiative rather than by the coöperative study and work of the entire teaching and administrative staff.

8. The need of and importance of differentiated lines of training appear, from reports, to be recognized by these colleges, but differentiation seems to be accomplished largely by election of courses on the part of students rather than by the establishment of definitely differentiated curricula.

9. Students are certificated, in accordance with law, at five levels: (1) at graduation from the high-school division of the training schools; (2) upon completion of the work of the freshman year; (3) upon completion of the work of the sophomore year; (4) upon completion of the work of the junior year; and (5) upon graduation with the bachelor's degree. Provision is made, however, for granting degrees to those who have not met the requirements for certificates.

10. From 35 per cent to 77 per cent of the courses in the several colleges receive professional treatment according to catalogue descriptions. However, it must be admitted that such evidence is not at all conclusive and that catalogues generally give very slight information as to the actual conduct and treatment of courses.

11. The place of the training school in the professional preparation of teachers is acknowledged by the Texas colleges, as evidenced

by the fact that each has provided facilities of that character. However, it is plain that the enrollments of college students have increased much more rapidly than the size of the training schools. The result is that facilities are at present very inadequate for giving a thorough program of observation, participation, and student teaching to all candidates for certificates.

12. The degree of correlation actually obtaining between the training school and the subject-matter departments can hardly be determined by objective means. Visits to each institution, together with ten years of teaching and supervisory experience in one of them, lead to the opinion that there has been little concerted effort toward making the work in the training schools an integrated part of the whole task of each of the colleges. A majority of the subject-matter teachers seem to have no more knowledge of or contact with the training school than would be expected of teachers in a liberal arts college. This should not be interpreted as an adverse criticism of the teachers or as implying a state of friction. It is rather an indication of integrated curriculum work yet to be done.

13. Each institution has undertaken to serve the public schools by recommending qualified teachers to school boards and superintendents seeking to fill positions. Records for this purpose are kept with varying degrees of completeness and accuracy. There is some indication that work of this kind has developed slowly under the pressure of demands from the field and that it has not been aggressively prosecuted by means of efficient administrative organization.

14. Records of positions into which students are placed, and of calls received from the public schools, as they are beginning to be developed, should prove useful guides in the construction of curricula.

Proposals

A commendable feature that is revealed by a study of the curricula of the Texas teachers colleges is an awareness on the part of their staffs of problems that are vital to professional institutions. Their growth during the past decade, from the standpoints of enrollments, physical plants, and collegiate rank, has been rapid. That their curricular patterns and content have been noticeably influenced by academic tradition and custom presents no new phenomenon in the development of professional schools for teachers. It must be remembered also that all institutions of collegiate rank in the state, even junior colleges, are offering work leading to teachers' certificates, and that the certificate laws require the very minimum of differentiated and professional curricula. If past growth is any prediction of future development, the teachers colleges will come to occupy a more important place in the educational system of the commonwealth. It is predicted, however, that their increasing importance will be in direct proportion to the energy and vision they employ in becoming definitely professional institutions. With these ideas in mind the following suggestions for improvement of curricula are offered:

1. That a central commission be established in the state to study the professional curricular requirements demanded by the needs of the state as a whole. The staffs of the teachers colleges should be largely represented in such a group, and reasonable provision should be made for expenses. Such a commission would likely be of most service if organized under the authority and with the sanction of the State Board of Education.

2. That the staff members in each college be organized, as auxiliary to the coördinating commission, under competent leadership to study the curricula of their own institution and to make their findings available to the central commission. Such procedures would serve to eliminate a considerable proportion of institutional and departmental autonomy which automatically delays unity and effective harmony in constructing and administering training curricula to meet the needs of the state.

3. Through such administrative arrangements for arriving at more unitary and clearly defined purposes, that critical attention be given:

a. To the curricular patterns to be employed in the training process.

b. To the types of teachers that can be most economically and effectively trained at each institution to meet the requirements of the public schools.

c. To preserving such a degree of practical contact with developing public school conditions as will insure the greatest usefulness of the colleges, and the largest possible success of their product.

d. To the desirability, under existing conditions in Texas, of establishing curricula leading to a single professional degree, thereby eliminating work which does not qualify students to enter the teaching profession.

4. That more sharply differentiated curricula be developed; attention being given, however, to preserving broadening contact with

the major fields of human culture. The establishment of more definitely differentiated curricula would likely result in reducing the number of independent term courses, or thirds, in all departments—especially in the field of education.

5. That careful planning be given to programs for preparing teachers in such of the special fields as the demand of the public schools justifies. Among these fields, physical education and health, social and citizenship training, industrial and commercial arts, music and fine arts, and auditorium activities will likely claim serious attention.

6. That many of the extracurricular activities which have been available to students at their option be made integral parts of curricular requirements in order to prepare for the "all-round" service which the schools expect.

7. That provision be made in all curricula for a more extensive contact with training school facilities. This would involve:

a. Directed observation in the third term of the freshman year.

b. Continued observation supplemented by participation and distributed student teaching in the sophomore year.

c. A continuation of distributed student teaching during the junior year to afford practical contact with different grade levels in the elementary school or with several subject-matter fields in the high school.

d. A minimum period of one school month during the early part of the senior year devoted to concentrated student teaching, during which the student would be given the responsibility, under guidance, of all the duties of a teacher both inside and outside the classroom.

e. Provision for professional integrating courses to follow the period of concentrated practice.

8. As auxiliary to recommendations under 7, that more active provision be made for coöperative activity on the part of each member of the teaching staff in connection with the participation and practice work of students.

9. That the responsibility of recommending students and alumni to teaching positions be centered at each college in one individual who should be ranked as a member of the administrative staff and that he be provided with adequate facilities for assembling complete records. The data collected by this officer should serve as a basis for a continuous study of the output of each institution and as a guide to the arrangement of curricula. The same individual could properly

be expected to serve as a liaison officer between the training institutions and the schools they serve.

10. That the broader and more intensive contacts with training facilities, together with an aggressive prosecution of the work of placement and follow-up, should result in more pronounced professional treatment of courses in all curricula.

CHAPTER V

THE NEED OF TEACHERS IN TEXAS IN RELATION TO A PROGRAM OF TEACHER TRAINING

The purpose of this chapter is to direct attention to the importance of an accurate knowledge of a state's need of teachers; to review some of the important studies which have been made of that problem; to present such facts as were obtainable in regard to the need of teachers in Texas; and to draw conclusions which seem justified and which have value for proposals looking toward a stable program of teacher preparation for the State of Texas. Efforts directed at balancing the supply of teachers with the demand are justifiable only when it is clear that such procedure will result in more efficient schools and better advantages for the children of the state. The personal welfare of teachers is not the primary consideration. Teachers are not private practitioners as are physicians, lawyers, and engineers but are public servants whose compensation and terms of service are fixed by those delegated to represent the public. Legal sanctions in America have established the status of public schools as state rather than local institutions.[1] The responsibility for preparing workers for the schools seems clearly to attach to the state and has been generally accepted by the states of the Union. The maintenance of a balance between the number prepared and the needs of the schools is, therefore a matter of simple economy. A committee of the American Association of Teachers Colleges has declared that the answer to the question of teacher supply and demand holds the key to the whole problem of teacher training.[2] Dr. Buckingham maintains that every state owes it to its schools and citizens to be studying this problem and that the work can be done most efficiently by a state department of education.[3]

[1] Cubberley, E. P. *State School Administration.* Houghton Mifflin Company, Boston, 1927.

[2] Pittenger, L. A. and Others. Digest of the report of the committee authorized by the American Association of Teachers Colleges at the Atlantic City meeting to make a study of the supply, demand, training, and certification of teachers. Mimeographed report to the meeting in Detroit in 1931.

[3] Buckingham, B. R. "Research in Teacher Supply and Demand," *Educational Administration and Supervision,* Vol. XV. No. 4, pp. 259-68.

The director of research of the National Education Association has directed public attention to the importance of information concerning the demand for teachers and the available supply.[4] Ten to twelve years ago there was a real shortage of persons who were certificated to teach. Since that time enrollments in teacher-training institutions have been increasing much more rapidly than has the number of teaching positions. During the same time the average length of teaching tenure has substantially increased. The number of students enrolled in all types of institutions which train teachers was reported to be more than half a million in 1928, a number which represented an increase of more than 400 per cent over the number in training two decades ago. During the same period the number of teaching positions has increased by approximately 35 per cent.[5] In addition to recruits coming to the profession from the schools there are considerable numbers who obtain teaching licenses in several states by taking examinations without having satisfied definite training prerequisites.[6] The effect of such conditions on the efficiency and progress of the public schools is of fundamental importance. It is generally conceded that untrained teachers, if such are certificated, tend to supplant those with proper preparation unless preventive measures are set up. The continuance of the extremely meager salaries prevailing in many communities over the nation will never attract professionally trained teachers. The problem of the teacher needs of the schools is receiving national attention in the teacher-training survey which is being carried on with the direction of the Federal Office of Education.[7]

The problem of securing and maintaining a desirable balance between a state's need of teachers and the available supply is a responsibility which properly belongs to well-informed and vigorous state educational administration. It cannot be solved by local effort. Two important considerations demand continuous study of the problem and serious attempts at its solution. First, the expenditure of state funds to train large numbers of teachers in excess of the needs of the schools can hardly be justified from the standpoint of practical

[4] Norton, John K. "Teacher Supply and Demand," *The New York Times,* July 27, 1930, Sec. 3, p. 7.

[5] Frazier, Benjamin W. *Teacher Training, 1926-28.* United States Bureau of Education Bulletin, 1929, No. 17, pp. 15-16.

[6] Cook, Katherine M. *State Laws and Regulations Governing Teachers' Certificates,* United States Bureau of Education, Bulletin, 1927, No. 19.

[7] Judd, Charles H. "A National Survey of Teacher Training," *The Journal of the National Education Association,* Vol. 19, No. 9, pp. 291-92, Dec., 1930.

economy. Furthermore, it has been demonstrated that the indiscriminate training of persons to teach tends to result in financial support of training institutions which is not sufficiently adequate or stable to insure their ability to meet the best-known standards. Second, the character and efficiency of the public schools are affected by conditions of the teacher market. A large oversupply of teachers, especially if they are not definitely prepared for the work to be done, will eventually result in a depreciated type of teaching service. As a corollary to that consideration it should be remembered that the distinctive quality and general advancement of the teaching profession could not be maintained under conditions of a largely excessive supply. The character and status of the personnel of any profession very definitely determine the character of the service rendered by that profession. It may be concluded, therefore, that an accurate knowledge of teacher demand is an important requirement in planning teacher-training facilities and that the state should establish such facilities primarily for the purpose of supplying the demand and not necessarily to give training to all who wish to take up teaching as a vocation or as an avocation.[8]

Several factors enter to complicate the problem of balancing teacher supply and demand. (1) The committee of the American Association of Teachers Colleges, whose report has been referred to, found that many states have not collected data on which to base studies of the problem. Several years are required to assemble complete data of that nature. (2) Standards of preparation must be set up by which to determine who are qualified teachers. (3) Certification laws are involved as an important factor in establishing standards of qualifications. (4) Salaries paid to teachers affect the level of qualifications, as determined by amount of training which may be reasonably demanded. (5) In turn salaries are profoundly influenced by the administrative plan used in the state. Systematic salary schedules based on the best that is known in that field can scarcely be expected in a state whose schools are administered by a very large number of practically autonomous district boards. (6) The whole matter of fiscal support of public education in the state is closely associated with the problem of supplying qualified teachers in suitable numbers to meet the needs of the schools.

Interest in the problem of teacher demand and supply appears to have attracted the attention of research students most noticeably dur-

[8] New York State Education Department, Educational Measurements Bureau, *Teacher Demand in New York State* (Mimeographed). 1929.

ing the past decade—since 1920. Eliassen and Anderson[9] in their report of studies in that field since 1924 list 119 titles, 50 of which were primary studies. The others were discussions of the problem, or mere editorial comment. Serious efforts to secure the facts in regard to the general demand for teachers and the available supply have been found in the following states: Ohio, New York, California, Indiana, New Jersey, Wisconsin, Colorado, Vermont, Massachusetts, Pennsylvania, Rhode Island, Illinois, Missouri, Arkansas, Minnesota, North Carolina, Connecticut, West Virginia, Michigan, and Texas. Partial or limited investigations have been made in other states. State departments of education have not engaged largely in such studies but have left them, in the main, to personal or institutional research.

A general feeling that the supply of teachers is becoming excessive apparently provides the motive for the interest being shown in the problem.[10] Times of economic depression are accompanied by increased enrollments at teacher-training institutions and by greater numbers of applicants for teaching positions. The earlier studies reported by Eliassen and Anderson show a frequent undersupply of teachers, while those made more recently present data to indicate an oversupply or a general tendency in that direction. The undersupply recently found has been in specific fields or subjects and suggests the need of better adjustment and guidance as to kinds of training rather than the necessity of encouraging greater numbers to enter the profession. A very prevalent idea found also in the literature has been expressed by the Commissioner of Education in the following words: "No one has been so bold as to say that there is an oversupply of well-trained teachers."[11] There is a distinction, therefore, to be made between the number of legally certificated teachers and the number who have had training equivalent to commonly accepted minimum standards. These standards have been described by Buckingham as follows:

> We believe that the system whereby teachers may qualify for the classroom by taking one year of professional training beyond the high school cannot be abandoned too soon. No competent educator of our acquaintance

[9] Eliassen, R. H. and Anderson, E. W. *The Supply of Teachers and the Demand,* Educational Research Bulletin, College of Education, Ohio State University, Vol. IX, No. 16, pp. 440-46, Nov. 5, 1930, Columbus, Ohio.

[10] Whitney, F. L. *Teacher Demand and Supply in the Public Schools,* Colorado State Teachers College, Education Series No. 8, pp. 1-2, Greeley, Colo., 1930.

[11] Cooper, William John. "Some Teacher Problems," *National Republic,* Vol. XVII, p. 35, May, 1929.

regards the system of county normal schools in any state as anything but a makeshift. We think too that even the two-year course is insufficient, though as a minimum requirement it may be a stopping place toward something better. In the long run the dignity of teaching and the professional basis on which it should rest will require four years of preparation beyond the high school. This amount of training is now customarily thought of as a minimum for induction into a truly professional career.[12]

The oversupply so frequently reported doubtless included all who are legally certificated to teach, regardless of qualifications as measured by preparation for the profession. The surplus as thus determined is gradually growing.

Many different general methods and techniques have been employed in attempting to reach conclusions as to the demand for teachers and the available supply. As would be expected, not all results are strictly comparable. Techniques used appear to be determined by conditions in particular states and by the resources at the command of the investigator. Eliassen and Anderson[13] distinguished four general and eleven specific techniques utilized in the studies they examined. The study of the problem in Ohio, published by Buckingham in 1926, was made with financial assistance from the Commonwealth Fund and has served as a guide for several subsequent investigations. The state's need of new teachers was determined by finding the number of new teachers actually appointed in the schools of the state in a typical year. Newness was classified as follows:[14]

- I. Newness to the state
  - A. Inexperienced (Type 1)
  - B. Experienced
    - 1. Outside the state (Type 2)
    - 2. In the state but with interval of at least six months (Type 3)
- II. Other types of newness
  - A. Location
  - B. Rank
  - C. Type of school

The New York study also secured data as to the actual number of

[12] Buckingham, B. R. *Supply and Demand in Teacher Training.* Bureau of Educational Research Monographs, No. 4, p. 4, Ohio State University, March 15, 1926, Columbus, Ohio.

[13] Eliassen, R. H. and Anderson, E. W. *Op. cit.*, pp. 440-46.

[14] Buckingham, B. R. *Op. cit.*, p. 9.

teachers employed during one year, but classified new teachers into twelve groups as follows:[15]

1. Those who began teaching in the fall of the year studied but had not taught during the previous year.
2. Those who began teaching in the middle of the typical year but did not teach during the first half of it or any part of the preceding year.
3. Those who began their teaching in the fall of the typical year, but had not taught during the latter half of the preceding year.
4. Those who began in the middle of the typical year, had not taught the first half of that year, but had taught all or part of the preceding year.
5. Teachers who came from private schools to public schools in the fall of the typical year.
6. Those from private schools who began to teach in public schools in the middle of the typical year.
7. Teachers from outside the state who took their first positions in New York in the fall of the typical year.
8. Those from outside who began to teach in the middle of the year.
9. Those who were new to the kind of position they took at the beginning of the typical year.
10. Teachers who took new kinds of positions in the middle of the year.
11. Those who were new with respect to the type of school but not with respect to the kind of position in the fall of the typical year.
12. Those who were new with respect to type of school in the middle of the year.

These studies and others take the actual experience of the schools as a measure of their teacher needs. The wide variations found in the requirements of different kinds of positions and types of schools are interesting and significant. It seems entirely possible for a state to have too many teachers qualified for certain kinds of work or types of schools and too few for others. In studying teacher turnover in the State of New York, Elsbree found the per cent of turnover to vary inversely with the size of the community. Cities of less than 5,000 showed 17.40 per cent and those of more than 50,000, 6.52 per cent. In villages the range was from 3.03 per cent to 42.38 per

[15] Coxe, W. W. *Teacher Demand in New York State*, pp. 1-2 (Mimeographed). State Education Department, Albany, N. Y., 1929.

cent. The average rate of turnover of high-school teachers (15.40 per cent) was noticeably higher than that of elementary teachers (9.37 per cent). Among teachers of separate high-school subjects the turnover was found to be as follows: commercial, 9.91 per cent; history and civics, 11.08 per cent; mathematics, 11.14 per cent; English, 11.59 per cent; modern languages, 12.81 per cent; Latin, 14.29 per cent; other subjects, 16.19 per cent; science, 17.13 per cent.[16] While these figures do not represent proportions of teachers who were new to the state, they are interesting when compared with the findings of the State Education Department for the year following, 1926-27. The report shows that 12.9 per cent of the total number of elementary teachers and 12.7 per cent of the high-school teachers were new to the state.[17] Estimates in New Jersey indicate that approximately 14 per cent of elementary teachers and at least 20 per cent of high-school teachers were new to that state in the same year.[18] In Arkansas it was found that 24.6 per cent of rural teachers and 21.3 per cent of teachers in towns and cities were new in 1924-25.[19] The per cent of replacements among teachers in Colorado in 1926-27 was 11.1.[20] In Kentucky a study published in 1925 shows that approximately 10 per cent of city teachers and 25 per cent of teachers in rural schools were new employees.[21]

The facts just summarized suggest some interesting considerations. Actual experience indicates a greater demand for teachers in some states than in others and in certain types of communities as compared to other types within the same state. The question naturally arises: Is experience as it should be? From the standpoint of educational efficiency and fairness, no sound reason can be offered for imposing annually a large proportion of new recruits upon the schools of the open country and small communities. Indications are that teachers are not doing the kind of work for which they were trained.

[16] Elsbree, W. S. *Teacher Turnover in the Cities and Villages of New York State,* Chap. II. Contributions to Education, No. 300. Bureau of Publications, Teachers College, Columbia University, 1928.

[17] Coxe, W. W. *Op. cit.,* p. 21.

[18] Bagley, W. C. *Professional Education of Teachers in New Jersey.* (Unpublished study, 1928.) Figures are derived from Trabue, M. R. *Supply and Demand of Teachers in New Jersey.* Fort Orange Press, Albany, N. Y., 1928.

[19] Grant, J. R. *A State's Teacher-Training Problem,* Chap. VII. George Peabody College for Teachers, Contributions to Education, No. 18. Nashville, Tenn., 1925.

[20] Whitney, F. L. *Teacher Supply and Demand in the Public Schools,* p. 63. Colorado State Teachers College, Greeley, Colo., 1930.

[21] Donovan, H. L. *A State's Elementary Teacher-Training Problem,* p. 49. George Peabody College for Teachers, Contributions to Education, No. 17. Nashville, Tenn., 1925.

In fact it is well known that numbers of individuals who follow secondary training curricula take positions in elementary schools and that it is the policy of many school systems to promote teachers from the elementary to the high school. Remedial measures are to be sought in progressive educational statesmanship which has been slow in making itself felt in a country where education developed from the desires and plans of the people, and where schools are generally regarded as local or community enterprises. The suggestion is made that the need of new teachers in any state could be much reduced by a centralized administrative system that would place teaching on a more professional basis. However, until such statesmanlike direction is secured actual experience in the matter of teacher needs appears to be the most reliable guide.

F. H. Ullrich during 1928-29 investigated the teacher supply and demand situation in Texas.[22] Information was secured from such records as were available in the office of the State Department of Education, and through questionnaires to school boards, superintendents, and placement offices of Texas colleges. The study revealed a general oversupply of persons certificated to teach in Texas. Among high school teachers the oversupply was especially acute in the fields of English, home economics, Spanish, and social science. The number seeking positions in elementary and rural schools was far in excess of the demand. Reports presented from county and city superintendents uniformly expressed the opinion that there existed a very large surplus of teachers. Their judgments were based on the number of applications received from those seeking teaching positions. As an example, six cities with a total teaching personnel of 4,210 received 15,300 applications in 1928. Similar conditions were shown by reports from the smaller school systems. Thirteen towns reported a total of 1,022 applications for thirty-five vacancies. Superintendents appeared to hold the opinion that the supply during recent years had been increasing much more rapidly than the number of available positions and that such conditions increased the difficulty of raising professional standards among the teaching personnel of any particular district. This study, however, calls attention to the fact that there was likely a shortage of persons possessing standard qualifications in the matter of academic and professional preparation. It was esti-

[22] Ullrich, F. H. "Combating the Problem of Too Many Teachers," *The Texas Outlook,* Vol. XIV, No. 3, March, 1930, pp. 33-35. Published by the Texas State Teachers Association, Fort Worth, Texas. Also in *The Nation's Schools,* Vol. V, Jan., 1930, pp. 31-36. Based on unpublished master's thesis in the University of Texas, 1929.

mated that if college or university graduation had been in force as a prerequisite for high-school teaching, there would have been a shortage of 1,215 teachers.

The task of public education in Texas is one of gradually increasing magnitude as measured by the number of children for whom teachers must be provided. Table 71 shows the scholastic population of the state by years from 1920 to 1930. In March of each

TABLE 71

SCHOLASTIC POPULATION OF TEXAS SINCE 1920

YEAR	POPULATION
1920–21	1,271,157
1921–22	1,297,991
1922–23	1,296,596
1923–24	1,304,200
1924–25	1,321,600
1925–26	1,340,083
1926–27	1,348,635
1927–28	1,370,082
1928–29	1,399,791
1929–30	1,426,859
1930–31	1,563,595

year a census is taken of children who will be of legal age on September first following. Until March of 1930 the ages included were 7 to 17, inclusive, but in 1930 the lower limit was extended to include the six-year-old children. The increase over the ten-year period amounted to 23 per cent as compared to the increase in general population of 24.9 per cent, as shown in Chapter I. The average annual rate of increase has been approximately 2 per cent. Negro children constitute slightly less than 17 per cent of the total scholastic population. In 1930 there were in Texas approximately 1,298,500 white children of legal school age.

When one considers the economic and industrial progress that has been made in Texas within recent years and the development of natural resources accomplished and in prospect, there seems reason to believe that the increase in scholastic population will continue at a rate no slower than that of the past ten years. Brenholtz,[23] in his study of population as a factor in the need for high-school teachers, predicted an average annual increase in the secondary-school population of one per cent for the decade from 1930 to 1940. Since the

[23] Brenholtz, Harold. *Population as a Potential Factor in the Need for Teachers for Secondary Schools of a State, with Special Application to California and Texas,* Chap. V. Doctor's thesis at the University of California, 1930. (Unpublished.)

number of children of elementary-school ages exceeds the number of those of high-school ages in the state,[24] and considering the probable general development in Texas, an estimate of 2 per cent average annual increase in the total scholastic population for the next decade may be regarded as conservative.

In 1929-30, 93 per cent of the white children of legal school age were enrolled in public schools. Table 72 shows the enrollment in elementary and high schools in the independent and common districts for a period of seven years. It can be seen that the high-school enrollment has steadily increased from year to year as has the elementary enrollment in the independent districts, with the exception of 1929-30, when there was a decrease of about 46,000. Enrollment in elementary schools of the common districts shows a steady decrease since 1924-25. This may possibly be explained by the rising percentage of urban population in the state. The common districts are largely those in the open country and are under county administration. The total enrollment in elementary schools of both classes of districts increased annually with the exception of the years 1925-26 and 1926-27 when there was a fraction of one per cent decrease. The average annual percentile increase in all elementary schools was 1.9 per cent, and in all high schools, 5.1 per cent. The average annual absolute increase was found to be 13,602 in the elementary schools and 8,116 in the high schools.

TABLE 72

ENROLLMENT OF WHITE PUPILS IN ELEMENTARY AND HIGH SCHOOLS

Year	Independent Districts		Common Districts		Total Independent and Common Districts	
	Elementary Schools	High Schools	Elementary Schools	High Schools	Elementary Schools	High Schools
1923–24	422,123	119,209	369,950	40,680	792,073	159,889
1924–25	443,572	128,569	392,736	44,275	836,308	172,844
1925–26	455,493	134,844	374,762	46,265	830,255	181,109
1926–27	474,382	139,927	354,976	46,521	829,358	186,448
1927–28	491,345	154,037	339,800	46,199	831,145	200,236
1928–29	598,781	163,476	335,294	46,822	834,075	210,298
1929–30	552,686	167,438	334,605	49,264	887,291	216,702

Average yearly increase in elementary-school enrollment during the 7 years, 13,602
Average yearly increase in high-school enrollment during the 7 years, 8,116

[24] *Twenty-sixth Biennial Report of the State Department of Education,* Austin, Tex., p. 399.

TABLE 73

PREDICTIONS OF GROWTH IN ENROLLMENT OF TEXAS ELEMENTARY AND HIGH SCHOOLS, 1930–37

SCHOOL YEAR	ENROLLMENT IN ELEMENTARY SCHOOLS (ADDING 13,602)	ENROLLMENT IN HIGH SCHOOLS (ADDING 8,116)
1930–31	900,893	224,818
1931–32	914,495	232,934
1932–33	928,097	241,050
1933–34	941,699	249,166
1934–35	955,301	257,282
1935–36	968,903	265,398
1936–37	982,505	273,515

It appears that enrollment in Texas public schools is increasing at a more rapid rate than is the scholastic population. It is predicted that the increase in enrollment will continue as schools are improved and as high-school advantages are made available to larger proportions of the population.

The predictions of enrollment shown in Table 73 are based on the average annual absolute increase during the preceding seven years rather than on the percentage increase. The predictions of high-school enrollment especially are considered conservative because of the comparatively recent policy of the state of providing high-school advantages, free of tuition charges, to all children.[25] This policy is the result of the following recommendation of State Superintendent Marrs:

> I am yet of the opinion that the State should make provision for the payment of high school tuition when it becomes necessary for a student to leave his home district in order to secure high school instruction. This tuition should not be paid by the parent. If there is equal educational opportunity for all the children of all the people, there can be no requirement for any parent to pay tuition, as the educational opportunity of the child would then depend upon the financial ability of his parent. This is not democracy! The State furnishes free elementary instruction through its available school fund and it also furnishes free college education to any student prepared to enter one of the State's higher institutions of learning but the State has never to any appreciable extent supported free high school education. Such legislation should be enacted as would make it possible for every child, regardless of his residence, to have access to a public free school.[26]

[25] *School Laws of Texas,* Bulletin No. 264, State Department of Education, Section 356, p. 123, Austin, Tex., Nov., 1929.

[26] Marrs, S. M. N. *Twenty-fourth Biennial Report of the State Department of Education, 1924-26,* p. 9. Austin, Tex.

Table 74 shows the number of white teachers, including superintendents, principals, and supervisors, employed in the public schools of Texas from 1924-25 to 1929-30, and the increase each year over the number of the previous year. Negro teachers constituted approximately 12 per cent of the total number employed. The average annual absolute increase in the number of white teachers amounted to 1,101 while the average percentage increase has been 3.4 per cent. Each year since 1926-27 approximately 20 per cent of all white teachers has been men. It appears that the number of white teachers

TABLE 74

NUMBER OF WHITE TEACHERS IN THE PUBLIC SCHOOLS, 1924–30

YEAR	NUMBER OF TEACHERS	INCREASE OVER PREVIOUS YEAR
1924–25	32,052	.....
1925–26	33,466	1,414
1926–27	34,434	968
1927–28	35,623	1,189
1928–29	37,048	1,425
1929–30	38,661	1,613

is increasing at a more rapid rate than is the scholastic population or the enrollment in the schools. A possible explanation of this increase is the extension of high schools and the steady growth in the enrollment in such schools. (See Table 72.)

In order to show certificate qualifications of teachers and tendencies toward improvement, Table 75 was prepared. Sixteen kinds of certificates are recognized in the state although fewer than that number are now issued.[27] For the sake of brevity, first grade and first class certificates were combined into those of first rank, as were those of second grade and second class into those of second rank. The permanent certificate represents the greatest amount of academic and professional preparation. The total number of superintendents, principals, supervisors, and classroom teachers is shown for each of two years in the independent and common districts. In the former type of district the classroom teachers show the greatest improvement in the per cent holding permanent certificates. Fifty-nine per cent of them held such certificates in 1927-28 and 67 per cent in 1929-30. The greatest improvement in this respect in the common districts is shown by the supervisors, and the principals' group is next

[27] *Laws, Rules, and Regulations Governing State Teachers' Certificates,* Bulletin No. 252, State Department of Education, Austin, Tex., 1929.

in degree of improvement. However, the small number of supervisors in common districts is noticeable. Second rank certificates seem to be disappearing from all groups of school employees. That decided and rapid improvement in the teaching personnel of a state can be accomplished through certification laws has been shown by Yeager in his study of development in Pennsylvania.[28]

TABLE 75

CERTIFICATES HELD BY PUBLIC SCHOOL WORKERS*

KINDS OF CERTIFICATES	INDEPENDENT DISTRICTS				COMMON DISTRICTS			
	1927–1928		1929–1930		1927–1928		1929–1930	
	No.	%	No.	%	No.	%	No.	%
Superintendents	853		936		108		162†	
Temporary, first rank	170	20	121	13	32	30	53	33
" second rank	—		—		—		—	
Permanent	683	80	811	86	76	70	108	66
Special	—		4	.04	—		—	
Principals	1,543		1,720		3,892		3,950	
Temporary, first rank	444	29	478	28	2,639	68	2,254	57
" second rank	2		1		140	4	124	3
Permanent	1,093	70	1,242	72	1,113	28	1,565	39
Special	4		—		—		7	.1
Supervisors	248‡		419§		7		12	
Temporary, first rank	32	13	30	7	2	29	—	
" second rank	—		—		—		—	
Permanent	128	50	145	35	5	71	11	91
Special	54	23	118	28	—	—	1	9
Classroom Teacher	17,641		19,804		11,127		11,375	
Temporary, first rank	6,764	38	6,186	31	8,037	72	7,785	68
" second rank	154	.8	137	.7	1,193	11	791	7
Permanent	10,622	59	13,248	67	1,897	17	2,791	24
Special	101	2	233	1	—		8	

* Data from: Marrs, S. M. N. *Twenty-fifth Biennial Report of the State Department of Education*, Austin, Tex., Jan., 1929.

Twenty-sixth Biennial Report of the State Department of Education, Austin, Tex., March, 1931.

† 1 with no certificate. ‡ 34 with no certificates. § 126 with no certificates.

The amount of training received in institutions of learning is the most common measure of the academic and professional qualifications of teachers. It cannot be proved, however, that this is an accurate measure of teaching ability since certain apparently natural characteristics affect teaching success, and since it is well known that the character and quality of training differ greatly among institutions. Nevertheless, formal training is recognized as essential. Table 76 shows such qualifications possessed by the personnel of Texas public schools for the years 1927-28 and 1929-30. Certain discrepancies are noticed

[28] Yeager, W. A. *State Certification as a Factor in the Training of Elementary Teachers-in-Service.* Kutztown Publishing Co., Kutztown, Pa., 1929.

TABLE 76

ACADEMIC AND PROFESSIONAL TRAINING OF PUBLIC SCHOOL WORKERS*

Workers	Independent Districts				Common Districts			
	1927–1928		1929–1930		1927–1928		1929–1930	
	No.	%	No.	%	No.	%	No.	%
Superintendents	771		923		178		80	
Graduates of high school and no school	221	28	136	14	100	56	19	25
" " 2-year college	157	20	146	16	29	16	21	25
" " college or university	393	52	641	69	49	28	40	50
Principals, high school	640		798		1,833		2,272	
Graduates of high school and no school	207	32	133	16	1,259	69	996	44
" " 2-year college	110	17	157	20	315	17	874	39
" " college or university	323	51	508	64	259	14	402	17
Principals, elementary	906		927		1,791		1,745	
Graduates of high school and no school	381	42	225	24	1,332	75	991	57
" " 2-year college	214	24	342	37	307	17	604	35
" " college or university	311	34	360	39	152	8	150	8
Supervisors, high school	80		78		22		4	
Graduates of high school and no school	21	26	19	24	12	54	1	25
" " 2-year college	13	16	1	1	3	14	2	50
" " college or university	46	58	58	74	7	32	1	25
Supervisors, elementary	125		155		1		9	
Graduates of high school and no school	41	33	41	27	—	—	1	11
" " 2-year college	33	26	40	26	1	100	5	56
" " college or university	51	41	73	47	—	—	3	33
Classroom teachers, high school	5,063		6,376		1,284		1,441	
Graduates of high school and no school	667	13	543	9	811	63	593	41
" " 2-year college	538	11	641	10	232	18	459	32
" " college or university	3,848	76	5,192	81	241	19	389	27
Classroom teachers, elementary	12,201		14,318		9,779		9,737	
Graduates of high school and no school	6,810	56	4,887	34	8,108	83	6,206	64
" " 2-year college	2,995	25	6,214	43	1,151	12	2,932	30
" " college or university	2,396	19	3,217	23	520	5	599	6

* Data from: Marrs, S. M. N. *Twenty-fifth Biennial Report of the State Department of Education* Austin, Tex., Jan., 1929.

Twenty-sixth Biennial Report of the State Department of Education, Austin, Tex., March, 1931.

The table reads as follows: Of the 771 superintendents in independent districts in 1927–28, 221 or 28 per cent had no training above high school graduation.

in the numbers of superintendents, principals, supervisors, and classroom teachers presented in this table and those presented in Table 75. It is likely that the discrepancy results from inaccurate and incomplete reports received by the State Department of Education. A general improvement in academic and professional training during the two years is revealed by the percentages. However, the following facts are significant in showing that Texas has yet a large task in bringing its teaching personnel up to recognized standards of preparation. In 1929-30, 14 per cent of superintendents in the independent districts and 25 per cent of those in common districts had no better than secondary school training. Sixteen per cent of high-school principals and 24 per cent of elementary principals in independent districts, and 44 per cent and 57 per cent, respectively, of principals in common districts did not exceed this low level. Nine per cent of high-school teachers in the former type of districts and 41 per cent in the latter had no training beyond the secondary level, while the same was true of 34 per cent and 64 per cent, respectively, of elementary teachers in the two types of districts. One fourth of the supervisors showed the same low status of training. An interesting fact discovered in this table is that high-school teachers had better qualifications than superintendents or high-school principals in the independent districts. A larger percentage of the teachers were college and university graduates and smaller proportions had low levels of preparation than was true of either superintendents or principals. Evidently factors other than preparation have entered into the selection of administrative officers. However, it is doubtful whether valid reasons can be proposed to explain such general differences in training between administrators and classroom teachers.

The literature dealing with teacher training and the practice in certain progressive states, and the literature of accrediting agencies, are in agreement that desirable minimum standards of preparation are as follows: two years of training above secondary school for elementary teachers; and four years, represented by the bachelor's degree, for high-school teachers, principals, supervisors, and administrators. Some writers suggest the desirability of a fifth year of training for superintendents. If such minimum standards are applied to the public school personnel of Texas, the results are as shown in Table 77, which reveals the number of persons in each class of the service whose training was less in 1929-30 than that demanded by the standards. A total of 18,083 public school workers was below the standard of training required by their positions. Evidently Texas

TABLE 77

NUMBERS OF THE PUBLIC SCHOOL PERSONNEL WITH LESS THAN STANDARD TRAINING, 1929–30

Superintendents	with less than 4 years of college training	322
High school principals	" " " 4 " " " "	2,160
Elementary "	" " " 4 " " " "	2,162
High school supervisors	" " " 4 " " " "	23
Elementary "	" " " 4 " " " "	87
High school teachers	" " " 4 " " " "	2,236
Elementary teachers	with less than 2 years of college training	11,093
Total	....	18,083

did not have a surplus of trained teachers in 1929-30, and will not likely have for some time.

TABLE 78

DISTRIBUTION OF AVERAGE ANNUAL SALARIES OF WHITE TEACHERS OF TEXAS, INDEPENDENT AND COMMON DISTRICTS, MEN AND WOMEN, 1929-30*

	Independent Districts		Common Districts	
	Men	Women	Men	Women
$ 400- 499				1
500- 599		20		13
600- 699	1	66	1	67
700- 799	1	191	7	73
800- 899	15	279	27	43
900- 999	28	213	46	27
1000-1099	56	124	48	16
1100-1199	54	56	38	3
1200-1299	80	20	22	2
1300-1399	100	12	16	2
1400-1499	93	4	5	
1500-1599	66	2	8	
1600-1699	98	2	5	
1700-1799	90	4	1	
1800-1899	93		7	
1900-1999	65		4	
2000-2099	40		2	
2100-2199	27		1	
2200-2299	14		1	
2300-2399	15		2	
2400-2499	12			
2500-2599	5			
2600-2699	3			
2700-2799	4		1	
Over 2799	4			
Total	967	993	242	247
Medians	$1583	$878	$1083	$741
Q_1	$1300.07	$784	$917	$671
Q_3	$1847	$988	$1259	$874

* Data from Marrs, S. M. N. *Twenty-sixth Biennial Report of State Department of Education.*

The table reads as follows: An average salary of $600-699 is paid to men by 1 independent district and to women by 66 independent districts. The same is the average salary paid to men by common districts in 1 county, and to women by common districts in 67 counties.

In discussing the raising of requirements, the United States Office of Education makes the following comment:

In the formulation of salary schedules teaching experience is often given more weight than training. Certification requirements, however, more often raise standards of training than of experience. The salaries paid teachers eventually determine the amount of training which it is economically feasible for teachers to acquire. Many State departments, however, have not taken full advantage of present possibilities for raising standards by means of increased certification requirements. The States that are the last to raise standards may be among the first to witness a lowering of salaries.[29]

Table 78 shows a distribution of independent and common school districts of Texas according to the average salaries paid men and women teachers. The median salary for men in the independent districts was $1,583 and in common districts, $1,083. For women the medians were $878 and $741, respectively. The range of salaries for men is seen to be much greater than that for women, and is especially noticeable in the independent districts. Average salaries as shown by the *Biennial Report of the State Department of Education* for 1929-30 are as follows:

Average salary of white men teachers in the entire state	$1518.71
" " " " women " " " " "	1002.43
Average salary of white men teachers in independent districts	1893.00
" " " " women " " " "	1174.10
Average salary of white men teachers in common districts	1009.94
" " " " women " " " "	699.03

Table 79 was prepared to throw additional light upon the school salaries of Texas and to determine how they compare with those in the country at large and in certain other states. For the sake of brevity the comparison was limited to cities in the 5,000 to 10,000 population group, which is deemed sufficient to show the relative position of Texas in the matter of salaries. Reports on which data are based came from 451 cities and are for the year 1930-31.[30] For all cities the median salaries were: elementary teachers, $1,303; junior-high-school teachers, $1,494; high-school teachers, $1,692; school janitors, $1,255. Median salaries in Texas for these four groups were: $960, $1,152, $1,371, and $680, respectively; less than the national medians by $343, $342, $321, and $575. The average salaries shown in Table 78 and the averages presented above include principals and administrative officers with teachers. Elementary and junior-high-school teachers in Texas were paid less than the national median for school janitors, and high-school teachers were paid only $116 more than that median. Compared with national medians, the medians for three other southwestern states, and those of four selected states, the salaries of Texas teachers are very low. This

[29] Frazier, B. W. *Teacher Training, 1926-28,* United States Bureau of Education, Bulletin, 1929, No. 17, p. 17.

[30] *Research Bulletin of the National Education Association,* Vol. IX, No. 3, pp. 191-97, May, 1931.

TABLE 79

MEDIAN SALARIES OF TEACHERS AS REVEALED BY REPORTS FROM 451 CITIES IN THE 5,000–10,000 POPULATION GROUP, FOR THE YEAR 1930–31

STATE	ELEMENTARY TEACHERS	JUNIOR HIGH SCHOOL TEACHERS	HIGH SCHOOL TEACHERS	ELEMENTARY TEACHING PRINCIPALS	HIGH SCHOOL PRINCIPALS	SCHOOL JANITORS
United States	$1,303	$1,494	$1,692	$1,854	$3,038	$1,255
Texas	960	1,152	1,371	1,391	2,283	680
Arizona	1,452	1,800	2,020	1,920	—	1,300
New Mexico	1,288	1,564	1,663	—	—	713
Kansas	1,194	1,450	1,482	1,488	2,750	975
New Jersey	1,578	1,955	1,970	2,300	3,800	1,535
Pennsylvania	1,420	1,540	1,731	1,663	2,756	1,257
New York	1,735	1,905	2,015	1,975	3,092	1,583
California	1,591	1,963	2,307	2,946	3,750	1,542

raises a serious question as to the amount of training it is economical and feasible for Texas teachers to secure. It is suggested, however, that the raising of training requirements will have to precede the raising of salaries. More than 18,000 teachers with substandard training may be expected to have a powerful effect in keeping salaries down. The low salaries of teachers in proportion to the expense necessary to secure standard training are emphasized when it is pointed out that the average income of gainfully employed persons in the United States is approximately $2,000.[31]

The collection of reports from each independent district and from each county by which to determine the exact number of new teachers employed in 1929-30 appeared to be beyond the resources available for this investigation. However, such reports were obtained from a sampling of districts and counties within the territory of each teachers college. The total number of teachers employed in the districts reporting were: in common districts and independent districts of less than 500 scholastic population, 764; and in the larger independent districts, 674. Table 80 shows the percentage of new teachers reported in each kind of district. About one-fifth of the teachers were new in the common and small independent districts, and 6.2 per cent in the larger independent districts. There was a total of 22,974 white teachers in the independent districts and a total of 15,687 in the common districts of the state in 1929-30.[32] Applying the per-

[31] *Ibid.*, p. 192.

[32] *Twenty-sixth Biennial Report of the State Department of Education*, pp. 495-96. Data from independent districts of less than 500 scholastic population are included with county superintendents' reports with data from common districts.

centages of new teachers to these totals, neglecting the small proportion coming from other states, suggests that Texas needs annually 7,812 new teachers in the public schools for white children. Another source of information was utilized which showed that 7.6 per cent of the teachers in the high schools of the state were new in 1928-29; and that 21.6 per cent were new to their positions that year.[33]

TABLE 80

PER CENT OF TEACHERS WHO WERE NEW IN A SAMPLING OF DISTRICTS AND COUNTIES, 1929–30

KIND OF DISTRICT	INEXPERIENCED (NEW) TEACHERS	FROM OTHER STATES	EXPERIENCED, SERVING FIRST YEAR IN PRESENT POSITION
Common districts	20.4	—	53.1
Independent districts less than 500	18.2	2.0	39.0
Larger independent districts	6.2	1.5	17.6

Considering the size of Texas, its steady development, and the extension of the educational opportunities which seems to be in prospect, the estimated annual need of teachers does not appear to be excessive when compared to similar needs found in other states. In Colorado the number needed annually, based on reports of newly appointed teachers in 1925-26, was found to be 1,050.[34] In Ohio in 1923-24 the number was placed at 4,447;[35] and in 1926-27 at 5,446.[36] The number needed in Missouri in 1930 was estimated at 4,850.[37] Based on reports of new teachers in 1926-27, the annual number required in New York State, exclusive of New York City, was placed at 6,197.[38] The number needed in Arkansas, outside of Little Rock, was estimated, on the basis of data for the year 1923-24, to be 2,500.[39] As illustrated by the figures for Ohio, the larger needs in all states are found in the more recent years.

[33] *Directory of Teachers in Texas High Schools,* Bulletin No. 248, Dec., 1928, State Department of Education. Seven thousand high school teachers are listed in this bulletin. No similar directory of elementary teachers is issued.

[34] Whitney, F. L. *Op. cit.,* p. 65.

[35] Buckingham, B. R. *Supply and Demand in Teacher Training,* p. 11, Table I.

[36] Myers, A. F. *A Teacher-Training Program for Ohio,* p. 68. Contributions to Education, No. 266. Bureau of Publications, Teachers College, Columbia University, 1927.

[37] *Eightieth Report of the Public Schools of the State of Missouri, Parts I and II,* p. 144. Issued by Charles A. Lee, state superintendent of public schools, Jefferson City, Mo.

[38] Coxe, W. W. *Op. cit.,* p. 6, Table II.

[39] Grant, J. R. *Op. cit.,* p. 46.

The Texas educational survey, made in 1924, found considerable variation in the average teaching tenure in different types and sizes of schools, and between men and women, as shown in Tables 81 and 82. The general average tenure of elementary teachers was 5.3 years; and of superintendents, principals, and teachers in all classes of high schools, 6.9 years, which agrees closely with the findings of the Division of Research of the National Education Association about a year earlier.[40] If six years be taken as the correct tenure, and since there are 38,661 white teachers, 6,443 new teachers would be needed in Texas for annual replacements. If the average annual increase in number of white teachers—1,101 (see Table 74)—continues, the state will need annually 7,544 new teachers. This method of determination leaves out of consideration the results of enlarging the high-school facilities as proposed by Superintendent Marrs's recommendation presented above. The annual need of teachers in Texas may be conservatively placed at 7,800.

From Tables 81 and 82 it is easily seen that teachers with brief experience are found in the small schools of the common districts and in the small high schools. This means a large turnover in

TABLE 81

EXPERIENCE OF WHITE TEACHERS IN ELEMENTARY SCHOOLS OF COMMON SCHOOL AND INDEPENDENT DISTRICTS *

CLASS	NUMBER	NO INFORMATION	AVERAGE YEARS TAUGHT
Men in one-, two-, and three-teacher schools—common and independent districts	609	3	4.8
Women in one-teacher common schools	556	7	3.0
Women in two-teacher common schools	1,006	28	3.5
Women in one-, two-, and three-teacher schools in independent districts	154	15	5.5
Men in four or more teacher schools, common and independent districts	341	12	9.1
Women in four or more teacher common schools	360	6	4.3
Women in four or more teacher schools in independent districts	5,050	118	5.3
Total women, all classes	7,621	206	5.3
Total men, all classes	950	15	5.2
Grand Total	8,571	221	5.3

* *Texas Educational Survey Report,* Vol. VIII, p. 153. The Texas Educational Survey Commission, Austin, Tex., 1925.

[40] Norton, J. K. *The Problem of Teacher Tenure.* Research Bulletin of the National Education Association, Vol. II, No. 5, Nov., 1924.

TABLE 82

YEARS OF EXPERIENCE IN TEACHING, SUPERINTENDENTS, HIGH-SCHOOL PRINCIPALS, TEACHERS *

		Class					
		1	2	3	4	5	6
Superintendents	Range	2–25	1–46	2–44	3–45	3–46	8–38
	Median	9	11	12	14	16	29
	Mean	10.3	13	14.4	15.9	18.6	25.2
Principals	Range	1–31	1–23	1–42	1–32	1–30	10–29
	Median	3	4	5	6	8	22
	Mean	4.6	5.4	5.9	7.3	10.2	19.7
Women teachers	Range	1–23	1–13	1–23	1–31	1–32	2–36
	Median	3	3	3	4	4	7
	Mean	4.1	3.9	4.4	4.5	5.1	8.5
Men teachers	Range	1–15	1–18	1–27	1–23	1–39	1–32
	Median	2	3	2	3	4	8
	Mean	3.7	3.9	4	3.6	5.3	9.6

* *Texas Educational Survey Report,* Vol. III, pp. 82 and 86.

Note: The six classes shown in the table are distinguished as follows:

Class 1 includes those high schools offering less than four years of work.

Class 2 includes those offering four years of work but less than 13½ affiliated credits.

Class 3 includes four-year schools offering 13½ or more affiliated credits, but with no more than five teachers.

Class 4 includes those schools of 6 to 10 teachers, offering more than 13½ affiliated credits.

Class 5 includes high schools of more than 10 teachers, excluding those in cities noted in Class 6.

Class 6 includes high schools in the cities of Austin, Beaumont, Dallas, El Paso, Fort Worth, Galveston, Houston, San Antonio, and Waco.

such schools, and it also means that inexperienced teachers are to be found in those schools in which there is little or no supervision. The facts presented reveal a spirit of unrest among the teaching population which causes many to be on the move annually, doubtless in an effort to improve their professional and economic status. Only in this manner can they hope to secure the compensation they must have in order to meet the expense of additional training. It appears impossible except in the large city systems to make a life career of teaching in one locality. These conditions are a natural result of the high degree of district autonomy found in Texas.

The number of persons certificated is the best general indication of the supply of teachers available each year. It is doubtful whether the number of graduates of teacher-training courses who actually teach could be accurately determined in Texas.[41] However, whether

[41] Whitney found it impossible to secure complete data in Colorado. See Whitney, F. L. *Op. cit.*, pp. 19-20.

graduates at any level teach or not, the fact that they are certificated definitely places them on the supply side of the teacher market. In Table 3, Chapter I, the number of certificates issued on the basis of credits earned in various types of colleges from 1919 to 1928 is shown. In Table 4, Chapter I, the total number of certificates issued during the ten-year period is given, together with the per cents based on examination and college credits each year. Attention is directed in that chapter to the fact that the proportion of those based on examination is steadily and rapidly decreasing. In 1928, 5 per cent were so based, and, as subsequent tables show, that percentage was reduced to 3.9 per cent during the biennium 1928-30.

TABLE 83

NUMBER OF APPLICANTS FOR STATE EXAMINATIONS AND NUMBER OF CERTIFICATES ISSUED THEREON *

	1928†	1929	1930†	TOTAL
No. of Applicants:				
Elementary	416	1,361	968	2,745
High School	105	496	353	954
No. of Certificates Issued:				
Elementary	204	257	284	745
High School	90	190	153	433
First Grade‡	—	1	—	1
Permanent Primary‡	—	2	—	2
Total No. Applicants	521	1,857	1,321	3,699
Total No. Certificates Issued	294	450	437	1,181

* *Twenty-sixth Biennial Report of the State Department of Education*, p. 92.
† The last four months of 1928 and the first eight months of 1930.
‡ Work completed before the 1921 law took effect.

Tables 83, 84, and 85 reveal certain interesting and significant facts in regard to certification of teachers in Texas during the biennium 1928-30. From the data of Table 83 it is seen that less than one third (31.9 per cent) of the applicants for certificates by examination were successful and that the number licensed by examination to teach in elementary schools greatly exceeded the number granted high-school certificates. Table 84 shows clearly that every college in the state is a teachers college, with the possible exception of the Agricultural and Mechanical College from which only 78 persons were certificated in 1929-30. The teachers colleges appear to be serving their professional purpose when it is noted that more than

TABLE 84

Texas Certificates Issued on College Credentials, 1929–30*

Name of College	Two-Year Elementary	Three-Year Elementary	Four-Year Elementary	Six-Year Elementary	Permanent Elementary	Two-Year High School	Four-Year High School	Six-Year High School	Permanent High School	Special	Kindergarten	Permanent†	Total
	Types of Certificates												
Texas State Teachers Colleges	56	631	1,156	211	1,021	737	462	440	860	143	13	54	5,784
Agricultural & Mechanical College			1	2		3	39	10	22	1			78
College of Industrial Arts			125	70	20	34	123	23	195	119	14		723
Texas College of Arts and Industries:													
School of Arts			11	11		3	1						26
Teachers College		9	93		95	19	25	6	21				269
Texas Technological College			119	53	1	74	121	17	92	24			501
University of Texas			102	78	14	44	169	28	165	52		6	658
Independent Senior Colleges:													
White			524	293	42	202	533	132	870	78	17	5	2,696
Colored			137	66	5	20	53	2	131	4			439
Junior Colleges:													
State			120	50	13	63	117		1				369
Municipal			197	142	12	75	79	3	6	4	2		520
Independent:													
White			276	103	26	134	182	2		5	1	2	731
Colored			256	97	5	29	29	8	2				426
Schools for special subjects				1						4			5
Total Texas Colleges	56	640	3,117	1,177	1,261	1,437	1,933	671	2,385	434	47	67	13,225
Out of State Colleges			117	359	13	60	149	53	136	68	5	28	1,043
Grand Total	56	640	3,234	1,535	1,270	1,497	2,082	724	2,571	502	52	95	14,268

* *Twenty-sixth Biennial Report of the State Department of Education*, p. 91.

† Based on college work earned prior to August 31, 1925.

twice as many persons received certificates based on credentials earned in that group as in any other group of colleges. There seems to be little specialization among the institutions as to the training of elementary and high-school teachers. All give the same types of training. Even the junior colleges provided credentials for a few permanent high-school certificates. Table 85 shows 34,979 as the total number of certificates issued during the biennium. That number, however, includes the certificates extended as a result of college work done in the summer, but persons with certificates so extended must be regarded as additions to the potential teacher supply.

TABLE 85

Total Number of Certificates Issued and Extended by Summer Work

Basis of Certificates Issued	1928*	1929	1930†	Total
State Examinations (Texas)	294	450	437	1,181
State Examinations (Other States)	4	15	4	23
Approved Colleges (Texas)	3,051	12,894	9,713	25,658
Approved Colleges (Other States)	335	959	684	1,978
Experience (Permanent First Grade)	99	364	276	739
Total	3,783	14,682	11,114	29,579
Number Extended by Summer College Work		2,587	2,813	5,400
Grand Total	3,783	17,269	13,927	34,979

* Last four months of 1928. † First eight months of 1930.

It is impossible to tell from Table 83 the number of Negro teachers certificated by examination, or from Table 85 the number whose certificates were extended because of summer study. However, in order to determine approximately the number of white teachers certificated in one year, it is assumed that 12 per cent of the total number of certificates granted were granted to Negro teachers. It is estimated, therefore, from data furnished by these tables that 16,262 white teachers were certificated in Texas in the year 1929-30. If 7,800 represents at all accurately the annual need of new teachers in the state, more than twice as many are being licensed as are needed to meet the demands of the public schools.

Summary and Proposals

1. Since 1920 a general interest has been shown by research students in the problem of determining the demand for teachers in relation to the available supply. Studies have been made in at least

twenty states, and the problem is being attacked on a nation-wide basis by current investigations under the general direction of the Federal Office of Education. The general opinion seems to prevail that the country has a surplus of persons certificated to teach, and that the time has arrived to take active steps toward raising the standards of preparation for the teaching profession.

2. Students who have attacked the problem of teacher demand and supply agree that its solution is beset with numerous difficulties and complications and that a State Department of Education is the agency most likely to possess the facilities and authority to secure accurate and complete data bearing on the problem.

3. The importance of capable and well-prepared teachers is emphasized in the following quotation from Thorndike: "A nation which lets incapables teach it, while the capable men and women only feed or clothe or amuse it, is committing intellectual suicide."[42] The professional fitness of the teaching personnel will be at the maximum and conditions in the schools will be most favorable when the supply of trained teachers is approximately equal to the demand.

4. The training of teachers for the public schools is a responsibility of a state just as truly as are the establishment and maintenance of public schools. Any state which appropriates funds for the preparation of teachers greatly in excess of the number needed by its schools is guilty of an unwise use of its resources. The right of a state to control the number of teachers trained at public expense and to set up standards of preparation for its public servants cannot be successfully contradicted.

5. It is doubtful whether adequate support for a state's teacher-training institutions can be obtained as long as the state attempts to give training to all those who apply for admission. It seems reasonable to believe that the financial needs of such institutions will be better cared for when their responsibility is known and limited to the training of such numbers as are needed to supply the known needs of the schools.

6. The size of the task of public education in Texas is steadily increasing as measured by the scholastic population, the enrollment in the schools, and the number of teachers employed. The scholastic population is increasing at the rate of about 2 per cent annually and in March of 1930 was 1,563,595. Approximately 17 per cent of that number were Negroes. The average annual percentage increase in the

[42] Quoted by Buckingham, B. R. *Supply and Demand in Teacher Training*, p. 3.

enrollment of white elementary schools during the seven years prior to 1930 was 1.9 per cent; and in high schools, 5.1 per cent. The average annual absolute increase in the number of white teachers employed was 1,101 and represented an average percentage increase of 3.4 per cent.

7. Improvement in the qualifications of the teaching personnel of Texas public schools during the past few years is noticeable. The proportions of those holding the better ranks of certificates and with two years or more of college training have been increasing. However, if four years of preparation on the college level is accepted as a desirable minimum standard for high-school teachers, principals, supervisors, and superintendents, and two years as a minimum for elementary teachers, 18,083 members of the public school personnel had substandard training in 1929-30.

8. The salaries of teachers and principals in Texas are low compared with medians for the country at large and for many other states. In cities with a population of from 5,000 to 10,000 the median salaries in Texas fall below the national medians as follows: salaries of elementary teachers, $343; of junior high-school teachers, $342; of high-school teachers, $321; of elementary principals, $463; and of high-school principals, $755. A distribution of salaries in all districts in Texas shows a low level for the entire state. The great differences in the salaries paid in the numerous districts are evidence of the lack of a state policy, and an indication of the great degree of district autonomy obtaining in the administration of the public schools.

9. The State of Texas needs annually about 7,800 new white teachers for replacements and to fill new positions made necessary by the growth of the schools and the extension of high schools. However, more than 16,000 white persons are being certificated each year. This means that the supply is being increased at more than twice the rate of increase in the demand.

10. It is evident that the State of Texas has no plan for supplying its public schools with teachers in suitable numbers or with proper qualifications. Under present procedure, teachers not infrequently attempt to do work for which they have no preparation whatever. Furthermore, teaching positions are open to competitive bidding which all too frequently results in the selection of applicants possessing the poorest qualifications. The damaging possibilities of such conditions are entirely obvious.

The data presented in this chapter constitute ample basis for the proposal that the State Board of Education authorize the collection of facts each year from which the teacher needs of the schools and the supply of teachers actually furnished by the colleges can be determined. Such information, collected for several years, would make possible reasonably accurate predictions of future demand and serve as a basis for planning training facilities to insure a proper supply of teachers for each type and kind of service. The State Department of Education should be furnished with facilities for such research as the active agent of the State Board. The annual teacher needs of independent and common districts for the following classes of teachers should be known: (1) kindergarten and primary; (2) intermediate; (3) junior high school by subject-matter departments; (4) high school by subject-matter departments.

CHAPTER VI

A STATE PLAN OF TEACHER TRAINING IN TEXAS

This chapter makes certain proposals designed to contribute to a definite program for the professional preparation of teachers for the public schools of Texas. It is possible that these proposals will be at variance with the ideas, plans, and practices of many educational institutions in the state, both public and private. However, they are based on facts disclosed in this and other studies and their purpose is to assist in developing a state plan which will secure most economically the maximum educational results for the commonwealth. The special interests and growth of no one particular group of institutions are of sufficient importance to interfere with or retard the progress of public education in the state.

Certain limitations appear to force themselves upon this monograph because of the fact that several problems, other than that of proper teacher-training facilities, must be worked out in order to provide Texas with a state system of public schools equal to the best. And many of them are closely related to the task of building up an efficient and well-qualified teaching personnel. Certain of these problems, therefore, can be merely outlined and their relation to a teacher-training program pointed out.

For several years it has been increasingly difficult for the state institutions of higher learning to secure appropriations in the amounts asked for. Prospects are that the situation in regard to financial support of these institutions will become more acute under the present system of raising revenue and with the present lack of a state plan to control them and their functions. The public schools have also been finding the state's contribution to their support increasingly more uncertain. Two general causes, supplemented by a third, may be assigned. First, the state is operating under an outgrown Constitution framed in 1875. Under it, methods of securing revenue are unscientific and unsuited to the needs of a growing commonwealth. The very inefficient methods used in granting state support to the public schools may be suggested as a contributing cause. Also, whatever planning is done concerning the support of higher institutions is done by the legislature and not by persons qualified to know the educational needs of the state. Second, the student load carried by both the schools and the colleges is steadily increasing as shown by enrollment figures. Such conditions point to the necessity of a careful planning of the state's educational policies. The state's resources are not without limit. Such planning must necessarily include a remaking of the state Constitution.

Texas has no real state system of public education. The present arrangement is in reality an aggregation of a large number of autonomous districts together with fourteen institutions of collegiate rank under the control of several boards of regents. Under such a set-up equality of educational opportunity for the children of the state is practically an impossibility and a lack of coördination among the colleges is certain. The establishment in 1929 of the present State Board of Education, composed of nine members appointed for overlapping terms, is a step toward the integration of the state's educational activities. However, the powers and resources placed with this board are as yet so limited as to make possible little constructive work.

The Texas educational survey made in 1924 showed the facts about the state's educational program. As a result of the findings of that survey the Legislative Committee of the Survey Commission prepared eleven amendments to the Constitution and twenty bills which were proposed to provide more nearly a state system of education.[1] These measures were declared to be interdependent, and were designed to accomplish four major objectives: (1) stabilization of the income of the schools; (2) improved and stabilized organization of the schools to the end of efficiency; (3) equalization of educational opportunity; and (4) equalization of the burden of supporting the educational program of the state. A comprehensive tax survey and a codification of the educational laws were also recommended. It is held that the accomplishment of these objectives is vitally important to the building up of a well-qualified and stable teaching personnel.

The Texas method of distributing state aid to local districts, involving as it does a large measure of what Mort[2] refers to as the "large fund method" although the fund is meager, together with sev-

[1] The official report of the Legislative Committee of the Texas Educational Survey Commission was published in the *Texas Outlook* (official organ of the Texas State Teachers' Association), Vol. X, No. 12, pp. 8 ff., Dec., 1926, Fort Worth, Tex.

[2] Mort, Paul R. *State Support for Public Schools.* Bureau of Publications, Teachers College, Columbia University, 1926.

eral schemes to reward local effort, may be expected to result in glaring inequalities in educational opportunities provided and in wide differences in teacher qualifications secured by various districts. The method can make no provision for state-wide minimum salaries. In fact, the procedures employed for distributing state funds, in conjunction with existing certificate laws, operate to defeat the realization of equivalence of educational opportunity and to encourage the employment of teachers having the minimum of training. The situation in Texas is such that the educational offerings provided by districts of only average wealth are far above those of the vast majority of the numerous common and small independent districts, and the school advantages offered by the centers of wealth are generally regarded as utterly impossible of attainment in the poorer communities. The result is that schools in which the greatest teaching skill is needed employ teachers having the poorest qualifications, and employ them at the lowest salaries.

In order to accomplish the objectives set forth by the Legislative Committee of the Survey Commission and at the same time raise the standards of the teaching profession, a fundamental reorganization of the state's plan of support and of administration appears to be absolutely necessary. It is suggested that an adaptation of Mort's plan be worked out for the State of Texas. That plan provides for a state-wide minimum educational program and considers all money invested by the state as an equalization fund to guarantee the advantages of the minimum program to every child, regardless of the type of community in which he lives. It also provides for an equalization of the cost of such a program without preventing local communities from exceeding the minimum standards if they so desire. However, it leaves out all schemes for using state funds to reward local effort as tending to destroy the effect of provisions for equalizing educational opportunity. To secure economy and efficiency the plan calls for large units of administration and contemplates the abolition of the inefficient and costly district system. Educational leadership on a state-wide rather than on a local basis would be encouraged under such a plan, and the way prepared for the operation of a program of teacher preparation that would be economical and that would insure trained teachers in all schools.

The improvement of teaching standards in Texas and the successful operation of a state teacher-training program will require a complete revision of the certification plan. The present plan, if it may be referred to as such, is in reality a patchwork containing many reactionary features which have the effect of lowering standards. It is suggested, therefore, that all certification laws now on the statute books be repealed and that the certification of teachers be placed in the hands of the State Board of Education. Concurrently with such action, the State Department of Education should be reorganized by placing at its head a State Commissioner selected by the State Board; and by creating a Division of Teacher Training and Certification under the supervision of a competent director. Under such a plan classes of certificates, and regulations governing their issuance, would be prescribed by the State Board of Education rather than by detailed statutes passed by the legislature. It is recognized that it would be impossible and unfair to insist upon a too radical and immediate raising of standards and that the validity of outstanding certificates must be protected. The following outline of certificate regulations is proposed to indicate the nature of standards which Texas may reasonably expect to attain within eight or ten years. In these proposals it is presumed that the curricula pursued by candidates for all classes of certificates shall be prescribed in fairly complete outline by the State Board of Education and adhered to by all colleges in the state whose credentials toward certification are accepted.

Outline of Proposed Certificate Regulations

General Features

1. Certificates obtainable by examination shall be discontinued and all certificates shall be based on training received in accredited colleges.
2. Certificates shall represent completion of specific training and shall not be blanket licenses to serve the public schools in just any capacity. For example, holders of high-school certificates shall not be eligible to teach in the elementary grades without first meeting the requirements for elementary certificates, and those eligible for administrative positions must be holders of superintendents' certificates.
3. The law establishing the new plan should authorize the State Board of Education to allow teachers already in service a liberal amount of time in which to meet the new requirements.
4. The State Board shall be authorized to issue such temporary special certificates as the facts at its command seem to indicate are necessary to prevent injustices and disturbances due to the inauguration of the new plan.

5. No permanent or life certificate, in the sense of those issued under the present plan, shall be issued. Any certificate in Texas shall be voidable if the holder thereof leaves, and fails to practice, the profession of teaching for a period of three or more consecutive years.
6. The State Board of Education shall set up regulations governing the reinstatement of such voided certificates.

Kinds of Certificates

1. *Superintendent's Certificate, First Grade.*

   To secure this certificate an applicant must satisfy the following requirements:

   a. Graduation from a standard college accredited by the State Board of Education for the training of teachers. Those who begin their college work subsequent to the inauguration of the new plan will be expected to follow the prescribed undergraduate curricula in public school administration.
   b. Five years' experience as superintendent, principal, supervisor, or teacher.
   c. In addition to the above requirements the applicant must have completed one collegiate year of graduate work in a recognized college or university, specializing in administration and supervision.

This certificate shall be valid for ten years, and renewable for life, subject to continued practice of the profession, upon presentation of evidence of seven years' successful administrative experience while holding this certificate, and twelve semester hours of additional professional training approved by the State Board of Education.

Superintendents' certificates shall be valid for such positions as: superintendent, assistant superintendent, director of research, and other administrative positions.

2. *Superintendent's Certificate, Second Grade.*

   An applicant for this certificate must satisfy the following requirements:

   a. Graduation from a standard college accredited by the State Board of Education for the training of teachers. During this college course the applicant must have followed the prescribed curriculum in public school administration.

b. Three years' experience as superintendent, principal, supervisor, or teacher.

Such certificate shall be valid for five years and renewable once for a similar period upon completion of fifteen semester hours of graduate work approved by the State Board of Education. This certificate may be converted into a superintendent's first grade certificate upon meeting the requirements therefor.

3. *Superintendent's Certificate, Third Grade.*

This certificate shall be issued as long as the facts in the possession of the State Board of Education indicate that it is needed, after which time it shall be discontinued. To receive this certificate an applicant must satisfy the following requirements:

a. Completion of not less than three-fourths of the work for bachelor's degree in a standard college accredited by the State Board of Education for the training of teachers. During this time the applicant shall follow the prescribed curricula in public school administration.
b. At least one year of public-school experience.

This certificate shall be valid for three years and shall not be renewable. Work done in meeting these requirements may be credited toward a superintendent's second grade certificate.

4. *High-School Principal's Certificate, First Grade.*

To secure this certificate an applicant must satisfy the following requirements:

a. Graduation from a standard college accredited for the training of teachers. The curricula followed must be those dealing with secondary education and supervision.
b. Five years' successful experience as high-school principal or teacher.
c. In addition to the above requirements the applicant must have completed one collegiate year of graduate work in a recognized college or university, specializing in the problems of secondary education.

This certificate shall be valid for ten years, and renewable for life, subject to continued practice of the profession, upon presentation of evidence of seven years' successful experience while holding this certificate, and the completion of twelve semester hours of additional professional training approved by the State Board.

5. *High-School Principal's Certificate, Second Grade.*

To secure this certificate an applicant must satisfy the following requirements:

a. Graduation from a standard college accredited for the training of teachers. The curricula followed must be those dealing with secondary education and supervision.

b. Three years' experience as high-school principal or teacher.

This certificate shall be valid for five years and renewable once for a similar period upon completion of fifteen semester hours of graduate work approved by the State Board of Education. It may be converted into a high-school principal's first grade certificate upon meeting the additional requirements therefor.

6. *High-School Principal's Certificate, Third Grade.*

This certificate shall be issued as long as the facts in possession of the State Board of Education indicate that it is needed, after which time it shall be discontinued. To receive this certificate an applicant must satisfy the following requirements:

a. Completion of not less than three-fourths of the work for bachelor's degree in a standard college accredited by the State Board for the training of teachers. During this time the applicant shall follow the curricula dealing with secondary education and supervision.

b. At least one year of teaching experience.

This certificate shall be valid for three years and shall not be renewable. Work done in meeting these requirements may be credited toward the high-school principal's second grade certificate.

7. *Elementary Principal's Certificate, First Grade.*

To secure this certificate an applicant must satisfy the following requirements:

a. Graduation from a standard college accredited for the training of teachers. The curricula followed must be those dealing with elementary education, the practices in elementary schools, and supervision.

b. Five years' successful experience as elementary-school principal or teacher.

c. In addition to the above requirements the applicant must have completed one collegiate year of graduate work in a recognized college or university, specializing in the problems of elementary education.

This certificate shall be valid for ten years, and renewable for life, subject to continued practice of the profession, upon presentation of evidence of seven years' successful experience while holding this certificate, and the completion of twelve semester hours, or the equivalent, of professional training approved by the State Board of Education.

8. *Elementary Principal's Certificate, Second Grade.*

To secure this certificate an applicant must satisfy the following requirements:

a. Graduation from a standard college accredited for the training of teachers. The curricula followed must be those dealing with elementary education and supervision.

b. Three years' experience as elementary principal or teacher.

This certificate shall be valid for five years and renewable once for a similar period upon completion of fifteen semester hours of graduate work approved by the State Board, and it may be converted into an elementary principal's first grade certificate by meeting the additional requirements therefor.

9. *Elementary Principal's Certificate, Third Grade.*

This certificate shall be issued as long as the State Board of Education considers that it is needed, after which time it shall be discontinued. To receive this certificate an applicant must meet the following requirements:

a. Completion of not less than half the work for bachelor's degree in a standard college accredited for the training of teachers pursuing the curricula in elementary education.

b. At least one year of teaching experience.

This certificate shall be valid for three years and shall not be renewable. Work done in meeting these requirements may be credited toward the elementary principal's second grade certificate.

10. *High-School Teacher's Certificate, First Grade.*

To secure this certificate an applicant must satisfy the following requirements:

a. Graduation from a standard college accredited by the State Board of Education for the training of teachers. The curricula pursued must deal with secondary education and must include majors and minors in three subject-matter fields. Not less than three full college years of work must be done in each major and minor, and the certificate will be valid for teaching these subjects only.

b. Five years' teaching experience, three of which must have been done in high school.

c. In addition to the above requirements the applicant must have completed one collegiate year of graduate work in a recognized college or university, giving special attention to the problems of secondary education and to the study of his major and minor subjects.

This certificate shall be valid for ten years and renewable for life, subject to continued practice of the profession, upon presentation of evidence of seven years' successful teaching experience while holding this certificate, and fifteen semester hours, or the equivalent, of additional training approved by the State Board of Education.

11. *High-School Teacher's Certificate, Second Grade.*

To secure this certificate an applicant must satisfy the following requirements:

a. Graduation from a standard college accredited by the State Board of Education for the training of teachers. The curricula pursued must deal with secondary education and must include majors and minors in three subject-matter fields. Not less than three full college years must be done in each major and minor, and the certificate will be valid for teaching those subjects only.

b. Two years' teaching experience or one year of apprentice teaching under the supervision of the college in which undergraduate work was done.

This certificate shall be valid for five years and renewable for a similar period upon completion of fifteen semester hours of graduate work approved by the State Board of Education, and it may be converted into a high-school teacher's first grade certificate by meeting the additional requirements therefor.

12. *High-School Teacher's Certificate, Third Grade.*

This certificate shall be issued as long as the State Board of Education considers that it is needed and shall then be discontinued. An applicant shall satisfy the following requirement:

a. Completion of two years' work in a standard college accredited by the State Board of Education for the training of teachers. The curriculum prescribed for these two years shall be followed.

The certificate shall be valid for the teaching of not more than four subjects, each of which the applicant has studied during the entire two years.

This certificate shall be valid for five years and shall not be renewable. Work done to secure this certificate, and teaching experience gained while holding it, shall be credited toward requirements for the high-school teacher's second grade certificate.

The holder of a high-school teacher's certificate shall be eligible to teach in a senior high school, junior high school, or senior-junior high school.

13. *Elementary Teacher's Certificate, First Grade.*

An applicant for this certificate shall satisfy the following requirements:

a. Graduation from a standard college accredited by the State Board of Education for the training of teachers. The curricula followed shall be those prescribed for the preparation of elementary teachers.

b. At least two years of successful teaching experience or one year of apprentice teaching under the supervision of the college in which undergraduate work was done.

This certificate shall be valid for ten years and renewable for life, subject to continued practice of the profession, upon presentation of evidence of seven years of successful professional experience while holding this certificate, and fifteen semester hours, or the equivalent, of additional professional training approved by the State Board of Education.

14. *Elementary Teacher's Certificate, Second Grade.*

An applicant for this certificate shall satisfy the following requirement:

a. Completion of three-fourths of the work for the bachelor's degree in a standard college approved by the State Board of Education for the training of teachers. The curricula followed must be those prescribed for the preparation of elementary teachers, which shall include not less than nine semester hours of practice teaching in the elementary grades.

This certificate shall be valid for three years and renewable for a similar period upon completion of fifteen semester hours of additional college credit approved by the State Board of Education. It may be converted into the elementary teacher's first grade certificate by meeting the additional requirements.

15. *Elementary Teacher's Certificate, Third Grade.*

This certificate shall be issued as long as the conditions in the schools of the state, in the opinion of the State Board of Education, make it necessary. An applicant for it shall satisfy the following requirement:

a. Completion of two years of a teacher-training course in a standard college accredited by the State Board of Education for the training of teachers. The curricula followed must be those prescribed for the preparation of elementary teachers, which shall include not less than three semester hours of practice teaching in the elementary grades.

This certificate shall be valid for four years and shall not be renewable. However, it may be converted into the elementary teacher's certificate, second grade, by meeting the additional requirements.

General Notes

1. Holders of high-school principals' certificates and elementary principals' certificates shall be eligible to hold positions as high-school and elementary supervisors, respectively.
2. The State Board of Education shall have authority to set up requirements to be met by holders of one class of certificate in securing a certificate of another class. To illustrate, requirements should be established under which the holder of a principal's certificate may qualify for a superintendent's certificate and, in so

doing, receive reasonable credit for work done in securing the former. Likewise, holders of elementary teachers' certificates should be allowed to qualify for high-school teachers' certificates, and those who hold teachers' certificates should be afforded opportunity to secure principals' certificates.

Control of Teacher Training by the State Board of Education

It is proposed that the State Board of Education, acting through the Division of Teacher Training and Certification of the State Department of Education, establish and administer standards for accrediting all colleges in the state whose credentials are accepted as the basis for certificates. Colleges which do not meet such standards in full should not be recognized as teacher-training institutions. An adequate and well-qualified staff should be provided in the Division of Teacher Training and Certification to the end that effective supervision of the training of teachers may be accomplished. A college may qualify to issue credentials on which one or more classes of certificates are based and not be able to meet requirements to issue credentials for all classes.

The requirements established by the State Board of Education in Texas for the training of public school workers should not be lower than those contemplated by the current standards adopted from time to time by the American Association of Teachers Colleges, and in several particulars should be higher and more detailed. The present standards of the Association cover the following: (1) definition of a teacher-training institution; (2) requirements for admission of students; (3) standards for graduation; (4) size of faculty; (5) preparation of faculty; (6) teaching load of faculty; (7) training school and student teaching; (8) organization of the curriculum; (9) student health service and living conditions; (10) library, laboratory, and shop equipment; (11) construction and sanitary condition of buildings; (12) limits of registration of students; and (13) financial support. Information presented in previous chapters—dealing with student personnel, teaching staffs, and curricula—appears to furnish a basis for the suggestion that the Association standards should be exceeded by the Texas State Board requirements especially as to: (1) admission of students; (2) character of the preparation of the faculties; (3) training schools and student teaching; and (4) the organization and administration of differentiated curricula.

In view of the fact that there are at present in Texas such large numbers of persons legally certificated to teach, and the additional fact that a large number of colleges will seek to be accredited, it will likely be advisable in the near future to set up selective procedures for the admission of students to professional curricula in all accredited colleges. Mere graduation from high school is not a sufficient prerequisite to insure capable material from which competent teachers can be made. Again, the professional preparation of young people to serve the public schools requires faculty members who have had the advantages of professional training for that work and who are in sympathy with the needs and problems of the public schools. Exclusively academic preparation does not constitute sufficient qualification for staff members in a teacher-training institution. It is, therefore, proposed that the State Board requirements make it obligatory upon accredited colleges to staff their teacher-training departments with professionally trained people. It is generally known by students of teacher training that the minimum standards of the American Association of Teachers Colleges in regard to training schools and student teaching are far short of the best practice found in this country and in Europe. It is very urgently proposed that the requirements to be met by accredited colleges in Texas specify completely that adequate training schools for observation and participation be provided, and that a sufficient number of student-teaching centers be secured to permit every student before graduation to have at least one half of a semester of concentrated practice under proper supervision. Finally, the State Board requirements in Texas should set forth, in much greater detail than do the standards of the Association, the contents and sequence of the differentiated curricula to be established in all colleges seeking to be accredited. While minor variations in curricula might well be permitted, there seems to be no fundamental reason for great differences among corresponding curricula in institutions within the same state. The State Board of Education should, however, encourage progress in curriculum construction in the accredited colleges, and should recognize constructive work done by any institution in that field.

Functions of the State Colleges

With the plan of centralized control of teacher training and certification as outlined in the foregoing discussion the problem arises as to the status and functions of the state teachers colleges and of the other state institutions of higher learning. It has been shown that at present all these institutions are undertaking to prepare teachers. In fact the present tendency is for each institution to attempt in general whatever the others are doing, in what appears to be a competition for students. There is no controlling agency other than the policies of the several boards of regents and the separate appropriations which are obtained from the legislature. This study is not concerned with state policies in higher education other than that of teacher training. The following proposals are, therefore, limited to the functions of the teachers colleges and to the teacher-training activities of the other institutions. As has been pointed out in a previous chapter, the ends of state economy and the interests of the public schools will be best served by preparing the proper number of teachers to meet the needs of the schools. The proposed Division of Teacher Training and Certification should, therefore, be given the responsibility of making a continuous study of the demand for and supply of teachers in the state to serve as the basis of a state program.

Since the state is already committed to the policy of maintaining distinct institutions for the purpose of training teachers, it appears to be a matter of simple economy and efficiency to center that particular function in the seven teachers colleges. It would be difficult to justify state appropriations to maintain teacher-training departments in other state institutions except as they can be shown, by a study of teacher supply and demand, to be necessary to supplement the supply furnished by the teachers colleges or to provide special teachers not trained by them.

Under such an arrangement several plans are possible for the organization of the work of the teachers colleges. (1) The first two years might be devoted to a general junior college program and a three-year course of professional training, including differentiated curricula, begun with the junior year. Admission to the professional curricula should be on a selective basis. The last three years of this program should be devoted exclusively to the preparation of teachers. (2) The present four-year program might be maintained with professional preparation of teachers as the exclusive and only purpose. Students should be admitted on a selective basis and the number limited whenever conditions of the teacher market indicated such limitation to be necessary. A fifth or graduate year might be added by the State Board of Education in certain institutions as soon as the facts derived from the study of the demand for teachers showed the necessity for it. (3) The teachers colleges might be given a dual function and be permitted to offer a liberal arts program parallel to a four-year program of professional preparation for teaching. (4) A junior liberal arts program might be offered during the first two years along with a four-year program of professional teacher-training curricula. Under this plan and the third, provision should be made for a clear distinction between the two groups of students. Those who upon entrance select the liberal arts courses should be required to satisfy the professional requirements of the first two years before being granted admission to the professional curricula of the junior and senior years. (5) The present plan, summarized as follows, might be continued. It is a mingling of liberal arts courses and professional courses with very little differentiation in the professional curricula. Students take the required courses in education who have no intention, according to their own admission, of making teaching their profession. There is no selection or limitation of the students admitted. In fact, evidence seems to indicate that there is a rather definite policy of building up larger and larger enrollments, and of meeting the needs of all those who apply for entrance. No distinction between the truly professional students and the others is possible.

The plan adopted in Texas should aim at certain well-defined objectives. The state is no longer a pioneer commonwealth although it appears to be steadily developing and the need of a carefully wrought plan is evident. These objectives are proposed in the interest of state economy and educational efficiency. (1) The public schools should be supplied with the proper number of well-prepared teachers and a genuine profession of teaching should be built up. (2) The teachers colleges should have clear-cut functions and responsibilities. (3) Their financial support should be adequate and sufficiently stable to permit a proper discharge of such responsibilities. This would allow them to adopt progressive salary schedules which would make it possible for them to compete with other institutions in obtaining faculty members, and would provide rewards for efficient service together with sabbatical leaves of absence to encourage continued study on the part of their teachers. Such financial support would also make possible the operation of a retirement plan which will be more necessary as the colleges grow older. Stable financial support would permit the planning of capital outlay investments to cover a period of years to meet predetermined needs. (4) It is contended that it is entirely possible to know the teacher needs of the state with sufficient accuracy to permit the adoption of a definite plan covering the work and functions of the teachers colleges. This will in turn permit the working out of a plan of adequate and stable financial support which would be more economical, from the standpoint of state expenditures and services rendered, than the haphazard method which is in use at present.

Realization of these objectives would be practically impossible under several of the five possible plans suggested for the organization of the work and functions of the teachers colleges. The first plan, which suggests a five-year program, involves higher standards of teacher preparation than those contemplated by the proposed certificate regulations, and these standards are as high as probably will be reached during the next decade. It also involves the indeterminable task which would accompany the junior college program unless selective and limited admission were made applicable to the junior college. However, the plan as suggested would make possible the use of the junior college years for guiding and finding purposes to assist in a more accurate selection of those admitted to professional training. To accomplish that purpose it is doubtful whether enrollment should be limited at all.

Adoption of the third plan, which suggests a complete dual function, or the continuance of the present procedure, would prohibit the determination of a definite load for the teachers colleges. Unless the work expected of these institutions can be determined with fair accuracy, no plan of stable financial support is possible. The dual function would also lead to a number of administrative complications. The effect of such a plan upon the character of the professional curricula and upon the quality of the output is at present not completely known. Neither is it certain that the educational needs of the state require that the teachers colleges do the work of liberal arts colleges. However, tendencies shown in appropriations during the past few years indicate rather clearly that the state is not inclined to provide adequate funds for such a program.

The fourth plan suggested would be accompanied by most of the disadvantages and uncertainties just mentioned in connection with the discussion of the third. They might perhaps show themselves in lesser degree with a plan which calls for a liberal arts program only through the junior college years. Nevertheless, to insure proper support of the program of professional training would likely require an accounting system capable of keeping separate records for the two functions of each institution. It would probably be wise to place no arbitrary limit on the enrollment of the junior college, but such limit should in time be made to apply to the professional school. Certain members of the teaching profession in Texas have expressed the opinion that the time has arrived to make some selection among those applying for training.[3] In view of the fact that the teachers colleges have been serving students who seek liberal arts courses and pre-professional preparation for medicine, law, and other professions, it is probable that a reorganization will need to make sufficient concession to expediency to retain the junior college feature. This, however, should not be allowed to hamper the development of the professional work in these colleges.

The second plan suggested, which would make the teachers colleges strictly professional schools for the training of teachers, appears to be the ideal arrangement. The four-year program should be continued and a fifth year added in certain of the colleges when conditions in the teaching profession seemed to demand it. Under such a plan these institutions would be free to develop and make their peculiar contribution to the progress of education, unhampered by academic traditions and unrestrained by traditional influences. It is certainly true that the professional preparation of teachers for the schools of the next generation should be a peculiar and distinctive form of higher education. When the number of teachers needed for the various levels and kinds of positions is determined, the student load and curricular offerings of strictly professional schools could be assigned with fair accuracy, and the funds necessary for their proper support could be planned for a period of years. With the state's teacher-training activities committed exclusively to the teachers colleges, as far as is possible to meet teacher needs, every element of competition with other institutions would be removed from these professional schools and their administrative officers would be relieved of the rôle of lobbyist which they have been compelled to assume during each session of the legislature. The state would get what it paid for and would pay for no more teacher preparation than it needed. The public schools would improve as the result of a better trained and more professional teaching personnel.

[3] North Texas State Teachers College, Bulletin No. 95, "Cooperative Planning for Teacher Training Standards in Texas," *1931 Conference Proceedings*, pp. 59-71, May, 1931.

Summary

In this chapter the attempt has been made to offer certain proposals designed to improve the training of teachers for the public schools of Texas and to raise the level of the teaching profession. They have been based on facts disclosed by this study and upon information obtained from the literature in the field of teacher training. The following proposals have been made:

1. Adopt a modern system of state taxation in order to obtain sufficient revenue to finance a state system of public education. Without doubt Texas has the wealth to support a system of schools equal to the best in America.
2. Revise the plan of state educational administration by increasing the powers and responsibilities of the State Board of Education.
3. Adapt Mort's plan of state support for public schools to the conditions and needs in Texas, thereby equalizing the educational opportunities offered in all communities and also equalizing the burden necessary to support the program. The abandonment of the costly and inefficient district system would be effected under this plan.
4. Reorganize the State Department of Education by placing at its head a State Commissioner of Education. Create within the Department a Division of Teacher Training and Certification under the supervision of a competent director. Grant sufficient funds for the support of the Department to secure the best professional ability obtainable and to maintain an adequate staff.
5. Require the Division of Teacher Training and Certification to make continuous studies of the supply of and demand for teachers in the state.
6. Repeal all existing certification laws and empower the State Board of Education to issue all certificates, to designate the classes and grades of certificates to be issued, and to establish regulations governing their issuance. An outline of proposed regulations has been presented.
7. As part of the certification plan, make it the duty of the State Board of Education to set up requirements to be met by every college which seeks to be accredited for the training of teachers. These requirements should not be lower than those contemplated by the standards of the American Association of Teachers Colleges, and in several respects should be much more complete and

specific than the present standards. The principal details of differentiated curricula leading to the various classes of certificates should be included in the requirements.

8. Place with the State Board of Education sufficient authority over the budgets of the state's institutions of higher learning to insure the concentration of teacher training in the seven teachers colleges. Appropriations for that purpose should be granted to other institutions only when it is known that their teacher product will be necessary to supplement the supply of teachers furnished by the teachers colleges.
9. Give the State Board of Education power to fix the status and functions of the teachers colleges in accordance with the educational needs of the state as revealed by continuous studies prosecuted by the State Department of Education. It was suggested that ideally these institutions should confine their activities exclusively to the professional preparation of teachers. However, as a concession to custom, it is possible that they should be allowed to offer a general junior college program, at least for a time, in conjunction with their professional work.
10. Provide for a permanent committee composed of staff members from each teachers college to advise with the Division of Teacher Training and Certification on certificate requirements and professional curricula.

BIBLIOGRAPHY

AMERICAN ASSOCIATION OF TEACHERS COLLEGES, *Ninth Yearbook,* 1930.

ARMENTROUT, W. D. *Student Teaching in State Teachers Colleges.* Colorado State Teachers College, Greeley, Colo., 1928.

Atlas of the World, 1924. Funk and Wagnalls Company, New York.

BAGLEY, W. C. *Professional Education of Teachers in New Jersey.* Unpublished study, 1928.

BAGLEY, W. C., ALEXANDER, THOMAS, AND OTHERS. *Report of the Survey Commission of the Louisiana State Normal Colleges.* State Department of Education, Baton Rouge, La., 1924.

BENSON, C. E. *Output of Professional Schools for Teachers.* Warwick & York, Inc., Baltimore, 1922.

Biennial Reports of the Board of Regents, 1927-1929. Texas State Teachers Colleges, Austin, Tex.

BRENHOLTZ, HAROLD. *Population as a Potential Factor in the Need for Teachers in Secondary Schools of a State, with Special Application to California and Texas.* Doctor's thesis, University of California, 1930. (Unpublished.)

BRIGGS, T. H. *The Junior High School.* Houghton Mifflin Company, Boston, 1920.

BROGAN, WHIT. *The Work of Placement Offices in Teacher-Training Institutions.* Contributions to Education, No. 434. Bureau of Publications, Teachers College, Columbia University, 1930.

BUCKINGHAM, B. R. "Research in Teacher Supply and Demand." *Educational Administration and Supervision,* Vol. XV, No. 4. April, 1929, pp. 259-68.

BUCKINGHAM, B. R. *Supply and Demand in Teacher Training.* Bureau of Educational Research Monographs, Ohio State University, Columbus, Ohio, 1926.

BUREAU OF EDUCATION. *Statistics of Teachers Colleges and Normal Schools.* Bulletin, 1929, No. 14. 1927-1928.

BURKS, BARBARA STODDARD. "The Relative Influence of Nature and Nurture upon Mental Development." *Twenty-seventh Yearbook of the National Society for the Study of Education.* Part I, 1928. Public School Publishing Company, Bloomington, Ill.

CARNEGIE FOUNDATION FOR THE ADVANCEMENT OF TEACHING. *The Professional Preparation of Teachers for American Public Schools.* Bulletin No. 14, 1920, New York.

CHANDLER, PAUL G. "The Quality of Instruction in Teachers Colleges," pp. 136-41. *Ninth Yearbook of the American Association of Teachers Colleges,* 1930.

CHARTERS, W. W. and WAPLES, D. *Commonwealth Teacher-Training Study.* University of Chicago Press, 1929.

COFFMAN, L. D. *The Social Composition of the Teaching Population.* Contributions to Education, No. 41. Bureau of Publications, Teachers College, Columbia University, 1911.

COOK, HARRIS. *The Training of State Teachers College Faculties.* George Peabody College for Teachers, Contributions to Education, No. 86. Nashville, Tenn., 1930.

COOK, KATHERINE M. *State Laws and Regulations Governing Teachers' Certificates.* United States Bureau of Education Bulletin, No. 19, 1927.

COOPER, WILLIAM JOHN. "Some Teacher Problems." *National Republic,* Vol. XVII, May, 1929.

COUNTS, GEORGE S. *The American Road to Culture.* The John Day Company, Inc., New York, 1930.

COXE, W. W. *Teacher Demand in New York State.* State Department of Education, Albany, 1929.

CUBBERLEY, E. P. *State School Administration.* Houghton Mifflin Company, Boston, 1927.

Dallas Morning News, Dec. 16, 1929; Feb. 21, 1931. Dallas, Tex.

Denton Record-Chronicle, Feb. 21, 1931. Denton, Tex.

DEXTER, EMILY S. "The Relation Between Occupation of Parent and Intelligence of Children." *School and Society,* Vol. XVII, pp. 612-14, June 2, 1923.

DIVISION OF FIELD STUDIES, INSTITUTE OF EDUCATIONAL RESEARCH, TEACHERS COLLEGE, COLUMBIA UNIVERSITY. *Preliminary Report on Publicly Supported Higher Education in the State of Missouri.* Jefferson City, Mo., 1929.

DONOVAN, H. L. *A State's Elementary Teacher-Training Problem.* George Peabody College for Teachers, Contributions to Education, No. 17. Nashville, Tenn., 1925.

EBY, FREDERICK. *The Development of Education in Texas.* The Macmillan Company, New York, 1925.

ELIASSEN, R. H. and ANDERSON, E. W. *The Supply of Teachers and the Demand.* Educational Research Bulletin, Vol. IX, No. 16. College of Education, Ohio State University, Columbus, Ohio, Nov., 1930.

ELSBREE, W. S. *Teacher Turnover in the Cities and Villages of New York State.* Contributions to Education, No. 300. Bureau of Publications, Teachers College, Columbia University, New York, 1928.

EVENDEN, E. S. "The Critic Teacher and the Professional Treatment of Subject Matter," *Report of Ninth Annual Session of Supervisors of Student Teaching.* Warwick & York, Inc., Baltimore, 1929.

EVENDEN, E. S., STRAYER, G. D., and ENGELHARDT, N. L. *Score Card for Physical Plant of Normal Schools and Teachers Colleges.* Bureau of Publications, Teachers College, Columbia University, 1929.

FILES OF *The Texas Outlook.* Monthly publication of the Texas State Teachers Association, Fort Worth, Tex.

FRASIER, G. W. and WHITNEY, F. L. *Teachers College Finance.* Colorado State Teachers College, Greeley, Colo., 1930.

FRAZIER, B. W. *Teacher Training, 1926-28.* United States Bureau of Education, Bulletin No. 17, 1929.

FREEMAN, F. N., HOLZINGER, K. J., and MITCHELL, B. C. "The Influence of Environment on the Intelligence, School Achievement, and Conduct of Foster Children." *Twenty-seventh Yearbook of the National Society for the Study of Education,* Part I, 1928. Public School Publishing Company, Bloomington, Ill.

GARRISON, N. L. *The Status and Work of the Training Supervisor.* Contributions to Education, No. 280. Bureau of Publications, Teachers College, Columbia University, 1927.

General and Special Laws of the State of Texas: 38th Legislature, 1923; 40th Legislature, 1927; 41st Legislature, 1929. Secretary of State, Austin, Tex.

GRANT, J. R. *A State's Teacher-Training Problem.* George Peabody College for Teachers, Contributions to Education, No. 18. Nashville, Tenn., 1925.

HAGGERTY, M. E. and NASH, H. B. "Mental Capacity of Children and Parental Occupation." *Journal of Educational Psychology,* Vol. XV, No. 9, 1924.

HAMILTON, F. R. *Fiscal Support of State Teachers Colleges.* Contributions to Education, No. 165. Bureau of Publications, Teachers College, Columbia University, 1924.

HILL, C. M. *A Decade of Progress in Teacher Training.* Contributions to Education, No. 233. Bureau of Publications, Teachers College, Columbia University, 1927.

HILLEGAS, M. B. Editor, *The Classroom Teacher.* The Classroom Teacher, Inc., Chicago, 1927.

HOLLIS, E. V. "Why They Teach." *Educational Administration and Supervision,* Vol. XV, No. 9, 678-84, 1929.

HUBBARD, FRANK W. *Teacher Demand and Supply in the Public Elementary and Secondary Schools of the United States.* National Education Association, Washington, D. C., 1931.

HUDELSON, EARL. *Class Size at the College Level.* The University of Minnesota Press, 1928.

HUMPHREYS, H. C. *The Factors Operating in the Location of State Normal Schools.* Contributions to Education, No. 142. Bureau of Publications, Teachers College, Columbia University, 1923.

JUDD, CHARLES H. "A National Survey of Teacher Training." *Journal of the National Education Association,* Vol. 19, No. 9, pp. 291-92, Dec., 1930.

LEDLOW, W. F. *Protestant Education in Texas.* Unpublished doctor's thesis, University of Texas, 1926.

LEE, CHARLES A. *Eightieth Report of the Public Schools of Missouri,* Parts I and II. Jefferson City, Mo., 1929.

MAGEE, H. J. *Unit Costs of Salaries in Teachers Colleges and Normal Schools.* Contributions to Education, No. 489. Bureau of Publications, Teachers College, Columbia University, 1931.

MANGUN, V. L. *The American Normal School, Its Rise and Development in Massachusetts.* Warwick & York, Inc., Baltimore, 1928.

MARRS, S. M. N. *Biennial Reports of the Texas State Department of Education.* Austin, Tex., 1929-1931.

MCCONNELL, W. J. "Social Cleavages in Texas, A Study of the Proposed Division of the State." *Studies in History, Economics and Public Law,* Vol. CXIX, No. 2, Columbia University, 1925.

MCMULLEN, L. B. *Service Load in Teacher-training Institutions.* Contributions to Education, No. 244. Bureau of Publications, Teachers College, Columbia University, 1927.

MEADER, J. L. *Normal School Education in Connecticut.* Contributions to Education, No. 307. Bureau of Publications, Teachers College, Columbia University, 1928.

Minutes of the Council of Deans, Texas State Teachers Colleges. (Unpublished.) 1926, 1928.

Minutes of the Council of Presidents, Texas State Teachers College, Austin. 1920-29.

MOFFETT, M'LEDGE. *The Social Background and Activities of Teachers College Students.* Contributions to Education, No. 375. Bureau of Publications, Teachers College, Columbia University, 1929.

MORPHET, EDGAR L. *The Measurement and Interpretation of School Building Utilization.* Contributions to Education, No. 264. Bureau of Publications, Teachers College, Columbia University, 1927.

MORT, PAUL R. *State Support for Public Schools.* Bureau of Publications, Teachers College, Columbia University, 1926.

MYERS, A. F. *A Teacher-Training Program for Ohio.* Contributions to Education, No. 266. Bureau of Publications, Teachers College, Columbia University, 1927.

North Texas State Teachers College. *Coöperative Planning for Teacher-Training Standards in Texas,* Bulletin No. 95, May, 1931.

NORTON, JOHN K. "The Problem of Teacher Tenure." *Research Bulletin of the National Education Association,* Vol. II, No. 5, 1924.

NORTON, JOHN K. "Teacher Demand and Supply." *New York Times,* July 27, 1930, Sec. 3.

PHELPS, SHELTON. "Some Phases of the Training of Faculty Members of Teachers Colleges." *Ninth Yearbook of the American Association of Teachers Colleges,* 1930.

PHILLIPS, FRANK M. *Per Capita Costs in Teacher-Training Institutions, 1927-28.* Bureau of Education Circular, No. 11, 1929.

PITTENGER, L. A. AND OTHERS. *Digest of Report of Committee on Supply, Demand, Training and Certification of Teachers.* Mimeographed report to the Detroit meeting of the American Association of Teachers Colleges, 1931.

PRYOR, H. C. *Graded Units in Student Teaching.* Contributions to Education, No. 202. Bureau of Publications, Teachers College, Columbia University, 1926.

RANDOLPH, E. D. *The Professional Treatment of Subject Matter.* Warwick & York, Inc., Baltimore, 1924.

REID, J. R. "The Certificate Pendulum." *Texas Outlook*, August, 1929. Texas State Teachers Association, Fort Worth, Tex.

REISNER, E. H. *Nationalism and Education Since 1789*. The Macmillan Company, New York, 1923.

Revised Statutes of Texas, 1925. Austin, Tex.

REYNOLDS, O. E. *The Social and Economic Status of College Students.* Contributions to Education, No. 272. Bureau of Publications, Teachers College, Columbia University, 1927.

ROSENLOF, G. W. *Library Facilities of Teacher-Training Institutions.* Contributions to Education, No. 347. Bureau of Publications, Teachers College, Columbia University, 1929.

Salaries in City School Systems, Research Bulletin of the National Education Association, Vol. IX, No. 3. 1930-31, Washington, D. C.

School Laws of Texas. Texas State Department of Education Bulletin, No. 264. Austin, Tex., 1929.

SMITH, J. W. *Survey of the Development and Needs of the North Texas State Teachers College.* Master's thesis, Southern Methodist University, Dallas, Tex., 1925. (Unpublished.)

Southwestern Bell Telephone Co. *Economic Survey of Texas.* St. Louis, Mo., 1928.

STEELE, ROBERT M. *A Study of Teacher Training in Vermont.* Contributions to Education, No. 243. Bureau of Publications, Teachers College, Columbia University, 1926.

STEVENS, E. B. AND ELLIOTT, E. C. "Unit Costs of Higher Education." *The Educational Finance Inquiry Reports,* Vol. 13. The Macmillan Company, New York, 1925.

STOKES, S. M. AND LEHMAN, H. C. "Intelligence Test Scores of Social and Occupational Groups." *School and Society,* Vol. 31, No. 794, pp. 372-77.

TAYLOR, WILLIAM S. *The Development of the Professional Education of Teachers in Pennsylvania.* J. B. Lippincott Company, Philadelphia, 1924.

Texas Almanac. Published annually by the *Dallas News,* Dallas, Tex.

Texas Educational Survey Report, Vols. III, VI, VIII. The Texas Educational Survey Commission, Austin, Tex., 1925.

TEXAS STATE DEPARTMENT OF EDUCATION. *Laws, Rules and Regulations Governing State Teachers' Certificates.* Bulletin No. 252, Feb., 1929. Austin, Tex.

———. *Directory of Teachers in Texas High Schools.* Bulletin No. 248. Austin, Tex.

TEXAS STATE TEACHERS COLLEGES. *Catalogues,* 1929 and 1930.

ULLRICH, F. H. "Combating the Problem of Too Many Teachers." *The Texas Outlook,* Vol. XIV, No. 3. Texas State Teachers' Association, Fort Worth, Tex.

UNIVERSITY OF TEXAS. *Catalogue of the Medical Branch,* Bulletin No. 3005, 1930.

WAGNER, JONAS E. "The Professional Status of Faculty Members in Pennsylvania Teacher-Training Institutions." *Educational Administration and Supervision,* Vol. XV, No. 3, pp. 202-11, 1929.

WHITNEY, F. L. "Organization, Cost and Scope of a Department of Research," *Ninth Yearbook of the American Association of Teachers Colleges*, 1930.

WHITNEY, F. L. *Teacher Demand and Supply in the Public Schools.* Colorado State Teachers College, Education Series No. 8, 1930. Greeley, Colo.

WHITNEY, F. L. *The Intelligence, Preparation and Teaching Skill of Normal School Graduates in the United States.* University of Minnesota, 1922.

WORKS, GEORGE A. *College and University Library Problems.* American Library Association, Chicago, 1927.

YEAGER, W. A. *State Certification as a Factor in the Training of Elementary Teachers.* Kutztown Publishing Co., Kutztown, Pa., 1929.